An Idealist View of Life

'Science is a system of second causes, which cannot describe the world adequately, much less account for it.' Radhakrishnan explores in *An Idealist View of Life* the modern intellectual debate and the vain attempts to find a substitute for religion. He discusses, drawing upon the traditions of East and West, the nature and validity of religious experience. Finally, he creates a fine vision of man's evolution and the emergence of higher values. The range of subject combined with the author's own living faith, undogmatic and free of creed, makes this book a philosophical education in itself.

An Idealist View of Life

RADHAKRISHNAN

INDUS

An imprint of HarperCollins *Publishers* India

INDUS
An imprint of HarperCollins *Publishers* India Pvt Ltd
7/16 Ansari Road, Daryaganj, New Delhi 110 002

Published by Indus 1994

First published 1932

ISBN 0-04-141009-2

Typeset in 11/13 pt Palatino by
Print Line
S-343, Greater Kailash II
New Delhi 110 048

Printed in India by
Ahad Enterprises
2609 Baradari Ballimaran
Delhi 110006

To S. R. K.

NOTE

This book is largely based on lectures delivered by the author in 1929 and 1930 at the University of Manchester and University College, London, under the auspices of the Hibbert Trustees.

CONTENTS

CONTENTS

CHAPTER I

The Modern Challenge to Religion

I. What is idealism?

Idealism is an ambiguous word and has been used to signify a variety of views. An 'idea' is taken as a particular mental image peculiar to each individual and attempts are made in the Buddhist Vijñānavāda (mentalism) and English empiricism to reduce all knowledge to ideas in this sense. Whatever is real in the universe is such stuff as ideas are made of. Ideas or images are regarded as self-contained existences and not as avenues of the apprehension of a world which is at once more ideal and more real than themselves. The term 'idea' has also been used to signify the universal notion, which is not an existent here and now, but a quality of the existent which is shareable by other existents and knowable by other minds. While Berkeley's first statement is more of a mentalism holding that existence consists either in perceiving or being perceived, his modified view with its emphasis on 'notions' brings it under the second type. For Kant, knowledge is an extension of a sense-manifold by means of the categories of thought. While his main intention is to regard the categories as the means by which the world that extends beyond the given datum reveals itself to the finite mind, there is, however, the implication that the categories are only subjective and ideal while reality is an uncategorized, unidealized world with which we are face to face in immediate perception. These different tendencies are developed in later thought. While Hegel and his followers look upon reality as built up out of relations of thought, modern realists are more insistent upon the sense-manifold. Though reality for the Hegelian idealists is a dialect of ideas, no modern philosopher believes that the world of experience is constituted by mere ideas. For Croce, however, reality is mental activity. Even the conceptions of a something which is external, mechanical and natural are data furnished to mind by itself.[1] Mind is immanent in all cognitive experience as an active process which gives objective form to knowledge. It does not stand in a transcendent relation to an extraneous object which it passively contemplates. There is a third sense in which the term 'idea' is used. When we ask with reference to any thing or action, 'what is the idea?' we mean, what is the principle involved in it, what is the meaning or the purpose of its being, what is the aim or value of the action? What is it driving at?[2] This idea or value is the operative creative force. An idealist view finds that the universe has meaning, has value. Ideal values are the dynamic forces, the driving power of the universe. The world is intelligible only as a system of ends. Such a view has little to do with the problem whether a thing is only a particular image or a general relation. The question of the independence of the knower and the known is hardly relevant to it. Nor is it committed to the doctrine that the world is made of mind, an infinite mind or a society of minds. Idealism in the sense indicated concerns the ultimate nature of reality, whatever may be its relation to the knowing mind. It is an answer to the problem of the idea, the meaning or the purpose of it all. It has nothing in common with the view that makes reality an irrational blind striving or an irremediably miserable blunder. It finds life significant and purposeful. It endows man with a destiny that is not

1 See H. Wildon Carr: *The Philosophy of Benedetto Croce* (1917), pp. 12, 18.
2 See J. H. Muirhead: *The Real and the Ideal.* University of California Publications in Philosophy, vol. 8, 1926.

limited to the sensible world. When Touchstone asks Corin in *As You Like it*, 'Hast any philosophy in thee, shepherd?' Shakespeare means by philosophy not a system of abstract thought or a technical discipline of the schools but an attitude of mind which can best be described as 'idealistic'. Have you that spiritual dimension to your being, that mood of reflective inquiry and self-contemplation, that anxiety of mind to know the things spiritual in which is the true dwelling-place of man? Or do you belong to the race of unreflective people who are satisfied with business or politics or sport, whose life is dull prose without any ideal meaning? Philosophy is understanding, contemplation, insight, and a philosopher can find no rest until he gains a view or vision of the world of things and persons which will enable him to interpret the manifold experiences as expressive, in some sort, of a purpose.

An idealist view of life is not expressed in any one pattern. It is many-coloured and its forms are varied; yet underneath all the variations and oppositions there are certain common fundamental assumptions that show them all to be products of the same spirit. It has had a long and continuous history both in the East and in the West. The fountain-heads of the Vedas, including the Upaniṣads, in the East and Socrates and Plato in the West, set forth this creed in broad and flexible terms. The realistic systems of Hindu thought, the Nyāya and the Vaiśeṣika, the Sāṁkhya and the Yoga, and the Mīmāṁsā are not in serious disagreement with the fundamental intention of the idealist tradition of the Upaniṣads, viz. the inseparability of the highest value from the truly real. The absolute is reality, consciousness and freedom--*sat, cit,* and *ānanda.* In the West, from Socrates and Plato to Bradley and Alexander,[1] the idealist outlook of an ultimate

1 I mention Alexander advisedly to show that the modern opposition between realism and idealism in epistemology has

connection of value and reality is maintained. For Plato, the meaning of the universe is the realization of Good. The universe exists for that purpose.

In a sense, as Hegel said, all philosophy is idealistic. In contrasting appearance and reality, fact and truth, existence and essence, it is led to admit an ideal world beyond the phenomenal. Even absolute materialism is idealism, though of a crude kind, for the matter to which all existence is reduced is not a concrete actuality but an abstract idea. Modern physics reduces the world of immediate experience to one of shadows and symbols. Ions, electrons, ids are not observable phenomena and yet are posited as real since they fulfil the requirements of thinking. However anxious we may be for a return to the concrete, we find it difficult to reduce the real to the concrete. Ideas are always with us since they are an essential part of the real, and if we interpret them as ideals or values, an idealist view of the universe results. If we are not carried away by the noise of the controversy among the philosophical sects, but watch the deeper currents which are shaping them, we seem to find a strong tendency to insist on the insights of idealism, though, of course, the language and the style are different. Idealism today has to reckon with our problems and help us to face them. The stage seems to be set for a fresh statement.

Such a restatement can have little meaning for those who have not sounded the depths of the difficulties and discrepancies which a changing world is forcing on us. Though they are all too obvious, it is sometimes necessary to insist on the obvious. To know what the problem is, is quite as important as to know the answer to it. In a sense philosophy helps us to solve the problem by making us conscious of it. What are the main factors operative today in our life and

little to do with the main problem of idealism.

thought? It is to a brief consideration of these that I wish to devote this first chapter.

2. Scientific method

Among the new forces that have made our world so different from what it was the most important is natural science, which has imposed its methods and conclusions on us and altered the very atmosphere in which we live, move and think. The strict method of science requires us to believe a proposition only when we are in a position to prove it. Whenever statements are made, it is our duty to find out whether they are capable of verification by those who will take the trouble to investigate them. Religion, on the other hand, consists, according to Freud, 'of certain dogmas, assertions about facts and conditions of external (or internal) reality which tell us something that one has not oneself discovered and which claim that one should give them credence.'[1] 'If we ask on what their claim to be believed is based, we receive three answers which accord remarkably ill with one another. They deserve to be believed, firstly, because our primal ancestors believed them; secondly, because we possess proofs which have been handed down from this period of antiquity; and thirdly, because it is forbidden to raise the question of their authenticity at all. Formerly this presumptuous act was visited with the very severest penalties and even today society is unwilling to see anyone renew it. In other words, religious doctrines are "illusions"; they do not admit of proof and no one can be compelled to consider them as true or to believe in them.'[2] If the astronomical arguments of our ancestors of 2000 B.C. are not accepted by us, there is no reason why we should

1 *The Future of an Illusion*, E. T. (1928), p. 43.
2 *Ibid.*, pp. 45-46, 55.

give greater authority to their religious views. The authoritarian method breaks down on critical analysis. When authorities conflict, we are compelled to go beyond authority. The authority is commended to our acceptance on the ground that the author possessed superior opportunities of knowing the truth through other sources of knowledge. But when, for example, the New Testament and the Qu'ran conflict, we cannot assume that the author of one had better opportunities of knowing the truth than the other. We must turn to some other criterion, e.g. the rationality of their contents. The supernatural nature of religious authority will have to be given up.

The spirit of free inquiry and the right to think for oneself, which is not necessarily to think unlike others, have come to stay and the defenders of authority do not openly persecute the critically minded and are often anxious to appeal to reason in support of authority.

If for science truth is something we are getting nearer and nearer to as time goes on, for religion it need not be different. Why should we think that only in religion truth is something handed down from the past which we have to guard jealously lest we should stray further away from it? The golden age is in the future vision, not in a fabled past.

Our scientific theories which supersede earlier ones are only links in a long chain of progressive advances likely in time to be themselves transcended. Their only justification is their adequacy for the relevant facts. They are temporary resting-places in the search for truth and there is nothing absolute about them. Religion on the other hand claims to be absolutistic. Its truths are said to be unalterable and our duty is to defend them. Such truths, if any, belong to heaven; our truths are always provisional and tentative.

Science demands induction from facts and not deduction from dogmas. We must face the facts and derive our conclusions from them and not start with the conclusions and then play with the facts. Reasoning in religion is only a rearrangement of our prejudices. We are Hindus or Christians mainly because we are born Hindus or Christians and our fathers bore those labels. In science, the procedure is different. The modern temper insists that the scientific attitude of veracity and self-detachment must spread to all human affairs. The assumption of religion that God, the author of the universe, is the benevolent father of us all is an open invitation to explain away the difficulties and discomforts of life as delusions of the mind. The tendency of religion to mistake desires for facts, to take the world to be what we should like it to be, to reserve a certain part of life as falling outside the scope of ordinary knowledge is the direct opposite of empirical science.

Science insists on the reign of law. If law works everywhere and through all time, there is nothing mysterious or miraculous about the world. Only the uneducated believe that demons cause diseases and priests cure them. The world is a cosmos, an ordered whole. While in the West this conception was suggested by the astronomical discoveries of the fourth centry B.C., in India the order of the universe, the *rta*, is accepted as early as the Vedic Period. We need not be much disturbed by Professor Eddington's view of the 'final overthrow of strict causality' which he infers from the principle of indeterminacy with reference to the quantum theory. Eddington suggests that many of the laws of physics are statistical and no prediction about the behaviour of particular electrons can be made but only about their behaviour in the mass. If natural processes are themselves indeterminate, if something like freewill is to be put at the basis of ordinary events of nature, if strict determinism fails us anywhere, then all scientific enterprise will have to be abandoned. The continual search for cause and explanations is decisive proof that causality is the one thing scientists believe in, however formidable the exceptions may seem to be. The appearance of indeterminacy may be due to an element of error in our observations. It may be admitted that scientists are actually using for purposes of predicting phenomena theories which they are not able to reconcile or understand completely. It only means that further work of exploration is necessary, since there are facts whose laws we have not yet been able to discover. But all this does not justify us in saying that there are facts to which no laws apply. For that would mean that there are facts which have no nature of their own. They would be an ultimate exception to the concept of the rationality of the real. For all practical purposes strict determinism is a cardinal feature of natural science. At a time when we were not sure about the orderedness of the universe, when our science was still allied with magic, an animistic interpretation of nature was possible. Today such a view is out of the question. Special providence is the antithesis of order.

The seventeenth century scientists, Descartes, Kepler, Galileo and Newton, who had the vision of the world as a great machine allowed, however, that the mechanism was one contrived by God and worked in obedience to the precise laws of his mind. The traditional god who reigned in the heavens as never a despot ruled on earth, yielded to one whose sovereignty was bound by well-established laws. The eighteenth century scientists were more rigorous in their logic and so refused to allow any interference from outside with the mechanically ordered universe. Their god was conceived as external to the system, as one who does not function in regard to the world. He reigns but does not govern. In ancient Greece, Epicurus, though he was convinced that nothing that happened on earth, whether in the history of the cosmos or the life of humanity, was due to divine influence, did not abolish the gods altogether. He left them in the empty spaces between the worlds where they took no notice of us, though we in our weakness regarded them as beautiful objects of adoration and mistook their elegant ease for eternal life.[1] A god who always works by law is not easily distinguishable from one who never works at all. A non-functioning, ornamental deity cannot remain for long a vital force. Deism lapsed into scepticism. If a god is unnecessary for working the world machine, he does not seem to be quite necessary for starting it.

Besides, the need for religious mystery diminishes as the scope of scientific explanation extends. We generally indent on the hypothesis of God when knowledge reaches its limits. Popular use of expressions like 'it is an act of God', 'God only knows', shows how ignorance is the source of the knowledge of God. God is the name we tremblingly give to the unseen and the inexplicable. He is the 'sanctuary of ignorance', an indication of incomplete knowledge. The realm of mystery before which man feels humble slowly withdraws its frontiers. We can know the world and live our life without feeling our utter dependence on unknown forces.

Modern materialism is not so much the result of rational philosophy as of the startling triumphs of modern science. The view of the universe revealed by modern science--especially mathematics, physics and astronomy--does not seem to be less favourable to a mechanical hypothesis.

3. *Achievements of science*

Modern physics is transforming our old conceptions matter. The ultimate constituents are not atoms but positive and

1 'The blessed and immortal nature knows no trouble itself, nor causes trouble to any other, so that it is never constrained by anger or favour. For all such things exist only in the weak' (Bailey: *Epicurus: The Extant Remains* 1926 , p. 95).

negative electric influences, which are alike in the magnitude of their charge, though differing fundamentally in the mass, the positive being 1,845 times heavier than the negative. The ninety-two different elements are determined simply by the difference between the number of positives and negatives that are found in the nucleus. A change in this difference is enough to bring about a transmutation of these elements as in radio-activity. It is sometimes asserted that the new conception of matter has ended the old materialism. If this means that the old atomic theory is impossible, it is quite true; but if it means that the contrast between spirit and matter is diminished in any way, it is altogether untrue. If the mechanical theory is otherwise well-grounded, the analysis of the atom into electric energy does not touch it.

Astronomy has falsified the old little snug universe of Ptolemaic thought with a comfortable chronology of six thousand years. We cannot believe that the earth was brought into existence by a divine fiat on a certain Tuesday in the year 4004 B.C. Astronomy has stretched out space to infinity where distances are measured by light years and brought down the earth from its exalted place as the centre of the universe to the insignificant position of a small planet in a single solar system surrounded by innumerable other systems stretching off without end into cold stellar regions. The universe is far bigger than we ever dreamed of. The great sun on which our earth attends is but a speck among some hundred thousand million stars which form our stellar system and this great system in turn is but one of millions of such systems which fill space, and yet the wonder is that it is not improbable that space itself is finite so that a ray of light can perhaps travel round it and come back to its starting-point.[1]

1 Jeans: *The Universe Around Us* (1929).

A purely mechanical explanation is offered for the whole show. The unity of nature suggests to science a unitary ground of existence, with which all things when fully traced can be connected, but this unitary being need not be regarded as intelligent. Lifeless matter particles careered about for countless millions of years and in their interaction created myriads of nebulae, of suns, and eventually our solar system, including earth, sea, air and land. Sir James Jeans tells us that our solar system is only a cosmic freak due to the chance passage of an inconspicuous star in the neighbourhood of an equally inconspicuous nebula.[1]

What is life in our solar system? It exists on earth and may possibly exist in Venus and Mars, and yet its great importance on earth seems to distort our general view of the universe. From the cosmic perspective life is a by-product, a minor detail in a large scheme with no definite or direct relations to our hopes and fears. It exists only in our solar system and even there perhaps only on our planet. Life, which is such a merely local and superficial peculiarity, cannot be the end of the universe, as some of us are inclined to believe.[2] There must be a relevant relation between purpose and output, end and means. The stars in their courses are plainly about some other business.

It was long held that the mechanical view, while adequate in the realm of matter, fails us when we come to organic life. The delicate adjustments of the bodily organs

1 Those who are instructed in the main facts of astronomy can appreciate the unconscious humour of Genesis i. 16, 'And God made the two great lights, the greater light to rule the day, and the lesser light to rule the night; and he made the stars also.'
2 'It seems incredible that the universe can have been designed primarily to produce life like our own; had it been so, surely we might have expected to find a better proportion between the magnitude of the mechanism and the amount of the product.' (Jeans: *The Mysterious Universe* (1930), pp. 5-6).

to the functions they serve, the eye for seeing and the ear for
hearing, seem to require a different explanation. But the
carefully selected illustrations of design, contrivance and
adaptation used by Paley and Butler to prove the reality of
God conceived as a gigantic craftsman, are now shown to
be the working of the principle of adaptation to environment. Nature in her blind thirst for life has filled the earth
with innumerable types. The offspring of living organisms
are never exactly alike. They vary slightly both from the
parents and from one another. Variations which help the
individuals to live more easily tend to survive. Those individuals which do not share these variations pass out. By
a continuous piling up of small variations spread over a long
period of time, Darwin held, a new species is produced.
Though this view has suffered modifications in detail--
variations are said to be discontinuous and far from gradual
or by minute stages--the general theory is not much disturbed. The story of continuous development through the
whole of animate nature suggests the working of an automatic mechanism. No principle outside the natural world is
needed to account for it. In a closed world governed by
uniform laws, no spiritual principle can interfere. The elaborate
pictures given in our ancient Scriptures of the defeat of God's
original intention by a host of fallen angels or the attribution
of the countless woes of ages to the erroneous choice of an
imaginary chief which involved the whole of posterity in
ruin and corruption do not have any semblance of truth for
those familiar with the larger concepts of development
through countless centuries. We cannot be sure that species
move on to higher stages of development in orderly sequence. Ever so many degenerate and some die out altogether. No sooner has some form of existence perfected
itself than it proceeds to decay. The progress we have
achieved is the result of the terrible method of trial and

error. Struggle and suffering, disease and death are such pregnant facts that if there is any ruling power in the universe, it may be fate or chance or careless gods, but in no case a beneficent providence. Man is nothing more than the latest of a long series of living creatures, and he did not arrive on this planet faultless and finished but is being slowly ground into shape by the shocks of circumstances. The half men of the Paleolithic age, the Neanderthal and the Piltdown bones show how near the apes primitive men were. Anthropomorphism loses its point when the rise of humanity is seen to be a curious accident and its career a mere episode in cosmic history. The history of humanity measured against the inconceivably long vista of time is but the twinkling of an eye. Human beings confirmed to an infinitesimal part of space seem so far removed from the main plan of the universe. We cannot be certain that man is the last and the supreme utterance of life. The chain may well extend to other links which may be as different from him as he is different from the amoeba. Man is a relatively recent arrival on earth. He has possessed and governed it for less than a thousandth part of its existence. Gigantic reptiles and dinosaurs ruled it for millions of years and might have thought that they would continue for ever. Man today regards himself as the final triumph of biological evolution and has come to stay!

Man may be another unsuccessful experiment which the Unknowable, not quite certain of its direction, is making. Even if the evolution of life on earth does not proceed higher than the human species, science threatens us with a possibility of its extinction. The solar system, we are told, is like a clock which is running down and its processes are irreversible. Though it may not stop in our own day, its eventual doom can hardly be averted.[1] Scientific evidence seems to

1 Sir James Jeans says: 'Neither the sun nor any other star can continue radiating away its mass at such a rate for ever . . . The

suggest that the universe which has crawled by slow stages into its present shape is making for a condition of universal death.

The values for which we struggle are only a flash in the pan and will disappear sooner or later. The cosmic process is but a weaving and unweaving of forms in which the values we cherish find precarious and brief embodiment. Ethical principles are but general rules for the guidance of human conduct and owe their significance to the developing society in which they arise. Our sense of duty is at bottom the 'herd instinct' which is found even among animals. In obedience to this instinct the interests of the individual are subordinated to those of the group. The authority of conscience is of purely social origin and does not require any reference to a supernatural power. There is not a single human act which society has not at one time approved and at another condemned. Though standards change, life seems to be meaningless without them and so the myth or morality is invented. And science tells us how the illusion is born. Morality is a working arrangement and its sanction is social necessity. As morality is a matter of convention, society has a right to alter or amend it, if it judges such modifications in the line of its interests. There is no God commanding us into a prescribed mode of behaviour. Ethical rules are objective only in the sense that they are independent of this or

sun loses 250 million tons of mass every minute, and there is no known source of replenishment which can supply new mass to it at even a small fraction of this rate. The sun possesses enough mass to continue to radiate at its present rate for 15 million million years. Actually the sun can look forward to a longer life than this, for as a star ages, the rate at which it radiates away energy and so the rate at which it spends its mass continually diminishes. When allowance is made for this senile tendency to parsimony, we find that stars such as our sun continue to shine for some hundreds of millions of millions of years' (*Astronomy and Cosmogony*, 2nd Ed., 1929, pp. 417-418).

that individual and not in the sense that they are unconditional commands or that they assume that 'good' is an unanalysable and ultimate quality.

The case for theism from the moral side is questioned. If
we argue from our moral aspirations to their ultimate fulfilment, we assume as a premise what requires to be proved,
viz. that the world is reasonable, that it is teleologically
ordered, and that is the very proposition we wish to prove.
Man's sense of duty as revealed in his conscience or his idea
of a perfect being does not warrant the necessity for a moral
being or God.

Spengler tells us that cultural units are comparable to
plant growths. They pass through the stages of growth,
blossoming and decay. Call it destiny or collective soul, an
immutable law governs the rise and fall of races and cul-
tures. History circles in as fixed orbits and with as predeter-
mined a movement as the stars themselves.

In the light of our present knowledge of man's history and
the vastness of the cosmos it seems anomalous, if not absurd, to imagine that the earth or the human species or any
historic individuals in it form the centre of things. Our earth
is parochial and our citizenship on it a triviality. Geocentrism
in cosmology and anthropocentrism in philosophy and Bud-
dhocentrism or Christocentrism in religion are on a par.[1]
Man is the centre of all things only in the sense, as Professor
Eddington has pointed out, that he stands midway in size

1 The late Professor Troeltsch said that ascribing a central position
to Jesus in the history of mankind 'accords with the idyllic littleness
and narrowness of the world picture of antiquity or the middle
ages, with its few thousand years of human history and its
expectation of the return of Christ at the conclusion of the world's
history. But to the man of today it is strange and unintelligible, for
his general instinctive presuppositions do not accord with it'
(quoted by Rev. J. S. Boys Smith in the *Modern Churchman*, October
1928, p. 386).

between an atom and a star. He is almost exactly as much larger than an atom as a star is larger than a man. To those whose minds are dazed by the new knowledge of science, the orthodox theologians seem to be hike men talking in their sleep.

The detailed structural affinities between man and the higher apes and the astounding evidence of the blood test prove a close consanguinity between man and the anthropoids. The animal character of man is clear from the facts of his origin, prenatal development, birth, growth, decline and death. We cannot dismiss these facts as an elaborate jest on the part of nature simply to pull the legs of biologists. It is fairly certain that we are descended from the apes or their cousins.

That man is an animal among animals is neither new nor profound. But what is new is that he is nothing more than an animal. Professor Watson's behaviourist psychology affirms it. For him, psychology is only physiology with this difference, that while physiology is interested in the functioning of parts of the animal--for example, its digestive system, its circulatory system, its nervous system--behaviourism is intensely interested in what the whole animal will do from morning to night and from night to morning.[1] Man is an 'assembled organic machine ready to run.'[2] As for the

1 *Behaviourism* (1925), p. II.
2 'I mean nothing very difficult in this. Take four wheels with tires, axles, differentials, gas engine, body: put them together and we have an automobile of a sort. The automobile is good for certain kinds of duties. Depending on its make-up, we use it for one kind of job or another. If it is a Ford it is good for going to the market, for running errands. If it is a Rolls Royce, it is good for pleasure riding. In a similar way this man, this organic animal, this John Doe, who, so far as parts are concerned, is made up of head, arms, hands, trunk, legs, feet, toes and nervous, muscular and glandular systems, who has no education, and is too old to get it, is good for certain jobs.'*Ibid.*, p. 216.

soul and consciousness of traditional psychology Watson has no patience with them.[1] Language is a series of muscle twitchings. Thought happens as any other event does. It is a motor organization just like tennis playing, a form of behaviour consisting of subvocal movements of speech muscles. It is only silent speaking, 'talking with concealed musculature'. Thorndike's experiments on rats in mazes claim to show 'scientifically' that intelligence is nothing more than stimulus and response. Emotions are visceral reactions. There is no such thing as will. Man's capacity is confined to the reception of sensory stimuli and automatic reactions to them. The latter are determined entirely by the strength of the stimuli and the powers of the muscles and nerves they control. Man is merely a nexus between stimuli and responses. He is the most cunning of the animals. Mind is the body and man is a machine. Our thoughts have no consequence, our wills no efficacy.

Watson's behaviourism is immensely popular with the ordinary mind since it offers a scientific confirmation of its favourite prejudice, that all men are created equal. The distinction of superior and inferior men is declared to be untenable and everything is now a question of social and cultural

1 'This dogma has been present in human psychology from earliest antiquity. No one has ever touched a soul, or has seen one in a test-tube, or has in any way come into relationship with it as he has with the other objects of his daily experience. Nevertheless, to doubt its existence is to become a heretic, and once might possibly even have led to the loss of one's head. Even today a man holding a public position dare not question it.' Again, 'from the time of Wundt on, consciousness becomes the keynote of psychology. It is the keynote of all psychologies today except behaviourism. It is a plain assumption just as unprovable, just as unapproachable as the old concept of the soul. And to the behaviourist the two terms are essentially identical so far as concerns their metaphysical implications.' *Ibid.*, pp. 4 and 5.

environment.[1] All modification of inborn nature is due to the acquiring of conditioned reflexes. Moral determinism appeals to all since it gives an excuse for whatever we want to do. Personality is a thing we can see and shape into whatever form we please. Man the unpredictable, the free soul is a myth. We can make a god out of glands, if only we set about it.

Though we have a different emphasis in the new psychology associated with the names of Freud and Jung, it also upholds a kind of psychological determinism. Watson complains that Freud has 'resorted to Voodooism instead of falling back upon his early scientific training.' Freud's fault is that he sets up great claims for psychology as a study of consciousness. At any given moment of our waking life we are aware of a steady stream of stimuli of great variety which reach us by means of different sense-organs. These sense impressions along with their associated thoughts and images make up our consciousness. Beyond the threshold of this consciousness we have the store of facts and impressions from which we can select any at our pleasure. Some parts of this are more accessible than others but with effort even the most concealed can be revived. This is called the fore-conscious region as distinct from the first, which is the conscious. There is also a third region of the mind, called the unconscious, where the apparently lost experiences of our lives, the impressions received in our childhood and

1 All healthy individuals start out equal. Quite similar words appear in our far-famed declaration of Independence. The signers of that document were nearer right than one might expect, considering their dense ignorance of psychology. They would have been strictly accurate had the "clause at birth" been inserted after the word "equal". It is what happens to individuals after birth that makes one a hewer of wood and a drawer of water, another a diplomat, a thief, a successful man or a far-famed scientist.' *Behaviourism*, 217.

infancy, are stored up. Though we cannot lift them into the region of the conscious by any effort of ordinary thinking, they yet profoundly modify our behaviour. Psychoanalysts attempt to get information about the buried complexes in the unconscious region by means of free association and dream study. For the psychoanalysts the unconscious is the real mind. The buried complexes and the repressed factors are the dynamic elements, the driving forces of the mind.[1]

The bearing of these doctrines on the religious issue is profound. If 'the mind, the spirit and the soul are manifestations of the living brain just as the flame is the manifest spirit of the burning candle', when the brain is destroyed there is an end of it all. The gradual evolution of the human species under the influence of natural forces shows that man is of a piece with the rest of nature. His religious intuitions are only the dreams of a being with an ape pedigree. so cautious a thinker as Darwin observed in his *Autobiography* (1887): 'But then arises the doubt, can the mind of man, which has, as I fully believe, been developed from a mind as low as that possessed by the lowest animals, be trusted when it draws such grand conclusions?' The human mind is a product of the struggle for existence. It is a tool-making, food-seeking instrument which learns the right adjustment by a process of trial and error. Its working is experimental, its devices are utilitarian and its views tentative.

According to psychoanalysis, conscious reasoning plays an inconsiderable part even in highly advanced beings. And the most fundamental activities of the human mind are non-rational. Thinking is more rationalization than reasoning. We adduce reasons in support of opinions held on grounds other that the reason adduced. The personality of man is the

1 It is hardly fair to suggest that behaviourism and psychoanalysis represent the dominant schools of psychology. Psychologists do not seem to be quite agreed on what psychology affirms.

play-ground of instincts which are kept in check by repressive influences arising partly from the illusions of religious beliefs. If the depths of the unconscious contain the dynamic drives, then ethical striving and religious aspiration are only illusions.

Reason is, in many cases, used to defend the action of deep-seated instincts and desires. Religious reactions to imaginary beings are psychological functions of our irrational nature. Religious ideas are consoling devices produced by the mechanisms of projection and regression and do not refer to any objective reality. God is but a function of the unconscious. Quite in conformity with the doctrine of pansexualism, it is argued that religion in its beginning is 'a mere misrepresentation of sex ecstasy', and even higher religions are full of idealized sex emotions. The mystic experiences are the projections of the morbid cravings of the psychologically perverted. When we look upon God as a loving father, we have a regressive idea. In infancy and childhood we look to our parents to supply our wants and protect us from harm. When we grow to maturity we imagine that, as the parental providence governs the home, a patriarch king who knows and cares for us all paternally provides that things shall ultimately end happily for his children.[1] So even when we are faced by the stern facts of life, we delude ourselves into a state of sentimental security. Though you slay me, yet will I trust in you. We are grown-up infants and God is a sort of 'wet-nurse' to humanity.

The idea of God, which, the anthropologists say, has had

1 Cp. Jung: 'The idea of the masculine creative deity is the derivation, analytically and historically psychologic, of the "Father Image," and aims, above all, to replace the discarded infantile father transference in such a way that for the individual the passing from the narrow circle of the family into the wider circle of human society may be simpler or made easier.' *Psychology of the Unconscious* (1922), p. 29.

an unbroken sway from the most primitive ages of human history, is thus given a psychological explanation. Religious phenomena like the dread of God, the shame of the sinner and the feeling for salvation are similarly explained. Freud is definite that religion is an illusion incident to a particular stage in the psychological development of mankind. Society is in the process of casting it off, as its men of intelligence are rapidly outgrowing the stage of intellectual immaturity to which it belongs.[1]

At the moment there is great insistence on the psychological approach to religion. Though Wundt was the founder of the modern study of the psychology of religion, its chief representatives are from America, William James and Stanley Hall, Starbuck and Leuba, Coe and Pratt. Contributions of considerable value have come from Britain also.[2] Conclusions hostile to the reality of the religious object are asserted especially by those who are under the influence of the Freudian School. Leuba in his *A Psychological Study of Religion* contends that religious experience is a mere subjective state and its implication is an illusion very insistent, perhaps, but nevertheless, an illusion. The aberrant and the uneducated mistake the dreams which spring from below for the voice from above. The voice that reaches us from the heavens is obviously a human voice.[3] Its utterances are not messages

1 M. Reinach argues on independent grounds that the history of religion is nothing else than a history of illusions and errors which have played an important, though at times mischievous, part in human affairs, and the democracy of the future will have little to do with it. *Orpheus*, E.T. (1909), sec. 102.
2 Selbie: The *Psychology of Religion* (1924). Thouless: *An Introduction to the Psychology of Religion* (1924). Pym: *Psychology and the Christian Life* (1921).
3 Cp. Thomas Hobbes: 'To say (God) hath spoken to him in a dream is no more than to say he dreamed that God spoke to him. To say he hath seen a vision or heard a voice is to say that he dreamed between sleeping and waking.' *Leviathan*, Bk. 3, Ch. xxxii. Quoted

from visiting angels but clearly human postulates made by despairing souls for sheer self-preservation. When life around chills native zeal and integrity, supernatural assurances become popular. The feeling of certainty accompanying mystic visions is of doubtful value when the visions often conflict with one another. If the function of religion is to restore confidence when we are face to face with grave crises and are afraid of what is in store for us, then it works through suggestion and imagination. In the East and the West techniques calculated to develop the sensorial imagination have been fairly common among religious groups of a type.[1] If we fix our attention on the thought of a particular object, say the flames of hell, we actually feel after a time the scorching heat on the palms of our hands. It is through this method that we have seen in the course of our progress not only God but his enemy the Devil with his brood of witches and ghosts. 'All things are possible to him that believeth.' We can work ourselves up to the pitch of enlightenment.

Psychologists are interested in the discovery of the conditions that lead to the acceptance of fancies as facts but not in their truth value. We do not debate the truth of a detected illusion. As we describe the conditions by which *sati*, or witchcraft was once believed in by detailing scriptural authority, the weight of great names, the credulity of the common mind, etc., so do psychologists tell us about the conditions which favoured the acceptance of religion.[2]

in Barrat Brown and Harvey: *The Naturalness of Religion* (1928), p. 88.
1 The higher contemplative mystics both in India and Europe looked askance at ecstasies and dreams, visions and auditions.
2 The psychological approach to religion is not confined to psychologists. Mr Middleton Murry in his book on *God* (1929) says: 'God does not exist; but we shall never be able to do without Him, unless we know in ourselves the reasons why He was created.' According to him, the greatest seers like Jesus discover not the

Religion offers some compensation for the natural defects of the human spirit in the world and is an escape from the transiency, the uncertainty, the meaninglessness of a world to one where these defects are overcome by the presence of a God. In essence and actuality religion is the attempt of man to express his notion of a perfect being, a perfect world and the means by which he can be redeemed from the fact to experience of pure ideality. Gods are human beings as they would wish themselves to be.

Man's helplessness in the presence of nature makes him look up to supernatural sources of power and blessing. We adopt religion for its practical efficiency and not for getting into relation with the supreme spirit as the embodiment of the highest perfection.[1]

The French School of sociologists under the lead of Emile Durkheim emphasizes the part played by the social group

nature of God, but of themselves.

1 Dr Bouquet writes: 'A great deal of what is dealt with as religion in comparative text-books really seems to be primitive science, that is to say, attempts to account for the order and operations of a visible but pluralistic universe, rather than at establishing unselfish and disinterested relations with the one good god. Animism in its lower or higher forms is only a description of the forces of nature. The spirits, demons or deities, to employ Professor Leuba's phrase, are *used*. Human interest is for the most part secular. There is little or no devotion to the deity as an end in himself, as the embodiment of the highest moral and spiritual values. Sacrifices are offered by the ancient farmer for the same object that the modern one employs chemical manure and no other. It is precisely for this reason that in the famous dialogue *Euthyphro* finds it so difficult to answer Socrates when he asks, "What is the good of the cultus?" because Socrates has already cut away the connection between the gods and natural phenomena. The Parisian Catholic undergraduate makes a votive offering to the Immaculate Virgin for the success in his examination where the Cambridge Protestant merely employs a good coach. But is there any real difference in the dominant interest?' (Bouquet: *The Christian Religion and its Competitors To-day* (1925), p.14.)

in the origin and growth of religious conceptions. Religion
has been used from the beginning for carrying on the social
organization and conserving the secular values, for religious
sanctions seem to be more effective for keeping men loyal
and law-abiding than prisons and police courts. Religion is
the device to give an emotional stimulus to the socially
beneficent activities. As the social group is something over
and beyond the individuals whom it includes, its forms
possess for the individual a relatively independent or objective character. A typically social product like language is
not framed by the individual but is absorbed by him and yet
language is only a human product. Similarly religious belief
arises from the interaction of many minds and is only as
objective or as illusory as language itself. God, according to
this view, is not so much the projection of the cravings of
the individual as the product of society. Our sense of God
is due to the pressure of society on us.[1] An unapprehended
God is invoked in support of current ethics.

4. *Comparative religion*

As if the disorganization were not sufficiently decisive,
comparative religion and higher criticism which are relatively recent growths are making their own contributions.
Comparative religion enables us to study faiths other than
our own without condescension or contempt. It traces the
history of our ideas of God from the simple conceptions of
our remote ancestors who first formulated the experience
of the great environing mystery down to the living faiths.
Every mortal thing seems to have been deified. Powers of
nature, sun, stars, fire, water and earth, generative energies
were all made into gods. Hero-worship and human apotheosis

1 For an effective criticism of this theory, see Clement Webb: *Group
Theories of Religion and the Religion of the Individual* (1916).

added to the number. Our mental pictures of God are as varied as we are. The scepticism of Xenophanes, the first great student of comparative religion in Europe, is receiving daily confirmation.[1]

Anthropology, which moves with delight among golden boughs and totems, divine kings and heavenly twins, proves the lowly ancestry of many of our living gods. Some of the practices that have come down to us in the name of religion, anthropology traces to primitive ritual. The primitive peoples used to eat their gods in order to strengthen themselves and perhaps the Christian practice of eating Christ's body and drinking his blood is not unrelated to this old ritual. The stories recorded in religious literature are by no means divinely revealed, and if we still cling to them it only shows that errors die hard.

No god seems to be final and no religion perfect. There was a time when vast temples were built for Moloch and Baal, mighty in their own day with crowds of worshippers, gods who uttered commands and prohibitions interpreting which numerous priests spent their long lives. To doubt their power and presence was to be condemned as a heretic and thousands suffered death and persecution, but who is so poor today as to recognize them, much less do them

1 'Yes, and if oxen and horses and lions had hands and could paint with their hands and produce works of art as men do, horses would paint the forms of the gods like horses, and oxen like oxen, and make their bodies in the images of their several kinds! The Ethiopians make their gods black and snub- nosed, the Thracians say theirs have blue eyes and red hair.' Burnet: *Early Greek Philosophy*, 3rd ed. (1920), p. 119. Spinoza says: 'A triangle, if only it had the power of speech, would say that God is eminently triangular, and a circle would say that the Divine Nature is eminently circular, and in this way each thing would ascribe its own attributes to God and make itself like unto God, while all else would appear to it deformed.' *Correspondence of Spinoza*, ed. by Wolf (1928), p. 288.

reverence? What has happened to the Egyptian Ra and the Babylonian Shamash, to Isis and Ashtoreth, Zeus and Athene, Janus and Vesta, who ranked a few millenniums back with Yahveh himself, gods mentioned with fear and trembling and believed in by millions? Their day is done and their altars smoke no more. We can only smile at the naïveté of those who assume that while all other gods will pass away their own will abide for ever. The broken idols of the past seem to have no lessons for them. The history of religion is the record of the conflicts of contradictory systems, each of them claiming dogmatic finality and absolute truth, a claim made apparently absurd by the plurality of claimants.

If comparative religion tells us anything it is that every religion is moulded by fallible and imperfect human instruments, and so long as it is alive it will be changing. Spirit is growth, and even while we are observing one side of its life, the wheel is turning and the shadow of the past is twining itself into it.

A pathetic confidence in man as the type and exemplar of the universe led to the crude theories of animism which endowed almost anything animate and inanimate with human attributes. We credited stones with life and trees with passion. Even when we rose to clearer conceptions of human personality, the anthropomorphic tendency did not desert us. We endowed our gods with human passions and made them thunder forth wrath and vengeance for every trumpery misdeed. There is an assumption that the mind of man corresponds to cosmic reality.

5. *Higher criticism*

The scriptures which affirm the absolutism of religions and announce themselves as infallible, such as the Vedas and the Tipiṭaka, the Bible and the Qu'ran, are treated today

in the same critical and historical spirit as the Dialogues of
Plato or the Inscriptions of Aśoka. They are all human
documents written by human hands and liable to error. Not
merely religious scriptures but codes of custom and laws of
society, all these are supposed to have come from the gods.
Every people, Jew and Gentile, Greek and barbarian, attribute the first institution of their laws to the gods. We know
now that they all originated in the discordant passions and
the groping reason of human beings. Religious scriptures
are no exception. They are the conventions and devices
which seers of insight found it necessary to lay down to
enable men to live and live more abundantly. The scriptures
are products of history and some of their parts are forgeries,
or at least not so old as they were supposed to be. The case
for verbal inspiration is not seriously put forward. We cannot bring ourselves to believe that any of these scriptures is
the word of god. The higher and lower criticism of the
Christian scriptures tells us that the Bible contains elements
of myth, legend and floating tradition and exhibits a process
of growth with many levels of development. It is not to be
mistaken for a   historical narrative. A critical attitude is
fairly common among the thoughtful Hindus and Buddhists.
Their sacred books are analysed and their parts related to
their epochs. The Vedas are a literature rather than a single
book, containing writings of varied style, date and value.
Their inspired character does not imply divine dictation or
the super-session of the writer's normal powers. The different sections are held to contain the hopes and beliefs, the
fears and the imaginations of successive generations of
men. Their value is not determined by their hoary antiquity
or alleged divine dictation, but only by the nature of their
contents. Kang Yu We startled the Chinese world by pro-
claiming that the entire texts which tradition declared that
Confucius arranged and published as a holy inheritance for

the future were deliberate forgeries. His work on *The Reform
of Confucius* attempts to prove that the old writings of Confucius were not traditional and were not edited by him, but
that he had invented them all himself in order to lend an
historical background to his teachings, which were revolu-
tionary for his time.[1] Every revealed scripture seems to
contain in it a large mass of elements which scientific criticism
and historical knowledge require us to discard and there is
no reason why we should accept it at all. Truth is greater
than any revelation.

6. *Proofs for theism*

The so-called proofs for the existence of God are all
defective, if we mean by proof a demonstration as compelling to a rational being as the proof of a mathematical proposition. The ontological argument starts from the idea of
God as an absolutely perfect being. Such an absolutely
perfect being must exist, for non-existence would be an
imperfection and a more perfect being which exists could
be imagined. But such a proposition is opposed to the first
principle with which the argument started. Therefore God
exists. Kant points out that existence is not an attribute like
goodness or wisdom and cannot be involved in the conception of any idea in our minds. There are many things which
exist only in our imagination. We have an idea of a perfect
circle, but that does not mean that a perfect circle exists. The
idea of God is no exception and God's existence cannot be
deduced from the conception of God.

The causal argument is not more satisfactory. It proceeds
on a series of untenable assumptions: that the causal concept is valid, that it applies not merely to parts of the world
but to the world as a whole, that we can have a first cause,

1 Richard Wilhelm: *The Soul of China*, E.T. (1928), p. 77.

which somehow is an exception to the law of succession and that the first cause is God. An infinite series of causes and effects is not impossible to conceive. If causality is interpreted as meaning that the contingent implies the necessary, it begs the whole question. We take the world as created and then argue that it must have had a creator. If God is conceived as infinite, eternal and necessary, it is possible to look upon the world itself as infinite, eternal and necessary. Again, causality relates happenings in nature and we cannot by means of it go outside of nature and reach the creative source of things. The given world is a contingent fact. It is conceivable that there may be no world at all or only an irrational and fortuitous one. It is therefore conceivable that there may be no God. At best, for causality, God is only a contingent being. But the God of religion is an absolute being in no sense fortuitous. We have already seen that the moral argument fails since attempts are made to account for the development of the moral sense by a process of natural selection.

The argument from design is profoundly affected by the development of the theory of biological evolution. The question of the purpose of human life is irrelevant. Why should human life alone have a purpose and not animal life? The universe does not seem to have any definite purpose which it is attempting to realize. To be born, to live, to die and to begin all over again, until all things have disappeared as though nothing had ever been accomplished, such is the process of the universe, such its destiny. Even if the world lends itself to the realization of purposes, we cannot infer the reality of a purposing mind. We are thrown back on a naturalistic view with its insistence on mechanical determination, the insignificance of man, the irrelevance of personal immortality, the repudiation of personal freedom and the cosmic sanctions for moral standards and indifference

to a responsive spirit. While the intellectuals question the
foundations of religion and make it difficult even for the
religious-minded to entertain the larger hope, the idealists
dispute its practical value and efficiency.

7. *Practical inefficiency of religion*

By postulating a perfect god who is responsible for the
government of the universe, religion seems to take away the
edge from ethical striving. For Plato, the Good which is the
True and the Real shines everlastingly like the sun in the
high heaven. Man, dwelling in the cave of his ignorance,
bound in the chains of his stupidity and selfishness, takes
the shadows thrown upon the farthest walls by the light of
his own passions as realities, knows not that the Good is
there, the eternal source of all light and life. If his eyes are
cleared up, he will see the Real. There is nothing to fight
against except the doubts in his mind and the shadows of
his errors. What ought to be, already is. 'The consummation
of the infinite end,' says Hegel, 'consists merely in removing
the illusion which makes it seem yet unaccomplished. The
good, the absolutely good, is eternally accomplishing itself
in the world; and the result is that it need not wait upon us,
but is already by implication as well as in full actuality
accomplished.'[1] Religion is an *isness* and not an oughtness,
as Baron von Hügel loved to repeat. It is concerned with
what is actually environing and penetrating us and we are
saved if we recognize it. Religion insists on the apprehension of what already is and not on the achievement of what
is not. The realization of goodness is not a future contingency but an eternal and necessary reality. Such a view of
religion as adoration and not creativity makes us insensitive
to the woes of the world in which we live. By divorcing

1 Wallace's *Logic of Hegel*, E.T. (1892), pp. 351- 352.

eternity from time, spiritual realization from earthly life, we kill the only eternity of which we have knowledge, the eternity characteristic of intense living.

Salvation is interpreted as having a reference to the next world and not the building of the kingdom of God on earth. Religion is more world-fleeing than world-seeking or world-penetrating.

Religion asks us to separate the things of God from those of Caesar. Its principles should not be allowed to interfere with the free play of selfish impulse in a secular order If religion asks us to adopt brotherly love, avoid force, disregard wealth, the religious people seem to emphasize war, success and efficiency. Such a judicial separation between the two means the degrading of both the secular and the sacred. Religion is not doctrinal obedience or ritualistic display, but is self-sacrificing love and redemptive might. Those who tell us that we are not a nation of Christs and it is no use trying to imitate his example and seek martyrdom by disbanding our armies and scrapping our navies, that religion is not meant for practice, are helping to destroy religion altogether.

In the depths of religion there is ever a negation of life, a renunciation carried to the point of death itself. Great gods --a number of them and in all parts of the world--are said to have died for us and we are now called upon to die for them.[1] 'Know ye not that so many of us as were baptized unto Jesus Christ were baptized unto his death.' Paul's strictures on sex, expressed in the well-known words, 'For I would that all men were even as I myself', that is, celibate and continent, finds its parallel in other religious scriptures. Religious teachers the world over seem to reproach God for making us warm-blooded and not simply sexless neuters,

1 Sir James Frazer: *The Dying God* (1912).

bodiless ghosts. Human nature is regarded as a vile thing that must be hacked and twisted out of its shape in order to become endurable in the eyes of God. Religious men seem to have developed unduly the instinct for being unhappy. They seem to have a perverted ingenuity for finding out new contents for sin.[1] Religion with its 'Thou shalt renounce' is the direct opposite of the new commandment, 'Thou shalt enjoy', on which all our major and minor prophets are agreed.[2]

Religion believes that all needful truth is given to man and there is no need for further enquiry and search. It breeds the delusion that could inspire Tertullian's boast that the Christian mechanic will give a ready answer to problems that puzzled the wisest philosophers. Religion is suspicious of enquiry and criticism. The fear of knowledge is as old as the Garden of Eden. Prometheus who dared to steal knowledge and reveal it to men was chained to a rock. The story of Faust testifies to the wide-spread belief in the alliance between the men of knowledge and the powers of darkness. When we assume that we have the beginning and the end of all spiritual wisdom and direction for all time and all mankind, it becomes our duty to impose it on others by force

1 Bertrand Russell says: 'The qualities which make for happiness vary inversely in proportion to the amount of a man's religious belief.' Reply to Mr. Wood, *Literary Guide*, March 1929.
2 The new attitude to life is well brought out in the following extract from Professor Bateson's Presidential Address at the British Association in August 1914. 'Man is just beginning to know himself for what he is--a rather long-lived animal with great powers of enjoyment if he does not deliberately forego them. Hitherto superstition and mythical ideas of sin have predominantly controlled these powers. Mysticism will not die out; for these strange fancies knowledge is no cure, but their forms may change and mysticism as a force for the suppression of joy is happily losing its hold on the modern world. Returning to a freer or, if you will, simpler conception of life and death, the coming generations are determined to get more out of this world than their forefathers did.'

of arms or its subtler substitutes. In the name of religion men and women were put to death for not believing that evil spirits inhabit human bodies, for misunderstanding the mystery of the Trinity, for doubting the verbal inspiration of the scriptures and such other innocent departures from orthodox doctrines. Spiritual absolutism is responsible for the judicial murders of some of the divinest figures of antiquity. It exalts orthodoxy above holiness of life.

While the economic and political forces are bringing people closer together, religions are doing their utmost to maintain the inner barriers that divide and antagonize peoples. To the Hindus the Buddhists are heretics, even as the early Christians were atheists to the polytheistic Romans. Catholics would sooner see one an atheist than an Anglican. Religion engenders a great love for a great hate. Every religion has its popes and crusades, idolatry and heresy-hunting. The cards and the game are the same, only the names are different. Men are attacked for affirming what men are attacked for denying. Religious piety seems to destroy all moral sanity and sensitive humanism. It is out to destroy other religions, not for the sake of social betterment or world peace, but because such an act is acceptable to one's own jealous god. The more fervent the worship the greater seems to be the tyranny of names. By a fatal logic, the jealous god is supposed to ordain the destruction of those who worship him under names. The view that God has entrusted his exclusive revelation to any one prophet, Buddha, Christ, or Mohammad, expecting all others to borrow from him or else to suffer spiritual destitution, is by no means old-fashioned.[1]

1 The Bishop of London in his book on *Why am I a Christian?* published in the year 1929, says: 'That one little candle was put in our hands by the Child at Bethlehem, and it is the only candle there is in the world. I can say this, because I have been round the world, and have seen at close quarters the other religions of the world. They have certainly got no candle to light them on their way.'

Nothing is so hostile to religion as other religions. We have developed a kind of patriotism about religion, with a code and a flag, and a hostile attitude towards other men's codes and creeds. The free spirits who have the courage to repudiate the doctrine of chosen races and special prophets and plead for a free exercise of thought about God are treated as outcasts. No wonder that even the sober are sometimes tempted to think that the only way to get rid of religious fear, conceit and hatred is to do away with all religion. The world would be a much more religious place if all religions were removed from it.[1]

8. *Religion and politics*

The political side of modern civilization is derived from the Greek City State. With all its incomparable values the Greek mind had not a clear perception of the distinction between politics and religion, public duty and individual perfection. To it, Athens and Athene, later Caesar and God, were identical terms. The individual's highest good is in the service of the State. The Greek thinkers tried to distinguish between the good man and the good citizen and struggled to base the State on moral foundations. But they did not realize fully the claims of the individual soul and so identified the Church and the State. It is true that Socrates met his death in obedience to conscience and Aristotle allowed a few favoured individuals an inner life remote from the concerns of the City State. But all these fade into insignificance by the side of the great tradition that a man who does not participate in the civic life is either a god or a beast.

1 In one of Strindberg's plays, a nurse who is an ardent Christian seeks to convert a captain who is an atheist. She talks to him about the love of God. He replies, 'It is a strange thing that you no sooner speak of God and love than your voice becomes hard and your eyes fill with hate.'

When the Greek tradition got mixed up with the Eastern ideals of loving enemies, despising riches, taking no thought for the morrow and paying more attention to another world than this, confusion resulted which has not yet cleared up.

Religion today is a branch of statecraft, a plaything of politics. Our sense of worship is shifted to our country, which to most of us is a sacred symbol with its own creeds and ritual, demanding sacrificial living. The last war gave a pointed domonstration of the feeble claims of religion as compared with the imperious demands of patriotism.[1]

Where religion has not been herself the oppressor upholding darkness by violence, she lends her authority to the oppressors and sanctifies their pretences. That religion is worth little, if the conscience of its followers is not disturbed when war clouds are hanging over us all and industrial conflicts are threatening social peace. Religion has weakened man's social conscience and moral sensitivity by separating the things of God from those of Caesar. The socially oppressed are seduced by hopes of final adjustment in a celestial fatherland, a sort of post-mortem brotherhood. No wonder religion is condemned as a piece of capitalistic propaganda. The workers and wage-earners have come to discover themselves and are demanding an opportunity for a fuller and deeper life. Anxious as they are for a new social order based on justice and creative love, they stand out of

1 It is sometimes asserted that religion saved the Middle Ages from the curse of nationalism. See, however, Dr Coulton: 'One of the first steps of the newborn University of Paris, in the twelfth century, was to divide its students into nations, just as Bologna University separated them at perhaps an earlier date. At Oxford, nationalism was none the less baneful for dividing the Englishman, not from the continent, but from his fellow-Englishman born north or south of the Trent, or from the citizens of Oxford itself. Dr. Rashdall was probably right in surmising that there may be no single yard of its High Street which has not at some time run with a student's blood.' *Quarterly Review*, July 1931, p. 108.

religious organizations which preach contentment and *status quo*. The social revolutionaries contend that religion blocks the way to all progress. It is a bourgeois prejudice and superstition which must be rooted out at any cost.[1] Spiritually an external or ceremonial religion is good for nothing; materially it has failed to stop the strong man from exploiting his weaker brother; psychologically it has developed traits which are anti-social and anti-scientific. As for its aesthetic and meta-physical satisfactions, they can easily be fostered by the spread of science and art, morality and social service and a living faith in human brotherhood. Communism is the new religion; Lenin is its prophet and science its holy symbol.[2] Karl Marx's theory of communism transplanted into the mystic soil of Russia has become a religion practising sanctified methods for its propagation. The active agencies of the communistic parties, the Red Army, the schools, the press and the platform, are struggling to rid the country of all religion. The driving force of Bolshevism is faith, mysticism and willingness to sacrifice even unto death. It is moved by dreams of a new heaven and a new earth even as were the believers in Jewish apocalypse. If the socialist declares, 'We are not opposed to religion. Neither are we supporting it. We are simply cutting out religion. Our socialist idea of a universal brotherhood is more important than God or Jesus Christ or any

1 'Under the head of combating bourgeois prejudices and superstitions, the first place is to be taken by the fight against religion, a fight which must be carried on with all requisite tact and all caution, especially among those sections of workers in whose daily life religion has hitherto been deeply rooted.' *Towards a Communist Programme* (1921), sec 2 ff.

2 On the walls of the Moscow club-house are found such placards: 'Nobody knows when the world was made, but everyone knows that a new world was born in October 1918.' 'Take the gods out of the skies and remove capitalism from the earth. Make way for the youth of communism.'

religion,'[1] we must confess that he is more truly religious than most worshippers of God or Christ. It is no answer to say that these admirable ideas are found in ancient scriptures, for it is equally beyond doubt that the official exponents of religion dismissed them as too ideal for an unideal world. Religion has been given a fairly long trial and the socialist seeks for an opportunity to experiment with his new creed. He asks for a fair chance before he is judged. When he argues that if only socialism had, as organized religion has, huge establishments, temples, mosques and churches-- whole-time paid agents, thousands of honorary workers, millions of rank and file, it would put to shame the leaders of religion by making the world ring from end to end with the courageous gospel of fight against poverty and disease, war and crime, oppression and exploitation of every kind, we may or may not agree with his hope, we may dissent from his drastic methods of reform, but we cannot deny the force of the accusation that organized religion with all its resources, actual and potential, has failed. If it is still tolerated, it is due to ignorance and indifference, and we cannot afford any more to be either ignorant or indifferent.[2]

The age has lost the living sense of the truth which it once held. The spirit which revolted against divine rights and sanctified tyrannies in politics, which protested against the inequity of social abuses and established conventions, which, in the Reformation, expressed itself in the claim to determine the sense of the scripture and ritual, which gave to modern Europe in the Renaissance the free curiosity and the intellectual scrutiny of the Greek mind and the practical sense of equity of the Roman, is today expressing itself in

1 Quoted from Basil Matthews: *The Commonwealth of Youth* (1928), p. 65.
2 For an analysis of the present tendencies and future prospects of religion, especially in the Christian world, see Joad: *The Present and Future of Religion* (1930).

the demand for the sway of science and social idealism. Here is the truth of things which does not depend on any doubtful scripture or fallible human authority but which all who have the intellectual power to observe and honesty to judge will accept. A life of joy and happiness is possible only on the basis of knowledge and science.

9. *General unrest*

The present confusion and disorganization are not confined to Europe and America. Though there are fundamental distinctions between the East and the West, the striking feature at the moment is the extent to which the cultural life of the peoples is getting unified. Turkey is turning its back on Islam for the sake of national efficiency and progress.[1] What is true of Turkey is more or less true of other Moslem states, Persia, Egypt and Afghanistan. In China and India venerable structures built by the patience and effort of unnumbered generations are attacked from all sides. Religion is set down as the cause of our intellectual and national bondage, of our failure and lack of vitality. Many of the Indian leaders are convinced that orthodox fundamentalism, which is still the creed of the majority of the people, has cost us a lot in struggle and suffering, in stunted manhood and deformed spiritual growth. When we find men of undoubted piety range themselves against common sense and scientific knowledge, against the dictates of humanity and the demands of justice, all in blind obedience to laws whose infallibility is a myth, our leaders are getting tired of religion and think it is time we part with it. The country wants today not so much salvation from sin as social

1 Mustapha Kemal said in a speech to the convention of the people's party in the autumn of 1927, 'The provision in the constitution that Turkey is a Moslem state is a compromise destined to be done away with at the first opportunity.'

betterment which will transform the mass of people who are ill-fed, ill-clothed and ill-housed into a free community of well-regulated families, living not in luxury, but in moderate comfort with no fierce or unhealthy competition. Freedom is the rallying cry. It is inevitable that the challenge of freedom means often a rude handling of old loyalties and a hasty dismissal of venerable beauty in symbol and ceremony. But freedom asks for its price.

10. *The present need*

The present unrest, it is clear, is caused as much by the moral ineffectiveness of religion, its failure to promote the best life, as by the insistent pressure of new knowledge on traditional beliefs. There are a few intellectual snobs with whom it is a sign of accomplishment to ridicule religion. To care for religion is to be old-fashioned; to be critical of it is to be in the movement. A reading democracy which is necessarily imperfectly educated feels it its duty to reject traditional control when it does not understand the reasons for its claims. Scepticism does not cost us much. It is faith that requires courage nowadays. Besides these denying spirits we have the much larger number who have out-grown the faith but are unwilling to break away for fear of the pharisees. Our concern, however, is with those who find themselves while willing, yet incapable of belief. Their souls have grown more sensitive and so their difficulties are deeper and their questions more insistent. Their doubt is an expression of piety, their protest a kind of loyalty. In the depths of the human soul lies something which we ration-alize as the search for truth, a demand for justice, a passion for righteousness. This striving for truth and justice is an essential part of our life. We do not need an Aristotle to tell us that the pursuit of knowledge is our highest duty and the only permissible excesses are the excesses of the intellect. The disorders due to the disturbance of our minds are preferable to the bondage of the human spirit. This is not the first time in the history of the world that the age was felt to be transitional and religion held to be untenable. It is said-- though I cannot vouch for its authenticity--that the first words uttered by Adam to Eve as they stepped out of the gate in the garden of Eden were, 'We live in times of transition.' Every period is one of transition. Through discord and confusion lies progress. It *happens* in the sub-human level; it is *willed* in the human. The spirit of man can change the direction of the march. The invention of what is needful at a particular moment, of the device which will help us to adapt ourselves to the new situation has the same significance as the development at the right time of the new variation which alone is adapted to the altered conditions. At a time when humanity is struggling to rise from a state of subjection to authority to one in which perfect self- determination is possible, we need the assistance of creative minds. The prophet souls and not the priest minds, the original men of understanding and not the mechanical imitators of the inherited habits are needed to help our wandering generation to fashion a goal for itself. Prophecy is insight. It is vision. It is anticipating experience. It is seeing the present so fully as to foresee the future.

CHAPTER II

Substitutes for Religion

THOSE who are assailed by religious doubts are devising several ways to escape from the present confusion. In the absence of any definite direction from the leaders, they are taking to crude and amazing cults. They are finding substitutes for religion in Theosophy, Anthroposophy, Christian Science, New Thought and such other adventures of the human mind. But the more thoughtful are not satisfied with these sentimental substitutes and their constructive proposals range from dogmatic denial to dogmatic affirmation.

I. *Naturalistic atheism*

Lucretius, who took refuge in the high indifference of atoms storming through the void according to eternal law, has many followers today.[1] It is no use exaggerating the extent of the reaction against crude materialism. It still remains the belief to which most people tend when they begin to reflect, and many who are fascinated by the conquests of science do not leave it.[2] For the emancipated intellectuals--I hate the word highbrows--the universe is the product of unconscious, mechanistic energy towards which we cannot have any feeling of reverence or worship. Man is essentially a part of nature, and though his peculiarity is

1 'My own view of religion is that of Lucretius. I regard it as a disease born of fear and as a source of untold misery to the human race' (Bertrand Russell: *Rationalist Press Association Annual*, 1930).
2 See the article on 'Scientific Humanism' by Julian Huxley, *Contemporary Review*, July 1931.

that he thinks, it does not make him a privileged being. He is but a specific type among living forms, and it is quite possible that nature may produce a more exciting type with vastly superior powers, or extinguish all life. Whatever may happen, nature is not likely to be deeply stirred. Human beings are an accident, and they will shortly disappear in the cosmic upheaval which is destined to destroy this universe. We have felt in our pulses the pain and misery of the world, but the love and grace of God are only our dreams. The silence that answered Jesus' prayer in the garden of Gethsemane to spare the cup of sorrow and shame is all that the noblest of us can expect in the hour of doom. We are in the grip of nature, which did not ask us whether we would like to be. It gave us corruptible bodies and suffering hearts without asking whether or not we would like to have them. It selected for us the scene of our existence, the conditions of our life, and left us to discover what they are, but yet is quite ready to crush us if we ignorantly cross its purposes. If we scrutinize the truth of religion, this central fact comes out. In Christianity, for example, the salvation of man is mythical. The human individual, who is a victim at once of his own blindness and order of nature, cannot be saved. Since man cannot face this truth, he invents a divine force transcending the careless chaos, from whom salvation comes as an act of grace on the ground of pity. Strictly speaking, we cannot and do not deserve to be saved. In the spirit of Lucretius, Bertrand Russell exhorts us to give up the gorgeous consolations of religion and those dreadful thoughts of the invisible which had incited men to kill themselves and kill others. According to him, the future religion will consist of two parts: a worship of the ideal conceived merely as the ideal, and a worship of the actual merely as actual or existent. The first involves the goodness, but not the existence, of its object, and the second involves the existence, but not the goodness, of its object.[1] We must accept the universe as it is and expect nothing from it. It is more manly to believe in the actual and suffer it than revel in the absurd.

We cannot deny that there is an element of sublimity in this stoicism, which submits to the great laws of existence, necessity or chance, without inventing trivial consolations. But it is difficult to maintain an attitude of noble despair to an uncaring universe. From sublime stoicism to neo-paganism the transition is easy. If the universe is a huge machine, which goes on its way regardless of the hopes and fears of humanity, and if the human individual is but a sorry accident looked at from the cosmic perspective, there is no reason why we should add to the sum of human misery by denying ourselves the few precarious joys which life offers. While the stoic teaching is too modest in its promises and too difficult in its practice to attract large numbers, neo-paganism, which justifies and encourages the major temptations of the age, has multitudes of followers. But both stoicism and neo-paganism are ways of escape, devices adopted when we lose our faith in life. The one saving grace of life is, as Seneca said, though it has but a single entrance it has many exits and one can always choose the time and manner of one's going out.[2] Any moment we feel that the game is not worth the candle, we may return God, in the words of Ivan Karamazov, 'the entrance ticket'. In darkness there will be no disappointment. Pessimism is a strangely powerful creed, whose immense vogue is an indication that we are sick with despair. When Diogenes found the Greek liberties disappear under the Macedonians, he warned his

1 'The Essence of Religion', *Hibbert Journal*, October 1912.
2 Epictetus bade his disciples remember that after all the door is open; like boys at play when we are tired of the game we can decide to end it, and while this alternative remains, it is not fair to continue and complain.

compatriots to fear nothing, desire nothing, possess nothing, for then no malicious ingenuity of life can disappoint us.

Art and reflection are sometimes suggested as substitutes for religion. Russell exhorts us to 'cherish, ere yet the blow falls, the lofty thoughts that ennoble our little day'. In the age of Buddha in India and the past days of paganism in Europe, when the old sanctions and faiths were attacked, men sought and found in philosophy the consolations which traditional religion could no longer offer. If disinterested reflection reveals to us the hideous thing life is, we may at least dream a little and build within ourselves a shrine where we can worship our ideals. We can thus find imaginary satisfactions for our unfulfilled desires, and play in fancy the roles we have missed in life. Art becomes a sort of mental self-indulgence, a distraction that takes away the horrid taste of the real. The intellectual aristocrats of our time profess a creed which is a blend of the different views of naturalism, stoicism, paganism and pessimism.

As a substitute for religion the stoic-pagan creed is rather weak. We cannot live if we do not recover our faith in life and the universe. It is true that we should oppose a passionless disillusion to the lies which cripple our minds. Rationality is essential, but so is religion if disintegration is to be averted. It may be that religion does not rest on purely speculative grounds. But it is not enough to be logical. We have also to be reasonable. Loyalty to life requires us to know the creative mystery and serve it to the best of our power. If we feel ourselves to be unwanted in the universe, we may try to cover up our inner crisis by family attachments or civic duties, but the essential loneliness of the soul is worse than solitary confinement. The felt solitude of the human soul, its strange isolation in an incomprehensible world, breaks the vital rhythm that sustains the world. The prophets of disillusion call upon us to seek truth, create beauty and achieve goodness. We cannot strive for these ideals if we are convinced that we are unimportant accidents in a universe which is indifferent, if not hostile, to them. If the nature of the world is malign, our duty is to defy.

It is only fair to ask where the urge to do these noble things comes from. If the strivings after truth, goodness and beauty are a part of the cosmic plan, then it is not unfriendly to us. Russell admits, 'It is a strange mystery that nature, omnipotent but blind, in the revolution of her secular hurryings through the abysses of space has brought forth at last a child, subject to her power, but gifted with sight and knowledge of good and evil, with the capacity of judging all the works of his unthinking mother'.[1] We cannot leave this stupendous fact as a 'strange mystery. We set apart nature as a flat and lifeless background of irresponsible energy against which the drama of human life is played, and then insist on the contrast. If science teaches us anything, it is the organic nature of the universe. We are one with the world that has made us, one with every scene that is spread before our eyes. In a metaphor common to the Upaniṣads and Plato every unit of nature is a microcosm reflecting in itself the entire all-inclusive macrocosm. If there is law, if there is order in the universe, our life and consciousness are not accidents. We are solid with the world and are deeply rooted in it. We are not merely spectators of the universe but constituent parts of it.

Besides, the real is not so unsatisfying as we are asked to believe. It is not fair to blot out the lights and deepen the shadows. The world contains wonderful achievements of man, his heroisms and beauties, his imaginations and inventions. Even if the order of the world is created by our minds, our minds are a part of the universe. The ideals we cherish

1 *Mysticism and Logic* (1918). p. 48.

may be still remote and unaccomplished, but the fact is we possess the ideals, and love them so much as to condemn the world because it does not conform to them.[1] Our judgments of value, our convictions of truth, our appreciations of beauty, our experiences of love are the proof that we are not the products of merely physical forces. Those who plead eloquently for the maintenance of values cherish the dim hope that, after all, man is not a victim of the massive necessities, physical and economic, bound to their routine and entangled in their conflicts. He is an actor in the drama capable of forcing destiny and controlling the compulsion of things. The man who, even when conquered by the caprice of the world, remains unconvinced, points to his own innate dignity and superiority to nature.

The judgment on the world is passed on the unconscious assumption that the pleasure of man is the end of life. Egotism, legitimate when kept within bounds, is highly misleading when it produces the habit of taking oneself too seriously, as a sort of self-appointed judge of the universe. In complaining against the world, we are not seeking truth, and are lacking in the larger charity of the universe. If we look at life as it is, without ignoring or exaggerating any of its tendencies, we shall see that this stupendous movement

1 'We grant that human life is mean,' wrote Emerson, 'but how did we find out that it is mean? What is the ground of this uneasiness, of this old discontent? What is the universal sense of want and ignorance but the fine innuendo by which the soul makes its enormous claim?' Emerson is here paraphrasing Descartes' statement that we should not be conscious of finiteness if we did not have the idea of infinity all the time within us. A sense of spiritual want is a witness to our relation with spirit. 'What is strange,' Dostoevsky wrote in *The Brothers Karamazov*, 'what would be marvellous is not that God should really exist; the marvel is that such an idea, the idea of the necessity of God, could enter the head of such a savage, vicious beast as man. So holy it is, so touching, so wise and so great credit it does to man.'

is not at work for our private benefit. It has its own vast design, which it is seeking to fulfil, compared with which our highest aims are petty.

That the world is not a pleasure garden, but is full of pain and suffering, is not a new discovery. The prophets of religion admit this fact and account for it by *avidyā* or ignorance or original sin, in which humanity is said to be somehow implicated. They also imply that happiness can be attained by the right use of human personality. Happiness is not to be confused with pleasure. It consists in harmony, in unity with oneself, in the consciousness of an affirmative attitude to life, in the peace resident in the soul. Nature tends to perfect each thing or each species after its kind. Pain and suffering may be in the process, but if we are wise we will accept it all with joy and work for the consummation of each one's real nature. When a man seeks pleasure and avoids pain, he is on a lower level. The pursuit of truth and the striving after goodness may entail penalties and sufferings, even death of the body, and yet they may contribute to the greatness of the spirit which is real happiness.

After all, it does not seem to be a lonely or a love-starved universe. Even those engaged in the grim struggle of life may build up a sense of comradeship on the basis of respect for each other's suffering. Fellowship in suffering redeems the suffering as well.

Russell tells us that fear is the source of all religion. It only means that there is a lack of understanding between man and the universe around him. To understand life is to possess it as a whole in the unity of thought. Primitive man lived in vital unself-conscious union with nature. When his critical intelligence develops, a dualism is set up between man and the rest of reality. This dualism is the source of fear. Religion tries to remove fear, give us fearlessness, by restoring the lost unity between man and nature, the sense of communion with the All. Naturalism asks us to endure truth and reverence reality, but we cannot do so if there is a cleft between man and nature. Religion, by insisting on an organic connection between the world of nature and the world of values, delivers us from our isolation and transiency. It therefore takes us deeper than intellect, and re-establishes the vital relationship already at work between man and nature.

Atheism belongs to the intellect. When we sink back into the inmost core of our lives, we are compelled, whether we like it or not, to accept the universe. Atheism is contrary to the ultimate instinct of life. That life is good and is to be made the most of is the act of faith, the unanalysable ultimate for which no reasons could be given. All degrees of atheism belong to the surface of the mind. Life is much more exultant and mysterious than our intellects can comprehend. Russell's philosophy does not prove the failure of man, but only the inadequacy of intellect as against the truth that is proved in our pulses. The animal instinct which urges man to live and accept the world becomes a reasoned faith in him, that the nature around us is trustworthy and will respond to our efforts.

Russell and his followers protest against a supernatural world. If it is conceived as existent and not merely logically thought, then it must have active relations with the world in which we live. Miracles, incarnations, ascensions are invoked to bring the natural and the supernatural worlds into intimate union. If the two are bound together according to fixed laws, there is no reason why we should break up reality into the two opposite camps of nature and supernature. It is all nature; only we should not confine the term to the obvious facts and forces noticed by our imperfect science. The natural and the supernatural are a distinction within reality, and not between a world we know and another we do not know. If the supernatural is opposed to the natural, it is sometimes confused with the chaotic as distinct from the ordered. It is full of chance novelties and incalculable accidents. Such a kind of supernatural is repudiated by science. The true conception of the supernatural is however different. Nature has an order of its own. The supernatural is the natural in her true depths and infinity. It is not anything different from nature.

2. *Agnosticism*

Agnosticism admits the mystery and holds that we do not know and we cannot know. That which transcends us in none of our affair. Life has been compared in an old allegory to a bird that flies out of the darkness into a lighted chamber and, after flitting about there for some time, disappears into the darkness again. We know not the beginning of things, we know not whither they tend, we know just a part of their middle course. Why, then, should we worry about it all?[1] Even if the cosmic process has a purpose, we cannot know what it is. The agnostic does not deny that there is a reality behind the phenomena. If he does, then he is not an agnostic, for he knows that we know all the reality there is. If, on the other hand, he holds that there is something behind the phenomena, though we cannot be certain of its nature, even this is inconsistent with agnosticism, for he knows that there is something whose nature is such that it can never be known by us. We cannot be certain that we could not know any more of that of which we admittedly know so much that it is unknowable. To be ignorant is not the special perogative of man; to know that he is ignorant is his special privilege. The latter implies an ideal of knowledge which sets limits to one's ignorance as well as to knowledge. Besides, it is vain

1 Cp. *Bhagavadgītā*, II. 28.

to urge men to turn away from the pursuit of the real.

3. *Scepticism*

Some of those who are impressed by the variety of philosophical opinions are inclined to scepticism. They find all opinions interesting, and they are too cultured to have any convictions. Nothing is serious to them, neither art nor philosophy, neither politics nor religion. The world does not seem to have any purpose for the many little purposes that we may discover are so much in conflict with one another that we may well regard the world in its entirety as devoid of any purpose. The part of wisdom is to drift along confusedly, hoping for the best, expecting little and believing in nothing very much.

Scepticism thrives most in periods of transition. When the Hellenic culture and morality were breaking up under the impact of a wider civilization, the Sophists appeared. The age of the Buddha and the period of Śamkara in India were most friendly to the growth of scepticism.

Scepticism brings out the sense of loneliness in a world which is robbed of all point. Consistent scepticism is an impossible attitude. Hume tells us how he left his scepticism in his study at a safe distance from life. Though a sceptic is expected to doubt the possibility of knowledge, he always admits the truth of his own position. A scepticism which is in earnest with itself cannot rest in mere scepticism. It affirms the doubter and the doubt. It doubts because it has an ideal of certainty. As a method, scepticism is one thing, as a metaphysics, quite another. The famous sceptics of the world adopted it only as a method. Descartes travelled from doubt to dogma. Hume did not impugn knowledge. Balfour defended 'philosophical doubt' only to establish the 'foundations of belief'. Russell has faith in the method of

science.[1] It is difficult to find a sceptic who has not his
superstitions. Protestantism which began as a protest
ended as a religion. Today, many of those who deny God
are unable to dispense with ghosts. Negation is never mere
negation. We deny a thing because we believe something
else with which it is inconsistent. We discover the illusory
character of knowledge only by reference to something else
of which we claim to have knowledge. Generally, the sceptic is at war with the faith of his generation. The function of
scepticism is in relation to the dogmatism which it
criticizes.[2] But scepticism cannot be the final resting-place
of human thought. If the old faith has become impossible, a
new must be found. The sceptic is seeking for a way of life
which is worth following, a belief that might be honestly
held, and a social order in which we can find shelter. The
deepening of doubt is a sign of spiritual growth.

4. *Humanism*

   A more positive attitude is adopted by what is sometimes
called humanism. It holds that it does not matter what we
think about the ultimate nature of reality if only we are
prepared to do the proper thing. Religious theories may be
mere speculations. We cannot be sure what is true, or whether
anything is true at all. Life at any rate is something certain
and definite, and so let us occupy ourselves with the improvement of life. Humanism is a protest against naturalism
on the one side and religion on the other. The soul of man is

1 His *Sceptical Essays* (1928) is an eloquent plea for the application
  of the scientific temper to the problems of human life.
2 Socrates, when accused of heresy, declared: 'I do believe that there
  are gods, and in a higher sense than that in which my accusers
  believe in them.' Buddha believed in a god different from the
  popular ones in which his contemporaries trusted. To break down
  the images of the gods we worship is not always an act of unbelief:
  it is the announcement of a higher sense of God.

not a thing of nature; nor is it a child of God. Devotion to values would be inexplicable, if men were entirely products of nature. As against religion, humanism contends that this world is our chief interest and perfection of humanity our one ideal. The ultimate harmonious interrelation of all individuals with one another is the aim of humanism. Loyalty to the great community, as Royce said, is our highest duty. The humanist has no sympathy with all religious taboos which tend to drive away the blood from our veins. Morality is not meaningless self-mutilation. While excessive asceticism is encouraged by religion, humanism believes in balance and proportion. It is based on the Greek doctrine of harmony and the Roman sense of decorum.

Humanism is not to be confused with what is sometimes called the gospel of a good time. It does not admit that all modes of thought and activity are equally valid or justified by the mere fact of their existence. The composite self which is an unstable collection of diverse elements requires to be worked into a full and balanced whole. In the nature of things some propensities cannot be allowed full play, for when let go they create conditions in which the freedom of self-expression is curtailed. Besides, man is planted in a social environment which imposes limitations on his life. And these are not felt as a restriction, as the individual gets in return a sense of peace and satisfaction. Professor Irving Babbitt, of Harvard University, the leading representative of the American type of humanism, in his book on *Rousseau and Romanticism* (1919), admits that human society and its progress depend on the control which men exercise by means of the will over the natural human instincts. He recognizes an inner check which is the principle of inhibition. His quarrel with religion is due to his reading of religion as something which puts the principle of control outside man, while humanism places it within man. We can realize the humanist's ideal by means of the inner discipline without reference to any supernatural power.

Humanism, which is more a tendency than a system, has had a long history. In the East, Confucius held that the highest good was the proper maintenance of a well-balanced system of human relationships. 'Our moral being is the great reality (literally "the great root") of all existence, and the moral order is the universal law of the world.'[1] When the Brahmanical faith was undermined by its own ascetic excesses, Buddha insisted on the majesty of the moral law and mercy to all creation. The Greek view of life was essentially humanistic, with its insistence on measure, order and proportion. In the Renaissance we had a widespread revival of humanism. Kant defends a rational and ethical life as against a mystical religion.[2] Morality is, for him, a categorical imperative, a command about which there is nothing contingent or conditional. Our consciousness of moral obligation is something absolutely different from any other experience, and is ultimate and self-explanatory. The obligation of duty is one and the same for all rational beings. The absolute claim of the moral law on our obedience results in the recognition of the equality of all who are aware of a like claim upon them, who constitute a kingdom of ends, a spiritual commonwealth, in which the moral law is supreme. Kant's attitude to moral law is deeply religious, full of that feeling of awe and self-abasement, but it is not

1 Confucius, quoted in Rufus Jones: *New Studies in Mythical Religion* (1927), p. 180.
2 'The delusion that we can effect something by attempts at a supposed intercourse with God is religious fanaticism. Such a feeling of the immediate presence of the supreme being and such a discrimination between this feeling and every other, even moral feeling, would imply a capacity for an intuition which is without any corresponding organ in human nature.' Quoted in Selbie: *The Psychology of Religion* (1924), p. 247.

religion. The positivists identify religion with the service of humanity. The ethical movement is inclined to equate God with the moral ideal. The French school of Emile Durkheim and his followers treat religion as a social phenomenon.[1] Many of our sceptical thinkers today adopt humanism as the creed of common sense. It has a natural appeal to the human mind when it is uncertain of the source of life and its nature. It has its strongest representatives in America, where it is felt to be the only hope of salvation for a world dominated by the tyranny of scientific ideas and threatened by a mechanization of spirit. American humanism draws upon the Greek, the Buddhist and the Confucian traditions.[2]

Humanism seems to be religion secularized. The self-sufficiency of the natural man, the belief that the only values that matter are human values is the central faith of the humanists. Plato and Aristotle, from whom this faith derives its inspiration, are clearly aware that the deeper needs of the soul require to be satisfied.[3] We are not really

1 'The god of the clan, the totemic principle, can be nothing else than the clan itself, personified and represented to the imagination under the visible form of the animal or vegetable which serves as totem' (Durkheim: *Elementary Forms of Religious Life*, E.T., p. 206). According to Ames, religion is nothing more than 'the consciousness of the highest social values' (*Psychology of Religious Experience*, ch. viii).

2 'It is only proper that I acknowledge my indebtedness to the great Hindu positivist; my treatment of the problem of the One and the Many, for example, is nearer to Buddha than to Plato' (*Rousseau and Romanticism* (1919), p. xx). Professor P. E. More is a student of Plato and the Upaniṣads. See his *Shelburne* Essays (1904-1928) and the *Greek Tradition* (1904-1928). A section of American Unitarians distinguished themselves from the more conservative members of that body by adopting the creed of humanism. See Reese: *Humanist Sermons* (1927).

3 'While I have life and strength I shall never cease from the practice and the teaching of philosophy, exhorting anyone whom I meet and saying to him after my manner, you, my friend, a citizen, of

human if we do not feel that we are related to something
that transcends the finite and the conceivable. We want not
a mere improvement of the world, but an ideal transfiguration of it. If the humanists regard the enhancement of personality as the chief end of life, our personality cannot be
reduced to either physical manhood or economical well-
being, or instructed mind, or sensitive conscience. We cannot live up to the full height of our potential being without
drawing upon the deeper resources of spirit. The roots of
man's being are in the unseen and eternal, and his destiny is
not limited to the duration of his life on earth.[1] Humanism
is confessedly rationalistic, and ignores elements in life
which cannot be dealt with in intellectual terms. There is a
story about the visit of an Indian philosopher to Socrates.
Aristoxenes reports that Socrates told the Indian stranger
that his work consisted in enquiries about the life of men,

the great and mighty and wise city of Athens--are you not
ashamed of heaping up the greatest amount of money and honour
and reputation, and caring so little about wisdom, truth and the
greatest improvement of the soul, which you never regard or heed
at all?' (*Apology*, 29). In a recently discovered fragment of one of
Aristotle's lost dialogues, the inadequacy of mere economic
prosperity is well brought out. 'Be assured that the good of man
does not depend upon abundance of possessions, but upon the
right inner quality. Not even the body is regarded as in a happy
condition, merely because it is decked out in resplendent robes,
but only if, though wanting in finery, it is well developed and in
good health. Likewise one should call only that man fortunate
whose soul is ethically developed rather than the man who is rich
in outward possessions and is worth nothing in himself. Even a
horse is judged by its actual virtues. If it is a poor horse, it is not
rated higher because it has a gold bit in its mouth and a costly
harness on its back' (quoted by M. C. Otto: *International Journal of
Ethics*, January, 1929, p. 302).
1 Cp. Aristotle: 'We should not give heed to those who bid one think
as a mortal, but so far as we can we should make ourselves
immortal and do all with a view to a life in accord with the best
principles in us' (*Nichomachean Ethics*, 1177b.)

and the Indian smiled and said that none could understand things human who did not understand things divine.

Humanism demands a disciplined life and insists on wholeness and harmony. But it sets the moral and natural elements of man in sharp opposition. It is the essence of the moral will to check the free play of natural impulses and desires. If the dualism between man and nature is radical, the ideal of harmony cannot be attained. Besides, is the controlling will a mere negative check or has it any positive content? If it is the former, it has no content: if it is the latter, whence is its content derived? The higher will in man becomes identified with the spirit in him. Without the recognition of such a spiritual centre, which will help us to co-ordinate the variety of unlike elements of which human nature consists, our life will have no integrity.

In his *Nichomachean Ethics*, Aristotle lays down the golden mean, a balance between two extremes as the rule of life. He promises a fair share of earthly pleasures for a life of virtuous activity. And modern humanists adopt a similar view. It is not easy to determine what exactly is the mean between too much and too little. What is the course of self-respect which steers clear of slavish obsequiousness and arrogant airs? Where does decency lie between ascetic purity and sensual indulgence? When is violence not strength? Between the right and wrong it is not a mere quantitive difference. Aristotle himself admits that it is difficult to hit the mean though easy to miss it. We cannot apply a mere mechanical rule. We must develop a living adjustment, a sure taste in any concrete case. The difference between mechanical morality and true virtue is determined by the delicate insight into the realities of the situation. Aristotle recognizes that it is only the sense of something stable and unitary beneath the shifting experiences of life that can help us in seeing the right in any context. We must first gain

entrance into the kingdom which is not of this world if we
want to build it on earth. Enlightened humanism seems to
ignore this essentially non-wordly character of a truly spiritual life. Durkheim is not quite fair when he identifies
religion with social morality. In all religions where is a
trans-social reference. No religion can fulfil its social functions adequately if it is only social.

Virtue is not a mere balancing or nice calculation. An
ancient critic spoke of Aristotle as 'moderate to excess'. He
gives us good form and not a holy fervour, cold efficiency
and not constructive passion. For a balanced humanist,
non-violence is as much anti-social and unpractical as an
indiscriminate use of violence. The middle course may perhaps be the law of retaliation. Moral heroism is a jealous
god and not a judicious compromise. The saints aim at
righteousness, not respectability. They burn with a passion,
an adventurous enthusiasm that is reckless of life. Humanism lacks that indefinable touch, that *élan* of religion which
alone can produce that majestic faith whose creativity is
inexhaustible, whose hope is deathless, and whose adventures are magnificent. Those who keep their eyes close to
the ground and accept the counsel of the Delphic oracle to
follow 'the usage of the city' may conform to the code of
humanism, but they are not moral heroes. It is all the difference between being a gentleman and being a religious
man. It is more easy to be a gentleman than to be a Christian,
to have sufficient self-respect and self-control, to be decent
and good than to hunger and thirst after righteousness.[1] The

1 Dean Inge said recently that 'even a bishop would display
  Christian meekness if he were told that he had not behaved like a
  Christian; he would not be at all meek if he were told that he was
  no gentleman.' We may not like the version of the
  eighteenth-century epitaph, which describes a gentleman as
  'uniting a rational enjoyment of the pleasures of this world with a
  confident expectation of those of the world to come'. Cp. also

saints invariably overstep the boundaries. Their saintliness consists in overstepping. Socrates and Jesus overstepped the boundaries. Though they died for their love of truth and justice, they live for ever, echoes and lights unto eternity. They change the minds of men and illumine the otherwise dark pages of human history. Real love or will to good expresses itself in various forms, from sacrifice of oneself for one's neighbour to the acceptance of even those who offend us cruelly. All this is possible only if we do not sacrifice the mystical to the moral. The truly religious live out of a natural profundity of soul; their effortless achievements are not primarily directed to a refashioning of this world. Their faith is essentially life-transcending, and as a result, life-transforming.

However ingeniously we might plan and organize our society and adjust human relationships, so long as the world is what it is, the best of us cannot escape sorrow and suffering. Socialism cannot remove human selfishness. Even if we by some stroke of good fortune escape from the usual annoyances of life, we cannot free ourselves from death. Our bodily organism has in it seeds of dissolution. Mortality seems to be native to our world. Can humanism make death trivial and service significant? It is easy to ask us to draw on our capacity for endurance and heroism and go down into the valley, strong, alone and conquering, but when we are uncertain of the meaning of the world such advice is stupid. In the second book of the *Republic*, Plato tells us of an absolutely just man who yet passes for an unjust one, and suffers the most severe penalties with no hope of relief in this life and no expectation of reward in the next. When Socrates is asked whether such a one tortured on the rack and crucified can yet be happy, he answered in the affirmative,

Chesterfield's definition of decorum as the act of combining the useful appearance of virtue with the solid satisfaction of vice.

simply because he was not a mere humanist, but believed in the spirit in man and the significance of the world. Humanism has no consolation for those who bear in pain the burden of defeated hopes and suffer sorrow and contempt. Kant's chief argument for theism is that since the good man is often defeated on earth, we require a superhuman power to adjust virtue and happiness. When the foundations of life are shaken, when the ultimate issues face us demanding an answer, humanism does not suffice. Life is a great gift, and we have to bring to it a great mood; only humanism does not induce it.

When the humanist admits the ultimateness of the values, he is implicitly accepting the spiritual view of the universe. For him the ethical self is a power above the ordinary self in which all men may share, in spite of the diversity of personal temperament and to which our attitude must be one of subjection. The question is inevitable whether the ethical ideal is a mere dream or has the backing of the universe. Is man ploughing his lonely furrow in the dark or is there a transcending purpose that is co-operating with him in his quest for ideals, securing him against the ultimate defeat of his plans? Are the values mere empirical accidents, creations at best of the human mind, or do they reveal to us an order of being which is more than merely human, a spiritual reality which is the source of the significance of what happens in the temporal process? Does human life point beyond the contingent to another world, absolute and eternal though in contact with the human, and exerting a transforming influence on it? Professor Alexander is of opinion that the world of values arises as a secondary emergent product out of a simpler ultimate existent. For him values are incidents in the empirical growth of things, within what is really the primary reality of space-time'[1]. Alexander denies priority to value, but finds it difficult to account for the development of space-time without the postulation of a *nisus*. The *nisus* is not space-time. If it were it could not serve the purpose for which it is assumed; if, on the other hand, it is something that make space-time move on to higher forms, it is something different from space-time and prior to it. The principle of explanation seems to be space-time and the *nisus*, the void and God, to use Old Testament terminology. Kant's ethical theory shows that we glimpse the spiritual reality superior to the human by means of the ethical consciousness. Though Kant distinguishes religion from ethics as an independent activity of the human spirit, some-what subordinate to the ethical, his system as a whole sets right the balance. While virtue is good in its own right, it is not the whole good, which is virtue combined with happiness. Perfect virtue and perfect happiness are two sides of the unconditioned good which the practical reason sets before itself. Our moral consciousness is offended if there is a divorce between the two. Perfect happiness, however, is dependent on natural causes which do not seem to have any direct relation with virtue. A proper adjustment of happiness to virtue is possible only if we assume a divine being who is able to bring the cosmic into conformity with the moral and regulate the combination of happiness and virtue. Our moral consciousness *postulates* God, who is adequate to the realization of the *summum bonum*. Kant is convinced that this world is not all, and that the disproportion between the claims of virtue and the rewards of life will be set right. If we do not accept the postulate of God, we shall be faced by a dualism between the moral law which claims our allegiance and a universe which is apparently indifferent if not hostile to the

1 Space Time and Deity, vol ii (1920), p.134.

demands of morality. If the authority of the moral law is to be justified, if the ultimateness of man as a moral being is to be vindicated, then the world process which has resulted in the formation of human personalities has significance and the structure of things is spiritual. Humanism thus leads to a view of itself as rooted in a reality deeper and more comprehensive, in which it finds its completion. Humanism is concerned with value; religion relates value to reality, human life to the ultimate background against which it is set. However crude and misconceived the savage's religion may be, it gives him the security that the real is friendly to his values, and is not indifferent to his welfare. From the totemic principle of the savage to the absolute spirit of the philosopher, there is right through a confident belief that man is a fragment of the larger scheme of things which contains the secret of his life and his surroundings and exerts a mysterious power over his destiny.

The great humanists see the abiding element of the one in the infinite flux of the many. Plato admits the Immutable Idea and Aristotle the last Immaterial Form. In early Buddhism we have a religion which does not insist on an eternal God, and yet makes a strong appeal to the consciousness of evil, the need for holiness and the conquest of greed and sensuality. Early Buddhism had implicit trust in an eternal right that dwells in the constitution of things. The structure of the universe is ethical. It is *dharmabhūta*. Even Matthew Arnold, for whom religion was morality tinged with sentiment, believed in some kind of relation and response to 'the more than ourselves that makes for righteousness', the more than the finite and the finished, in submission to which is our peace. For the American humanists, Babbitt and More, humanism and religion are two stages on the same path. Naturalism is right in its insistence on man as body; humanism is right when it exalts man as mind; but man is not merely body or mind, but it is spirit as well. So humanism cannot do duty for an adoring life which is identified with the mind of God, and manifests itself in service and self-loss.

There is no conflict between religion and a reasonable humanism. The truly religious act in this world; the inner feeling of the relation between God and man is bound to issue in the service of humanity. While what matters is works or fruits of religious life, its social productivity, the most efficient servants of society are those who cultivate anxiously the interior life. A religion whose centre is man and not God is never a strong one.

5. *Religion and humanism*

The attacks of humanism and social idealism are directed against the force of reactionary ecclesiastical systems with their warnings of afterlife and future settlements. Thanks to the spread of the humanist revolt, religion is becoming more and more an instrument of social reform. Within the Christian Church we come across reformers who invoke the religion of Jesus for the programme of Moscow. We are reminded of Jesus's definition of those who called on his name and yet neglected to feed the hungry, and his declaration that what is done to the least of his brethren is done to himself, of St James' remark on religion pure and undefiled, and of St John's protest, 'He that loveth not his brother whom he hath seen, how shall he love God whom he hath not seen?' Harnack's works and Seeley's *Ecce Homo* proclaim a humanitarian type of Christianity. The vogue of Christian Science is due to its insistence on the practical character of Christ's mission. In India, under the influence of thinkers like Dayananda Sarasvati and Vivekananda, Gandhi and Tagore, a social gospel is becoming popular. The *Bhagavadgītā*, with its insistence on work, has become the most important Hindu Scripture. In religion accent is the vital thing, and it is now shifted to social reform. But we cannot forget that in essence religion is spiritual redemption and not social reform. Sanctity and holiness may imply service and fellowship, but cannot be equated with them.[1] Religion today has to fight not only unbelief and secularism, but also the subtler rival in the guise of social reform.

6. *Pragmatism*

Sometimes the modern challenge to religion is met by a somewhat pragmatist view. Pragmatism rejects absolute truth as a myth, and holds that all truths are human and relative. A truth is tested by the value of its consequences. In science, e.g., we adopt and act on suitable hypotheses even before they are tested and proved. Similarly we can make spiritual experiments in religion. We have to ascertain the value of religious views not by their objective truth, but by their ethical and spiritual results. It does not matter whether a particular dogma like the incarnation was realized in the person of Jesus or not, so long as the idea is a living reality in the community. The Christ of experience, the metaphysical and theological Christ, is not in any manner affected by the Jesus of history. When we say 'God is our father', we are not so much stating a truth about the nature of God as indicating a way in which we should act towards one another. Even if we do not believe, we must act as if we believed. It is useful to live as though there were a God. Social efficiency seems to require theistic belief. This view is traced to Kant's doctrine that the idea of God is a regulative one, a methodological fiction which helps us to regard

---

1 Cp. the criticism made of Renan's *Life of Jesus* by a French girl, 'What a pity that the story did not end with a marriage.'

objects of our thought as connected parts of a systematic whole.

In its insistence on the conative or teleological character of experience, and in its protest against the divorce of knowledge from practice in the concrete life of mind, pragmatism is quite in conformity with traditional idealism and its principle of the priority of the ideal. Its defect is in the narrow view of teleology which it adopts. The criterion of working must be applied in the larger context of the whole experience. The idea has value if it works not for a casual desire or temporary purpose, but for the whole relevant situation. It must satisfy critical intelligence. Profound needs of the soul seem sometimes to be satisfied by dangerous illusions. It we accept beliefs on the ground that they add to our mental health and happiness, many superstitions will become justified. The pragmatist seems to agree with the psychoanalyst in holding that religious beliefs compensate for the harshness of actual existence. If the object of belief were only imaginary, created in order to satisfy our needs, then the belief itself would in time wither away. We mean by God something more than the idea of God. The vital essence of religious conviction is that its faith is not a mere idea. If fictions helped many generations, it is because they were not known to be fictions. No man can worship permanently what is untrue. When we affirm that the only foundation of faith is the need or the desire of man to believe, we are expressing an ultimate unbelief. It is our duty to seek the truth, however uncomfortable and fugitive, instead of clinging to phantasies which are uplifting and consoling. God is not what a man wishes to be true for the sake of an easy time, but what he knows to be true, even though it means sacrifice and self-denial.

7. Modernism

What is called modernism is an attitude of mind whi ... is very ancient and is to be met with in all religions. Each generation is called upon to reconcile its experiences and fit them into a systematic scheme. Today the modernists are engaged in reconciling religious traditions with the new needs which have emerged in the process of development. In the Christian world, the modernists point out that even the central truths of Christianity are products of growth. The Jesus of the Gospels is different from the Jewish Messiah, the Greek Logos, or the Protestant Christ. The Jesus of the twentieth century bears the marks of Jewish piety, Greek philosophy, Roman legalism, German realism, and French logic. It is our duty to distinguish what is permanent from what is transitory in religious belief, and reconcile the permanent by means of re-interpretation with the new knowledge and aspiration. Dogmas are reduced to myths, miracles to legends, sacraments to symbols and sacred books to literature. Modernists are of all degrees, and it is impossible to deal with them all. One or two striking illustrations may be taken. Harnack's famous distinction between the religion of Jesus and the religion about Jesus gives a clue to liberal Protestantism. The suffering of Jesus is significant only if Jesus is a human sufferer. In submitting to suffering for the love of man, Jesus reveals God more than in other acts of his life. The statement, 'God so loved the world that he gave his only begotten Son', is a poetic representation of the simple intuition that to love is to suffer. The more we love, the more we suffer. Infinite love is infinite suffering. According to this view Jesus taught a higher ethics than a mere pharisaism. He is a man become God rather than God become man. The latter is as empty to the educated modernist as primitive magic is to the missionary.

Dean Inge claims that the Christian faith is a religion of
spirit and not one of dogma, which can be defended and
imposed. Religion is love and worship, not of what God did
or will do, but what he is doing today, revealed now as much
as ever, a light which the soul receives and reflects in more
or less of radiance according to its powers of feeling and
understanding. Jesus shows us the highest reflection of this
radiance in practical life. The religious truth is found in Plato
and the Upaniṣads. Its highest embodiment is in the life of
Jesus. So Dean Inge[1] claims that he is an adherent of the
Platonic tradition in Christian thought. Its characteristics
are 'a spiritual religion, based on a firm belief in absolute and
eternal values as the most real things in the universe--a
confidence that these values are knowable by man--a belief
that they can nevertheless be known only by wholehearted
consecration of the intellect, will and affections to the great
quest--an entirely open mind towards the discoveries of
science--a reverent and receptive attitude to the beauty,
sublimity and wisdom of the creation as a revelation of the
mind and character of the Creator--a complete indifference
to the current valuations of the worldling. The Christian
element is supplied mainly by the identification of the inner
light with the spirit of the living, glorified and indwelling
Christ.[2]

Professor Kirsopp Lake[3] dwells on the permanent characteristics of a pure religion of spirit and is indifferent to
Jesus' embodiment of them. His interpretation takes away
the distinctively Christian elements from Christianity and
effects its identification with a pure mysticism. The modernist attempt to relate the content of the faith to contemporary knowledge deprives the orthodox religion of its

1 *The Platonic Tradition in English Religious Thought* (1927), p. 9.
2 *Ibid.*, pp. 33-34.
3 *The Religion of Yesterday and of To- morrow* (1925).

distinctiveness and therefore does not have the sympathy of the multitudes who have also their rights in the matter. It is believed to be a sort of flat and vague aspiration after a higher life, somewhat academic and negative in character.[1] Since the modernists occupy a somewhat middle position, they are exposed to attack from both sides. The naturalists are dissatisfied since they feel that religion is getting a fresh lease of life by the modernist attempts. The traditionalists contend that by dragging into half light matters that would be safe in their obscurity, they are endangering religion itself. We must either leave them in obscurity and so lapse into faith or lead them forth into full light and thus accept secularism. Modernism seems to occupy an untenable half-way house.

8. *Authoritarianism*

The prophets of the new creeds seldom have an audience, much less a following. They have no bond of union except a common unbelief. In the confusion of counsels, the seeker is lost. He wants but does not get a standard to live by, an ideal transcending himself to which he can submit. Anarchy is the best support for authority. Despotism is next door to anarchy. Formless confusion carries us into the arms of fixed forms. Tired of the effort of thinking, frightened by the difficulties of doubt, we fall back on authority with a sigh of relief. It is a refuge from scepticism, if not its substitute. Liberty and reason are no doubt great ideals, but there can be no liberty without discipline and no reason without faith.

1 cp. Father Ronald Knox's caricature of the Modernist's prayer:
'O God, forasmuch as without Thee
We are not able to doubt Thee,
Help us all by Thy Grace
To teach the whole race
We know nothing whatever about Thee.'

The orthodox Christian Church, Catholic and Protestant, both take their stand on authority. It is authority that is exalted whether of Pope or of Council or of Book. Rome made Galileo recant, Calvin's Geneva might have burned him. Tennessee would have put him in prison.[1] The principle of free inquiry which lay behind the appeal to scriptural authority is still an unfulfilled ideal. The spiritual genius who can think out a religion for himself is one in a million. The large majority are anxious to find a shrine safe and warm where they can kneel and be comforted. For them it is a question of either accepting some authority or going without religion altogether. It is catholicism or complete disillusion. The leaders enlarge on the beauty and richness of the worship, the antiquity and order of the tradition, the opportunity for influence and service which the historic church offers. If we are not to languish as spiritual nomads, we require a shelter, and the church which is majestically one in creed, ritual, discipline and language, a corporation in which racial and national barriers are obliterated, a kingdom without frontiers, attracts the large majority.

The importance of authority and the value of tradition are

1 It is doubtful whether an infallible church or an infallible book is more favourable to real religion. However corrupt the church may be, it is a live organism responsive to the new influences. A book embodying a revelation supposed to be completed for all time to which no spiritual experience can add anything of value, is perhaps more damaging. It is true that Luther allowed to the individual liberty to examine the scriptures, and admitted that the General Council is not infallible. But Luther's logic ultimately ended in identifying truth with his own view of it. There is not in this matter much to choose between Catholic Authority and Protestant Orthodoxy. Nor can we be certain that the Protestant Reformation means the advance of a rational faith. It is arguable that there is far more intellectual strength in the mediæval scholastics than can be found in the emotional utterances of a Luther or a Calvin.

great. If we are not to lapse into individualistic rationalism and ultimate negation, if we are not to be led astray by our wandering whims, if our personal intuitions are to be guided by the accumulated wisdom of the race, only tradition can help us. It takes centuries of life to make a little history, and it takes centuries of history to produce a little tradition, and we cannot lightly set it aside. Mankind does not begin completely afresh with each individual. The first principles need not be proved by each of us. There is a body of accepted knowledge, a deposit of faith on which we can all draw. Though religion is in a sense each individual's personal affair, it is dependent on past tradition and grows out of it. But loyalty to tradition is one thing, and bondage to it quite another. Complete conformity is contrary to life. Only the dead are completely conforming. Progress is a law of life, and the power of change is essential to conservation. No tradition is final and absolute. The past helps us to reach more elevated heights from which, as the ages move, we may gain a clearer vision of the relations of God and man.

Authoritarianism is useful as a warning against the claims of scientific knowledge. There are aspects of reality where science is insufficient. It does not mean, however, that science and religion are opposed, and what the one affirms the other denies. 'If the wisdom of this world were really foolishness with God,' said Goethe, 'it would not be worth while to live three score years and ten.'[1]

In the wake of authoritarianism, which distrusts reason, superstition is growing stronger. All sorts of irrational ideas born of fear and ignorance are becoming fashionable. The sale of lucky mascots, the interest in astrology, and the faith in mediums show how near we are to the magicians and medicine men of ancient times. In some quarters religion

1 *Maxims and Reflections*, 618; *Goethe and Faust*, by Stawell and Dickinson (1928), p. 6.

itself is being transformed into a superstition, with the result that men of real piety and integrity of mind are repelled by it.[1] Strange esoteric sects, whose prophets believe themselves to be the only living recipients of divine revelation, are attracting the credulous.[2]

The problem facing us is whether we have faith in ourselves or not. If we have, we must possess the freedom to explore, the only limitation being that we should not interfere with others who are engaged in similar pursuits. Our faith is worth little if we are not sure that the individual will discover truth, through the exercise of his reason and conscience. Emerson said, 'God offers to every mind its choice between truth and repose; take which you please, you can never have both.' Respect for man requires us to possess faith that his powers of thought and spiritual discovery guided by his experience of the past will not lead him to error and confusion. There is the risk that we may be betrayed into error if we think freely, but the faith which does not face this risk is not true faith. Despotism and anarchy, an infallible authority and a disruptive subjectivism, are not the only alternatives either in politics or in religion. They are twin branches of one stem, complementary sides of experience which become opposed to each other when developed in fanatical abstraction. Neither is adequate to the fulness of human nature. The new authoritarian does not

1 Cf. Professor J. S. Haldane: 'The materialism with which orthodox theology is at present shot through and through is the whole source of the weakness of religious belief in presence of the sciences and of the alienation between religious belief and the sciences'(*The Sciences and Philosophy* (1929), pp. 311-312). Even the liberal schools are unwilling to shake off the materialism associated with theology in the way of supernatural revelations, interferences, miracles and such other superstitions. While scientific materialism is retreating, theological materialism is advancing.
2 See Ray Strachey: *Religious Fanaticism* (1928).

provide the forms into which men could throw themselves
with confidence and joy. The pioneers and the pathfinders
flouted authority and declared what their deepest being
found true. Each one of us has a superficial intellectual self
and a deeper individual one. A dynamic religion discovers
the individual and engages the depths in us. Our responses
then will not be of a routine character. The authoritarian
tickles us into acquiescence in the name of numbers. True
religion lifts us out of our ruts, treats us as individuals and
not units in a crowd. Those who are suspicious of free and
personal religion and wish to impose on all a divinely guar-
anteed dogmatic creed endanger the interests of truth and
stability which they are so anxious to conserve. Extremes
meet. Authoritarianism implies a sort of scepticism. In affirming that religion should be defended from human reason,
that its God should be approached with eyes coloured by
faith, that its systems should not be regarded too closely,
authoritarianism seems to harbour a secret scepticism. It
can have little appeal in an age remarkable for its criticism
of creeds of all shades.

Only those who have never known the meaning of doubt
can accept authority. The many thinking men who are still
hoping to discover a warrant for their faith which traditional dogmas cannot give, even when they undergo the violent
distortion of allegory and exegesis, can only be restive under
an authority that is merely external. The authoritarians
show a somewhat imperfect acquaintance with reality. When
John Wyclif and his followers translated the Bible into English about 1382, the study of the scriptures was no longer
confined to the priests who knew Latin, but was extended
to those who could read English. Every subsequent event
emphasized the equality of all men in the sight of God and
their right to serve God in their own way without dictation
from popes or priests. Even in backward India, the old days

in which the priest was often the only educated person in the village are over. An increasingly large number of people are familiar with the best thoughts of other religions and the great achievements of science. The intellectual classes are generally well informed, and if the priests are to interpret for them the momentous truths of spiritual life, they must appeal to their reason and persuade those whose minds are torn by doubt that the faith they are called upon to accept is a reasonable one. We cannot turn all men into machines even in religion. Dogmatic affirmation is as one-sided and unreasonable as dogmatic denial.

9. *Lack of the spiritual note*

I do not want to weary the reader by dealing with the many other ways of escape which our age is adopting, such as the cult of the superman, the worship of the eternal feminine, spiritualism, etc.[1] The different attempts to accommodate God to the modern mind are not quite successful in their ambition. Their one lesson is that, notwithstanding the transformation of life, the shifting of moral values and the preoccupations of the time, the primal craving for the eternal and the abiding remains inextinguishable. Unbelief is impossible. Along with a deep discontent with the standard forms of religion there is a growing seriousness about it. The forms are dissolving but the needs persist. The millions who neither dare to have a religion nor do without one are rushing hither and thither seeking for direction. The philosophical fashions of naturalism, atheism, agnosticism, scepticism, humanism, and authoritarianism are obvious and easy, but they do not show an adequate appreciation of the natural profundity of the human soul. In the Eastern religions, the energy of the depth of the soul is something

1 See Ferguson: *The Confusion of Tongues* (1929).

before which external existence pales into insignificance. While the tendency to emphasize the inward spirit as all that counts and treat life as an indifferent illusion is one-sided, to ignore spiritual life and confuse it with the physical or the vital is equally one-sided. If, in spite of our ethical culture and rationalistic criticism, we feel that our lives have lost the sense of direction, it is because we have secularized ourselves. Human nature is measured in terms of intellection. We have not found our true selves, and we know that we have not. It is a self-conscious age in which we live. Philosophers and professors of philosophy are speaking to us of what is wrong with us in the heavy tomes of a Keyserling or a Spengler and the slight pamphlets of the *Today and Tomorrow* series. Never was man's need to come to an understanding with life more urgent. We may be busy seeking for wealth, power and excitement, but we are no longer sure that it is all worth doing. We have no certain aims and no definite goals. Life is fragmentary and futile. Nothing means much or matters much. Anxious and enquiring minds are doubting and discussing, groping and seeking for the more precious meaning of life, its profounder reality, for the synthetic view which will comprehend the scepticism and the certainties, the doubts and the realities of contemporary life. Our division is profound and no organized religion is able to restore the lost unity. We are waiting for a vital religion, a live philosophy, which will reconstruct the bases of conviction and devise a scheme of life which men can follow with self-respect and joy.[1] Salvation is self-recovery, release from distraction.

1 Cp. 'Men think they can do without religion; they do not know that religion is indestructible, and that the question simply is, Which will you have?' (Amiel). Bernard Shaw lays down a dictum in *Back to Methuselah* (1921): 'Civilization needs a religion as a matter of life and death.

The *Bhagavadgītā* tells us that the trained understanding is
not distracted by details or divided in aims.[1] It has a sense
of the whole, an integrity of life, a stable anchorage which
helps us to face the gravest crises. It is the function of
philosophy to provide us with a spiritual rallying centre, a
synoptic vision, as Plato loved to call it, a *samanvaya*, as the
Hindu thinkers put it, a philosophy which will serve as a
spiritual concordat, which will free the spirit of religion
from the disintegrations of doubt and make the warfare of
creeds and sects a thing of the past.

1 ii. 41: Cp. 'If thine eye be single, thy whole body shall be full of light.'

CHAPTER III

Religious Experience and its Affirmations

I. *Philosophy of religion*

Philosophy of religion is religion come to an understanding of itself. It attempts a reasoned solution of a problem which exists directly only for the religious man who has the spiritual intuition or experience and indirectly for all those who, while they have no personal share in the experience, yet have sufficient belief that the experience does occur and is not illusory. The direct apprehension of God seems to be as real to some men as the consciousness of personality or the perception of the external world is to others. The sense of communion with the divine, the awe and worship which it evokes, which to us are only moments of vision or insight, seem to be normal and all-pervading with the saints. If philosophy of religion is to become scientific, it must become empirical and found itself on religious experience.

Before thinking can start there must be something thought about. Thinking does not produce its object but has it offered to it as a datum. If thought cuts itself away from the compulsion of fact, to that extent it ceases to be thought and becomes imagination. Just as there can be no geometry without the perception of space, even so there cannot be philosophy of religion without the facts of religion.

As we have seen, sometimes psychology of religion professes to serve as a substitute for philosophy and repudiates the validity of religious intuitions by tracing them to psychological factors as sub-conscious desires. To trace the psychological conditions of a belief is not to determine its validity. To say that our sense perceptions answer to reality, while spiritual intuitions do not, is for psychology a gratuitous assumption. Psychologically the experience we have of the world before us or of the British constitution or of the categorical nature of duty is on the same level as St Paul's vision on the road to Damascus or Augustine's in the Italian garden. In the experience itself no question is raised whether the object experienced is real or not. Professor Alexander says: 'It is for the worshipper as much a fact as a green leaf or the sun is for a dispassionate observer. The religious feeling and its object are given in one and the same experience.'[1] It is for philosophy of religion to find out whether the convictions of the religious seers fit in with the tested laws and principles of the universe.

It is sometimes urged that while the psychological experiences rationalized by science are more or less uniform for all observers, the data for philosophy of religion are diverse and discordant. Stones are hard and the sky is blue for all. But God is Buddha to some and Christ to some others. This difference means that the facts are more complex and require closer study. Just as we attempt to formulate in precise terms our sense experience in the natural sciences, even so philosophy of religion attempts to define the world to which our religious experiences refer. There is no reason why the intuitions of the human soul with regard to the ultimate reality should be studied in any other spirit or by any other method than those which are adopted with such great success in the region of positive science. When we speak of matter, life or mind, we refer to a certain type of experiences. Matter means a set of experiences with a certain definite character and we account for it by the hypothesis of electric energy or other kinds of resistance. The

1 *Hibbert Journal*, January 1928, p. 251.

same is true of life and mind. Religious experiences possess their own distinctive character and we seem to be in touch with reality other than that of matter, life or mind. We cannot say that we know matter, life and mind and not God or ultimate spirit. As a matter of fact, we do not not know precisely what matter or life is. We know that they are objects of experience though their real nature is hidden from us. So also we may not know the ultimate meaning of God, though we may know something about God or what answers to God in reality through religious experience. The creeds of religion correspond to theories of science. The physicist attempts to account for physical phenomena by the hypothesis of the electron and feels that his mental picture of it is like the real thing. However, we are realizing that it is simply impossible to form any picture at all of the ultimate nature of the physical world. The theories are symbolic and are accepted because they work. Similarly, we have certain experiences which we try to account for by the assumption of God. The God of our imagination may be as real as the electron but is not necessarily the reality which we immediately apprehend. The idea of God is an interpretation of experience.

Purely speculative theology which cuts itself off from religious tradition and experience and works from premises which are held to be universally valid cannot serve as an adequate philosophy of religion. The proofs of God's existence from premises of a general character yield not the God of religion but a supreme first cause or being who can be construed into the object of religious experience only if we start with the latter.[1] A category of thought with no basis in

1 'What in the end does the most complete teleology prove?' asks Kant. 'Does it prove that there is such an intelligent Being? No. It only proves that according to the constitution of our cognitive faculties we can form absolutely no concept of the possibility of

fact is not an experienced certainty. No stable conviction can be built on mere dialectic. Speculative theology can conceive of God as a possibility; it is religion that affirms God as a fact.

In dogmatic theology, on the other hand, the theologian regards himself as an expositor of traditional doctrine accepted as revealed and his task is limited to the elimination of contradictions in it. He takes his stand on one set of facts and ignores elements of reality that his scheme does not recognize. Within limits the theologian is allowed freedom to interpret doctrines and elucidate their implications, but his investigations should always confirm the dogmas. While the methods are optional, the conclusions are obligatory.

Philosophy of religion as distinct from dogmatic theology refuses to accept any restricted basis but takes its stand on experience as wide as human nature itself. It rejects the high *a priori* road of speculative theology and the apologetic method of dogmatic theology and adopts a scientific view of religious experience and examines with detachment and impartiality the spiritual inheritance of men of all creeds and of none. Such an examination of the claims and contents of religious consciousness, which has for its background the whole spiritual history of man, has in it the promise of a spiritual idealism which is opposed to the disintegrating forces of scientific naturalism on the one hand and religious dogmatism on the other.

2. *The essence of religion*

Religion has been identified with feeling, emotion and sentiment, instinct, cult and ritual, perception, belief and faith, and these views are right in what they affirm, though

such a world as this save by thinking a designedly-working supreme cause thereof' (*Critique of Judgment*, Bernard's E.T., p. 311).

wrong in what they deny. Schleiermacher is not wrong in saying that there is a predominant feeling element in the religious consciousness. Religious feeling, however, is quite distinct from any other kind of feeling. Nor is it to be identified with a sense of creaturely dependence; for then Hegel might retort that Schleiermacher's dog may be more pious than his master. If we assimilate religious experience to the moral consciousness, as Kant is inclined to do, we overlook the distinctive characters of the two activities. Religion is not mere consciousness of value. There is in it a mystical element, an apprehension of the real and an enjoyment of it for its own sake which is absent in the moral consciousness. Religion is not a form of knowledge as Hegel sometimes urged. While religion implies a metaphysical view of the universe, it is not to be confused with philosophy.

When Professor Whitehead defines religion as 'what the individual does with his own solitariness,'[1] he is urging that it is not a mere social phenomenon. It is not an apologetic for the existing social order; nor is it a mere instrument for social salvation. It is an attempt to discover the ideal possibilities of human life, a quest for emancipation from the immediate compulsions of vain and petty moods. It is not true religion unless it ceases to be a traditional view and becomes personal experience. It is an independent functioning of the human mind, something unique, possessing an autonomous character. It is something inward and personal which unifies all values and organizes all experiences.[2] It is

1 *Religion in the Making* (1926), p. 6.
2 When Croce declines to regard religion as an autonomous form of experience, and views it as an immature misunderstood form of philosophy, when Gentile treats it as a stage, though essential in our spiritual development, they are voicing their protest against the transcendental conceptions of God. The God before whose majesty we abase ourselves, or to whose love we surrender ourselves, is completely immanent, is the spirit in man objectified.

the reaction of the whole man to the whole reality. We seek
the religious object by the totality of our faculties and energies. Such functioning of the whole man may be called
spiritual life, as distinct from a merely intellectual or moral
or aesthetic activity or a combination of them. The spiritual
sense, the instinct for the real, is not satisfied with anything
less than the absolute and the eternal. It shows an incurable
dissatisfaction with the finiteness of the finite, the transiency of the transient. Such integral intuitions are our authority
for religion. They reveal a Being who makes himself known
to us through them and produces revolt and discontent with
anything short of the eternal.

3. *Personal experience of God*

All the religions owe their inspiration to the personal
insights of their prophet founders. The Hindu religion, for
example, is characterized by its adherence to fact. In its pure
form, at any rate, it never leaned as heavily as other religious do on authority. It is not a 'founded' religion; nor does
it centre round any historical events. Its distinctive characteristic has been its insistence on the inward life of spirit. To
know, possess and be the spirit in this physical frame, to
convert an obscure plodding mentality into clear spiritual
illumination, to build peace and self-existent freedom in the
stress of emotional satisfactions and sufferings, to discover
and realize the life divine in a body subject to sickness and
death has been the constant aim of the Hindu religious
endeavour. The Hindus look back to the Vedic period as the
epoch of their founders. The Veda, the wisdom, is the accepted name for the highest spiritual truth of which the
human mind is capable. It is the work of the *ṛṣis* or the seers.
The truths of the *ṛṣis* are not evolved as the result of logical
reasoning or systematic philosophy but they are the products

of spiritual intuition, *dṛṣṭi* or vision. The *ṛṣis* are not so much the authors of the truths recorded in the Vedas as the seers who were able to discern the eternal truths by raising their life-spirit to the plane of the universal spirit. They are the pioneer researchers in the realm of spirit who saw more in the world than their fellows. Their utterances are based not on transitory vision but on a continuous experience of resident life and power. When the Vedas are regarded as the highest authority, all that is meant is that the most exacting of all authorities is the authority of facts.

If experience is the soul of religion, expression is the body through which it fulfils its destiny. We have the spiritual facts and their interpretations by which they are communicated to o hers, *śruti* or what is heard, and *smṛti* or what is remembered. Śaṁkara equates them with *pratyakṣa* or intuition and *anumāna* or inference. It is the distinction between immediacy and thought. Intuitions abide, while interpretations change. *Śruti* and *smṛti* differ as the authority of fact and the authority of interpretation. Theory, speculation, dogma, change from time to time as the facts become better understood. Their value is acquired from their adequacy to experience. When forms dissolve and the interpretations are doubted, it is a call to get back to the experience itself and reformulate its content in more suitable terms. While the experiential character of religion is emphasized in the Hindu faith, every religion at its best falls back on it.

The whole scheme of Buddhism centres on Buddha's enlightenment. Moses saw God in the burning bush, and Elijah heard the still small voice. In *Jeremiah* we read: 'This is the covenant which I will make with the house of Israel after those days, saith the Lord. I will put my hand in their inward parts, and in their heart will I write it.' [1] Jesus's

1 xxxi. 37.

experience of God is the basic fact for Christianity: 'As he
came up out of the river he saw the heavens parted above
him and the spirit descending like a dove towards him: and
he heard a voice sounding out of the heavens and saying
"Thou art my beloved son. I have chosen thee".' According to
St Mark, the baptism in the Jordan by John was to Jesus the
occasion of a vivid and intense religious experience, so
much so that he felt that he had to go for a time into absolute
solitude to think it over.[1] He obviously spoke of the ineffable
happening, the sudden revelation, the new peace and joy in
words that have come down to us. He emphasized the
newness of the reborn soul as something which marks him
off from all those who are religions only at second hand.
'Verily I say unto you, among men born of women there hath
not arisen a greater than John the Baptist; but the least in the
Kingdom of God is greater than he.'[2] The vision that
came to Saul on the Damascus road and turned the per-
secutor into an apostle[3] is another illustration. Faith means
in St James acceptance of dogma; in St Paul it is the surrender of heart and mind to Christ; but in the Epistle to the
Hebrews, faith is defined as that outreaching of the mind by
which we become aware of the invisible world.[4] The life of
Mohammad is full of mystic experiences. Witnesses to the
personal sense of the divine are not confined to the East.
Socrates and Plato, Plotinus and Porphyry, Augustine and
Dante, Bunyan and Wesley, and numberless others, testify
to the felt reality of God. It is as old as humanity and is not
confined to any one people. The evidence is too massive to
run away from.

1 Mark I. 10.
2 See also Matt. xi. II.
3 Acts ix. 1-9.
4 See also I Cor. xiii. 12; Romans viii. 18-25; Rev. xxi. 22.

4. Character of religious experience

To study the nature of this experience is rather a difficult matter. All that one can hope to do is to set down a few general impressions. It is a type of experience which is not clearly differentiated into a subject-object state, an integral, undivided consciousness in which not merely this or that side of man's nature but his whole being seems to find itself. It is a condition of consciousness in which feelings are fused, ideas melt into one another, boundaries broken and ordinary distinctions transcended.[1] Past and present fade away in a sense of timeless being. Consciousness and being are not there different from each other. All being is consciousness and all consciousness being. Thought and reality coalesce and a creative merging of subject and object results. Life grows conscious of its incredible depths. In this fulness of felt life and freedom, the distinction of the knower and the known disappears.[2] The privacy of the individual self is

1 'In this intelligible world, everything is transparent. No shadow limits vision. All the essences see each other and interpenetrate each other in the most intimate depth of their nature. Light everywhere meets light. Every being contains within itself the entire Intelligible world, and also beholds it entire in any particular being . . . . There abides pure movement; for He who produces movement, not being foreign to it, does not disturb it in its production. Rest is perfect, because it is not mingled with any principle of disturbance. The Beautiful is completely beautiful there, because it does not dwell in that which is not beautiful' (*Enneads*, v. 8. 4).

2 'To have seen that vision is reason no longer. It is more than reason, before reason, and after reason, as also is the vision which is seen. And perhaps we should not here speak of sight; for that which is seen--if we must needs speak of seer and seen as two and not one--is not discerned by the seer, not perceived by him as a second thing. Therefore this vision is hard to tell of; for how can a man describe as other than himself that which, when he discerned it, seemed not other, but one with himself indeed?' (*Enneads*, vi. 9 and 10).

broken into and invaded by a universal self which the individual feels as his own.

The experience itself is felt to be sufficient and complete. It does not come in a fragmentary or truncated form demanding completion by something else. It does not look beyond itself for meaning or validity. It does not appeal to external standards of logic or metaphysics. It is its own cause and explanation. It is sovereign in its own rights and carries its own credentials. It is self-established (*svatassiddha*) self-evidencing (*svasamvedya*) self-luminous (*svayamprakāśa*). It does not argue or explain but it knows and is. It is beyond the bounds of proof and so touches completeness. It comes with a constraint that brooks no denial. It is pure comprehension, entire significance, complete validity. Patañjali, the author of the *Yoga Sūtra*, tells us that the insight is truth-filled, or truth-bearing.[1]

The tension of normal life disappears, giving rise to inward peace, power and joy. The Greeks called it ataraxy, but the word sounds more negative than the Hindu term '*Śānti*' or peace, which is a positive feeling of calm and confidence, joy and strength in the midst of outward pain and defeat, loss and frustration. The experience is felt as profoundly satisfying, where darkness is turned into light, sadness into joy, despair into assurance. The continuance of such an experience constitutes dwelling in heaven, which is not a place where God lives, but a mode of being which is fully and completely real.

However much we may quarrel about the implications of this kind of experience, we cannot question the actuality of the experience itself. While the profound intuitions do not normally occur, milder forms are in the experience of all who feel an answering presence in deep devotion or share

1 Ṛtambharatatrā prajñā (*Yoga Sūtra*, 1. 48).

the spell which great works of art cast on us. When we experience the illumination of new knowledge, the ecstasy of poetry or the subordination of self to something greater, family or nation, the self-abandonment of falling in love, we have faint glimpses of mystic moods. Human love perhaps takes us nearest to them. It can become an experience deep and profound, a portal through which we enter the realm of the sublime. 'My life, My all, My more,' said Sappho to Philaenis. To have one's heart and mind absorbed in love seems to unveil the mystery of the universe. We forget the sense of the outward world in our communion with the grandeur beyond. Religious mysticism often falls into the language of passionate love. It has been so from the Upaniṣads and the Song of Songs.

Since the intuitive experiences are not always given but occur only at rare intervals, they possess the character of revelation. We cannot command or continue them at our will. We do not know how or why they occur. They sometimes occur even against our will. Their mode of comprehension is beyond the understanding of the normal, and the supernormal is traced to the supernatural. Those who are gifted with the insight tend to regard themselves as the chosen ones, the privileged few. Conscious of a light which other men had not, they feel inclined to believe that the light has been directed on them and that they are not only the seekers but the sought. 'Only he who is chosen by the Supreme is able to realize it.'

If all our experience were possessed of intrinsic validity (*svataḥprāmāṇya*) there would be no question of truth and falsehood. There would be nothing with which our experience will have to cohere or to correspond. There would not arise any need or desire to test its value. All our experience will be self-valid, i.e. all reality will be present in its own immediate validity. But even the noblest human minds have only glimpses of self-valid experiences. The moments of vision are transitory and intermittent. We therefore do not attain an insight, permanent and uninterrupted, where reality is present in its own immediate witness. But we are convinced that such an ideal is not an impossible one.

So long as the experience lasts, the individual remains rapt in contemplation, but no man can rest in that state for all time. Life is a restless surge. Scarcely is the seer assured of the unique character of the experience than he is caught in the whirl of desire and temptation, discord and struggle. During the vision, its influence was so potent and overwhelming that he had neither the power nor the desire to analyse it. Now that the vision is no more, he strives to recapture it and retain in memory what cannot be realized in fact. The process of reflection starts. He cannot forget the blessed moments which have a weight for the rest of his life and give to his beliefs a power and a vividness that nothing can shake. The individual adopts an attitude of faith which is urged by its own needs to posit the transcendental reality. He affirms that the soul has dealings, direct, intimate and luminous, with a plane of being different from that with which the senses deal, a world more resplendent but not less real than the conventional one. The experience is felt as of the nature of a discovery or a revelation, not a mere conjecture or a creation. The real was there actually confronting us, it was not conjured out of the resources of our mind.[1] He claims for his knowledge of reality an immediate and intuitive certainty, transcending any which mere reason can reach. No further experience or rational criticism can disturb his sense of certainty. Doubt and disbelief are no more possible. He speaks without hesitation and with the calm accents of finality. Such strange simplicity and

1 Śaṁkara on *Brahma Sūtra*, i. I. I.

authoritativeness do we find in the utterances of the seers of the Upaniṣads, of Buddha, of Plato, of Christ, of Dante, of Eckhart, of Spinoza, of Blake. They speak of the real, not as the scribes, but as those who were in the immediate presence of 'that which was, is and ever shall be'. St Theresa says: 'If you ask how it is possible that the soul can see and understand that she has been in God, since during the union she has neither sight nor understanding, I reply that she does not see it then, but that she sees it clearly later, after she has returned to herself, not by any vision, but by a certitude which abides with her and which God alone can give her.[1]

In addition to the feeling of certitude is found the sense of the ineffability of the experience. It transcends expression even while it provokes it. It is just what it is and not like anything else. There is no experience by which we can limit it, no conception by which we can define it. The *Kena Upaniṣad* says that 'it is other than the known and above the unknown.'[2] As Lao Tze expresses it at the beginning of his *Tao Teh King*: 'The Tao which can be expressed is not the unchanging Tao; the Name which can be named is not the unchanging Name.'

The unquestionable content of the experience is that about which nothing more can be said.[3] Indian scriptures give cases of teachers who dispelled the doubts of their pupils by assuming an attitude of

1 James: *Varieties of Religious Experience* (1906), p. 409.
2 i. 3.
3 'There is an endless world, O my brother, and there is the Nameless Being, of whom nought can be said.
  Only he knows it who has reached that region: it is other than all that is heard and said.
  No form, no body, no length, no breadth is seen there: how can I tell you that which it is?'
                              (*Kabir*: Rabindranath Tagore's E. T., 76)

silence on this question.[1] When we hear enthusiastic descriptions about the ultimate reality, let us remember the dictum of Lao Tze that he who knows the Tao may be recognized by the fact that he is reluctant to speak of it.

Conceptual substitutes for ineffable experiences are not adequate. They are products of rational thinking. All forms, according to Saṁkara, contain an element of untruth and the real is beyond all forms. Any attempt to describe the experience falsifies it to an extent. In the experience itself the self is wholly integrated and is therefore both the knower and the known, but it is not so in any intellectual description of the experience. The profoundest being of man cannot be brought out by mental pictures or logical counters.[2] God is too great for words to explain. He is like light, making things luminous but himself invisible.

And yet we cannot afford to be absolutely silent. Though the tools of sense and understanding cannot describe adequately, creative imagination with its symbols and suggestions may be of assistance. The profoundest wisdom of the past is transmitted to us in the form of myths and metaphors which do not have any fixed meaning and therefore can be

1 Cp. Lao Tze: 'To teach without words and to be useful without action, few among men are capable of this.'
2 Cp. St Paul's words of his own experience in 2 Cor. xii. 2-4; also the following from Middleton Murry's *God* (1929). p. 36: 'What happenned then? If I could tell you that, I should tell a secret indeed. But a moment came when the darkness of that ocean changed to light, the cold to warmth; when it swept in one great wave over the shores and frontiers of myself; when it bathed me and I was renewed; when the room was filled with a presence and I knew I was not alone--that I never could be alone any more, that the universe beyond held no menace, for I was part of it, that, in some way for which I had sought in vain so many years, I belonged and because I belonged I was no longer I, but something different, which could never be afraid in the old ways or cowardly with the old cowardice.'

interpreted as life requires. The seers who were at least as wise and as subtle as ourselves, by letting their imagination work on experience, devised symbolic conceptions such as crossing the ocean of *saṁsāra*, ascending into heaven, meeting God face to face. Plato expressed his deepest convictions, which were incapable of proof, in the language of poetry, saying, 'Not this perhaps, but something like this must be true.' If we insist on interpreting these symbols literally, difficulties arise. But if we go behind the words to the moods they symbolize, agreement is possible.

The symbols and suggestions employed are derived from the local and historical traditions. An Orphic describes to us Charon and the spring on either side of the road and the tall cypress tree. The Vaiṣṇava speaks to us of the cowherd, the Brindāvan and the river Yamunā. The myths require to be changed as they lose their meaning with the lapse of time, but they are in no case to be accepted as literal truths. They require to be interpreted 'according to their meaning and not their lisping expression', as Aristotle suggests in speaking of Empedocles. Much of the rationalistic criticism of the sacred scriptures is due to a confusion between symbolic statements and literal truths. It is easy to prove that the world was not made in seven days or that Eve was not made out of Adam's rib. What they say is not scientifically true; what they mean is a different matter.

5. *Experience and the variety of expressions*

If all our experiences were adequately intuited at once, such immediate intuitions could not be doubted under any circumstances; but, as it is, we are compelled to relate our intuitive experiences with others and here we are obliged to employ formulas. The pedestrian function of consolidation and revaluation seems to be indispensable. The only way to impart our experiences to others and elucidate their implications for the rest of our life and defend their validity against hostile criticism is by means of logic. When we test the claim of the experience to truth, we are really discussing the claims of the forms or propositions in which the nature of the experience is unfolded. In the utterances of the seers, we have to distinguish the given and the interpreted elements. What is regarded as immediately given may be the product of inference. Immediacy does not mean absence of psychological mediation, but only non-mediation by conscious thought. Ideas which seem to come to us with compelling force, without any mediate intellectual process of which we are aware, are generally the results of previous training in traditions imparted to us in our early years. Our past experience supplies the materials to which the new insight adds fresh meanings. When we are told that the souls have felt in their lives the redeeming power of Kṛṣṇa or Buddha, Jesus or Mohammad, we must distinguish the immediate experience or intuition which might conceivably be infallible and the interpretation which is mixed up with it. St Theresa tells us that after her experience she learned to understand the Trinity. Surely she would not have recognized the revelation as that of the Trinity if she had not already known something of the Trinity.[1] Similarly, if Paul had not learned something about Jesus, he would not have identified the voice that came to him on the Damascus road as Jesus's. We must distinguish the simple facts of religion from the accounts which reach us through the depth of theological preconceptions. That the soul is in contact with a mighty spiritual power other than its normal self and yet within and that its contact means the beginning of the creation of a new self is the fact, while the identification of this

1 Evelyn Underhill: *Mysticism*, p. 132, 5th Ed.

power with the historic figures of Buddha or Christ, the confusion of the simple realization of the universal self in us with a catastrophic revelation from without, is an interpretation, a personal confession and not necessarily an objective truth. Something is directly experienced but it is unconsciously interpreted in the terms of the tradition in which the individual is trained. The frame of reference which each individual adopts is determined by heredity and culture.

Again, there is no such thing as pure experience, raw and undigested. It is always mixed up with layers of interpretation. The alleged immediate datum is psychologically mediated. The scriptural statements give us knowledge, or interpreted experience, a that-what. The 'that' is merely the affirmation of a fact, of a self-existent spiritual experience in which all distinctions are blurred and the individual seems to overflow into the whole and belong to it. The experience is real though inarticulate.

Among the religious teachers of the world, Buddha is marked out as the one who admitted the reality of the spiritual experience and yet refused to interpret it as a revelation of anything beyond itself. For him the view that the experience give us direct contact with God is an interpretation and not an immediate datum. Buddha gives us a report of the experience rather than an interpretation of it, though strictly speaking there are no experiences which we do not interpret. It is only a question of degree. But Buddha keeps closest to the given and is content with affirming that a deeper world of spirit penetrates the visible and the tangible world. Such a world certified as valid by the witness of perfect intuition exists beyond or rather within the world of multiplicity and change which the senses and understanding present to us. The primary reality is an unconditional existence beyond all potentiality of adequate expression by thought or description by symbol, in which the word 'existence' itself loses its meaning and the symbol of *nirvāṇa* alone seems to be justified. The only liberty in which Buddha indulges when obliged to give a positive content to it is to identify it with Eternal righteousness (*dharma*), which is the principle of the universe[1] and the foundation of all conduct. It is on account of it that we have the implicit belief in the worth of life.

The Hindu thinkers admit the ineffability of the experience but permit themselves a graduated scale of interpretations from the most 'impersonal' to the most 'personal'. The freedom of interpretation is responsible for what may be called the hospitality of the Hindu mind. The Hindu tradition by its very breadth seems to be capable of accommodating varied religious conceptions.

Hinduism admits that the unquestionable content of the experience is a *that* about which nothing more can be said. The deeper and more intimate a spiritual experience, the more readily does it dispense with signs and symbols. Deep intuition is utterly silent. Through silence we 'confess without confession' that the glory of spiritual life is inexplicable and beyond the reach of speech and mind. It is the great unfathomable mystery and words are treacherous.[2]

1 See Appendix to the writer's work on *Indian Philosophy*, vol. I, 2nd Edn. (1929).
2 Plutarch has preserved for us the inscription on a statue of Isis in the Egyptian city of Sais, which runs: 'I am all that hath been, and that is, and that shall be, and no mortal hath ever raised my veil.' Hooker in his *Ecclesiastical Polity* (i. 2) observes: 'Dangerous it were for the feeble brain of man to wade far into the doings of the Most High; whom although to know be life, and joy to make mention of his name; yet our soundest knowledge is, to know that we know him not as indeed he is, neither can know him; and our safest eloquence concerning him is our silence, when we confess without confession, that his glory is inexplicable, his greatness above our capacity and reach. He is above, and we upon earth. Therefore it

The empirical understanding is quite competent within its own region, but it cannot be allowed to criticize its foundation, that which it, along with other powers of man, takes for granted. The Supreme is not an object presented to knowledge but is the condition of knowledge. While for Buddha, who was ethically disposed, the eternal spirit is righteousness or *dharma*, in the strength of which we live and struggle, for many Hindu thinkers it is the very condition of knowledge. It is the eternal light which is not one of the things seen but the condition of seeing. The ultimate condition of being where all dualities disappear, where life and death do not matter since they spring from it, where spirit seems to enjoy spirit and reason does not stir, can be expressed only in negative terms. The Upaniṣads and Śaṁkara try to express the nature of the ultimate being in negative terms. 'The eye goes not thither nor speech nor mind.'[1]

There is a danger in these negative descriptions. By denying all attributes and relations we expose ourselves to the charge of reducing the ultimate being to bare existence which is absolute vacuity. The negative account is intended to express the soul's sense of the transcendence of God, the 'wholly other', of whom naught may be predicted save in negations, and not to deprive God of his positive being. It is the inexhaustible positivity of God that bursts through all conceptual forms. When we call it nothing we mean that it is nothing which created beings can conceive or name and

behoveth our words to be wary and few.'
1 *Bṛhadāraṇyaka Upaniṣad*, iii. 8. 8. For Śaṁkara it is *nirguṇa* (without qualities), *nirākāra* (without form), *nirviśeṣ ı* (without particularity), *nirupādhika* (without limitations). It is what it is. Isaiah's words are true, 'Verily, thou art a God that hidest thyself.' For Dionysius the Areopagite, God is the nameless supra-essential one elevated above goodness itself. St Augustine speaks of the Absolute, selfsame One, that which is.

not that it is nothing absolutely. The scriptures do not demonstrate or describe him but only bear witness to him. The three noteworthy features of spiritual experience are reality, awareness and freedom. If some parts of our experience come to us with these characteristics, it implies the possibility that all experience is capable of being received in the same manner. The consciousness to which all experience is present in its own immediacy, revealedness and freedom from anything which is not itself is the divine consciousness, that which is our ideal. We picture it as a glowing fire, a lucid flame of consciousness ever shining and revealing itself. In the divine status reality is its own immediate witness, its own self-awareness, its own freedom of complete being. There is nothing which is not gathered up in its being, nothing which is not revealed in it, and there is utter absence of all discord. It is perfect being, perfect consciousness and perfect freedom, *sat*, *cit* and *ānanda*. Being, truth and freedom are distinguished in the divine but not divided. The true and ultimate condition of the human being is the divine status. The essence of life is the movement of the universal being; the essence of emotion is the play of the self-existent delight in being; the essence of thought is the inspiration of the all-pervading truth; the essence of activity is the progressive realization of a universal and self-effecting good. Thought and its formations, will and its achievements, love and its harmonies are all based on the Divine Spirit. Only the human counterparts involve duality, tension, strain, and so are inadequate to the fulness of the divine. The supreme is real, not true, perfect, not good Its freedom is its life, its essential spontaneity.

6. God and self

While the fulness of spiritual being transcends our

categories, we are certain that its nature is akin to the highest kind of being we are aware of in ourselves. If the real were utterly transcendent to the self of man, it would be impossible for us to apprehend even dimly its presence. We would not be able to say even that it is 'wholly other'. There is in the self of man, at the very centre of his being, something deeper than the intellect, which is akin to the Supreme. God's revelation and man's contemplation seem to be two sides of one fact. The spiritual glimpses are prophetic indications of an undeveloped power of apprehension in the human mind as well as of an underlying reality with which it is unable to establish permanent contact without an adequate development of that power. There is a real ground in man's deepest being for the experience of reality. Man as a microcosm has relations with every form of existence. While the spiritual apprehension appears in the course of our ordinary life, it is not due to it. It has its source elsewhere though it exhibits its force on the plane of the ordinary consciousness. It is due to that part of the soul which is timeless being. The consubstantiality of the spirit in man and God is the conviction fundamental to all spiritual wisdom. It is not a matter of inference only. In the spiritual experience itself, the barriers between the self and the ultimate reality drop away. In the moment of its highest insight, the self becomes aware not only of its own existence but of the existence of an omnipresent spirit of which it is, as it were, a focussing. We belong to the real and the real is mirrored in us. The great text of the Upaniṣad affirms it--*Tat tvam asi* (That art Thou). It is a simple statement of an experienced fact. The Biblical text, 'So God created man in his own image; in the image of God created he him',[1] asserts that in the soul of man is contained the true revelation of

1 Genesis I. 27.

God. 'The spirit of man is the candle of the Lord.'[1] According
to Plato man is potentially a participator in the eternal mode
of being which he can make his own by living in detachment
from the fleeting shadows of the earth. In the *Theaetetus*
Socrates declares that we should strive to become 'like unto
the divine'. 'I and my Father are one.' 'All that the Father hath
are mine', is the way in which Jesus expressed the same
profound truth. It is not a peculiar relation between any one
chosen individual and God but an ultimate one binding
every self to God. It was Jesus's ambition to make all men
see what he was and know what he knew. In the Gospel
according to St Matthew, Jesus sums up the various ethical
demands in the general requirement: 'Be ye therefore perfect
as your heavenly Father also is perfect.' As Paul says, he
was the first-born among many brethren. Recognizing us all
as children of God and made in his image, Jesus shows us
by his own example that the difference between God and
man is only one of degree. St John spoke of the spirit as 'the
light that lighteth every man that cometh into the world,' the
'spirit that guides unto all the truth'. The phrase in I Peter of
a birth 'of the incorruptible seed by the word of God' refers
to the divine in man. Plotinus's last words to his physician
Eristochius are: 'I was waiting for you before that which is
divine in me departs to unite with itself the Divine in the
Universe'[2]. The Quakers believe in the divine spark or the
apex in the soul. Descartes asks: 'How could I doubt or
desire, how could I be conscious, that is to say, that anything
is wanting in me, and that I am not altogether perfect, if I
had not within me the idea of a being more perfect than

1 Proverbs xx. 27.
2 Witness also the last testament of Labadie: 'I surrender my soul
  heartily to my God, giving it back like a drop of water to its source,
  and rest confident in him, praying God, my origin and ocean, that
  he will take me into himself and engulf me eternally in the divine
  abyss of his being' (Inge: *Philosophy of Plotinus* (1918), vol. I, p. 12).

myself, by comparison with whom I recognize the defects of my own nature.'[1] According to Eckhart: 'There is something in the soul which is above the soul, divine, simple, an absolute nothing.... This light is satisfied only with the supra-essential essence. It is bent on entering into the simple ground, the still waste, wherein is no distinction, neither Father nor Son nor Holy Ghost, into the unity where no man dwelleth.' Augustine says: 'And being admonished to return into myself, I entered even into my inmost self. Thou being my guide, I entered and beheld with the eye of my soul, above the same eye of my soul, above my mind, the light unchangeable.'[2] St Catherine of Genoa says: 'God is my being, my life, my strength, my Beatitude, my Goal, my Delight.' 'All minds partake of one original mind', says Cudworth.[3] The individuals are the re-productions of an eternal consciousness according to Green. William James in his *Varieties of Religion Experience*, writes: 'The overcoming of all the usual barriers between the individual and the Absolute is the great mystic achievement. In mystic states we become one with the Absolute and we become aware of our oneness. This is the everlasting and triumphant mystic tradition, hardly altered by differences of clime and creed. In Hinduism, in Neoplatonism, in Sufism, in Christian mysticism, in Whitmanism, we have the same recurring note, so that there is about mystical utterances an eternal unanimity which ought to make a critic stop and think, and which brings it about that the mystic classics have, as has been said, neither birthday nor native land. Perpetually telling of the unity of man and god, their speech antedates language, nor do they grow old.' The immanence of God, the revelation of the meaning and mystery of life in the soul of man, is the

1 *Third Meditation.*
2 *Confessions*, vii. 10. See also vii. 32.
3 *Intellectual System*, iii. 62.

substance of the mystic testimony.

We generally identify ourselves with our narrow limited selves and refer to spiritual experience as something given or revealed to us, as though it did not belong to us. We separate the power of spiritual apprehension from the rest of our nature and refer to it as something divine. Such a separation is unfair to humanity. The insight of the best moments reveals the deepest in us. It is wrong to regard human nature as its very self when it is least inspired and not its true self when it is most. If our self finds in these moments of vision its supreme satisfaction, and is intensely alive while they last, then that self is our true self. We cannot limit our being to the physical or the vital, the customary or the conventional. The divine in us is the source and perfection of our nature.

The Divine is both in us and out of us. God is neither completely transcendent nor completely immanent. To bring about this double aspect, contradictory accounts are given. He is divine darkness as well as 'unencompassed light'. the philosophers with their passion for unity emphasize the immanent aspect, that there is no barrier dividing man from the real. The unity of man and God is the fundamental thesis of the great philosophic tradition which has come down to us from the Upaniṣads and Plato, Aristotle, Plotinus, Śaṁkara, Spinoza, Bradley and a host of others are witnesses to it.

Those who emphasize the transcendence of the supreme to the human insist on the specifically religious consciousness, of communion with a higher than ourselves with whom it is impossible for the individual to get assimilated. Devotional religion is born of this haunting sense of otherness. We may know God but there is always a something still more that seems unknown and remains unspoken. A profound impression of the majesty of God always remains with the devotee who is certain that we can never reach the divine level of glory. Some of the seers of the Upaniṣads, the author of the *Bhagavadgītā*, St Theresa, John of the Cross, represent this type. For them the experiences themselves are due to the grace of God. God speaks to us, commands us, comforts us, and we speak to him in praise and prayer, reverence and worship. There are many degrees in this personal relationship, from the feeling of utter humiliation to the communion with a supreme Love on whose grace the worst sinner can count.

There cannot be a fundamental contradiction between the philosophical idea of God as an all-embracing spirit and the devotional idea of a personal God who arouses in us the specifically religious emotion. The personal conception develops the aspect of spiritual experience in which it may be regarded as fulfilling the human needs. Man finds his rest and strength in the spiritual experience and so he knows the spirit as that which fulfils his needs. God is represented as possessing the qualities which we lack. In a sense the Freudians are not wrong when they assert that our religion is the projection of the desires of grown-up children. Justice, love and holiness are the highest qualities we know and we imagine god as possessing them, though these qualities exist in God in a different sense from their existence in us.

To compare the Supreme with the highest kind of being we know is nearer the truth than comparing him with anything lower. Though the supreme spirit in its essential aspect is the changeless noumenal reality, its representation in the form of a personal God who is the source, guide and destiny of the world seems to be the highest open to the logical mind. The difference between the Supreme as spirit and the Supreme as person is one of standpoint and not of essence, between God as he is and God as he seems to us. When we consider the abstract and impersonal aspect of the Supreme, we call it the Absolute; when we consider the Supreme as self-aware and self-blissful being, we get God. The real is beyond all conceptions of personality and impersonality. We call it the 'absolute' to show our sense of the inadequacy of all terms and definitions. We call it 'God' to show that it is the basis of all that exists and the goal of all. Personality is a symbol and if we ignore its symbolic character it is likely to shut us from the truth. Even those who regard personality as the ultimate category of the universe recognize that God is vast and mysterious, mighty and ultimate. [1]

Our myths and metaphors 'do him wrong, being so majestical', and the spiritual seers know it; it is their intellectual followers who ignore it.

In the history of thought we have had different interpretations of the spiritual experience, such as Buddha's conception that it is the reality which we are to accept with reverence; Aristotle's view of the Unmoved First Mover whose

1 Calvin says: 'God treats sparingly of his essence. His essence is indeed incomprehensible by us. Therefore let us willingly leave to God the knowledge of his own essence' (*Institute of the Christian Religion*).
A Bengali poet sings:
'I have searched the Vedas and the Vedāntas, the Tantras and the Mantras, yet nowhere have I found thy fulness.
'As Rāma thou dost take the bow, as Syāma the Black (Kṛṣṇa) thou dost seize the sword.
'O mother, mother of the universe, art thou male or female? Who can say? Who knows thy form?
'Nīlakaṇṭha's mind ever thinks of thee as chief of the Creators'
E. J. Thomson and A. M. Spencer: *Bengali Religious Lyrics*, 9. 78).
    A modern poet writes:
        'Some seek a Father in the heavens above;
        Some ask a human image to adore;
        Some crave a spirit vast as life and love;
        Within thy mansions we have all and more'
(G. Matheson, quoted in Bulcock: *Religion and its New Testament Explanation*, 1928, p. 278).

supreme perfection draws the universe towards himself as the beauty of the beloved draws the lover;[1] Spinoza's God who is that, than which nothing is more real, which we are called upon to love without expecting anything in return, a personal God who is a creature of moods and passions, an ethical God who is the highest good at which men aim, and a knightly god who begs of us the favour of helping him in his great designs. The monotheists are quite certain that the gods of the polytheists are symbolic if not mythological presentations of the true God, but they are loth to admit that their own God is at bottom a symbol. All religion is symbolic, and symbolism is excluded from religion only when religion itself perishes. God is a symbol on which religion cognizes the Absolute. Philosophers may quarrel about the Absolute and God, and contend that God, the holy one who is worshipped, is different from the Absolute which is the reality demonstrated by reason. But the religious consciousness has felt that the two are one.[2]

7. *The world a harmony*

Besides the affirmation of a spiritual reality which is variously interpreted and its consubstantiality with the deepest self of man, we have also the conviction of the unity of the universe. We see the one spirit overarching us. The earth and the sky, the world and the animals--all become suddenly strange and wonderful. For our eyes are opened and they all declare the presence of the one Supreme. The universe seems to be alive with spirit, aglow with fire, burning with light. All that there is comes out of life and vibrates in it. The Upaniṣad says: 'When all this is turned into the self, who is to be known by whom?' The supreme spirit is inescapable.

1 *Metaphysics*, A. 7.
2 Cp. Thomas à Kempis: 'He to whom the eternal word speaks is set at liberty from a multitude of opinions.'

It is 'above, below, behind, before, to the right and to the left.'[1]
The reborn soul is as the eye which, having gazed into the
sun, thenceforward sees the sun in everything', says Eckhart.
George Fox asks us to 'learn to see all things in the universal
spirit'. God is everywhere, even in the troubled sea of human
history, in the tragedy and injustice of the world, in its
suffering and sorrow. When we experience the harmony, the
discord with which we are familiar seems unreal.

   If the universe is essentially spirit, how do we account for
its appearance as non-spirit? If the experience gives us the
joyful awareness of the universe as a harmony, why do we
have the tension, the discord and the cleavage in the universe?
The world of science and common sense seems so different
from freedom of the self. Is it an illusion or is it a reality?
Those who are pragmatically inclined take the practical life
as the reality and treat spiritual experience as a mere dream,
so deep seems to be the division between them. Some of the
more careful trace the appearance of the multiple universe
to the limitations of human intelligence, *avidyā*, nescience.
The human mind, being what it is, tries to reconstruct the
universe from the intellectual point of view into an organic
whole. For the intellect, the unity is only a postulate, an act
of faith. For the spirit, the harmony is the experienced
reality. It belongs to the nature of things and we have had
partial and momentary premonitions of it, and we can work
up the harmony if we remember that the world of ordinary
experience is a feeble representation of the perfect world, a
combination of light and darkness, a reflection of the pure
idea in an incomplete material form. The hasty logic which
declares because the one is the real, the many are an illusion, is corrected in the view that the one reveals itself in
the many.

1 *Chāndogya Upaniṣad*, viii. 24.

8. *Self-recognition and the way to it*

If in spite of this identity or kinship between the soul and God the latter appears so far away, it is because the soul is immersed in what is alien to it, and finds it difficult to get at self-knowledge. Having drunk of the waters of Lethe (forgetfulness), man has forgotten his heavenly origin. He is an exile from heaven, clothed in what seems an alien garment of flesh. We have to discover the spirit in us by stripping off all that is extraneous to it. The assertion of the self as something other than the true reality of God is the fall or the original sin (*avidyā*). the obstacles to self-discovery are the stresses of the personal will and they can be overcome only by the replacement of the selfish will by an impersonal universalized will. The endeavour of religion is to get rid of the gulf between man and God and restore the lost sense of unity. It is a progressive attempt at self-realization, the lifting of the empirical ego into the transcendental place, mind in its immediacy into mind in its ideal perfection. A strict ethical discipline is insisted on. The apprehension of spiritual truth depends on the quality of the soul of him who sees,[1] and this quality can be raised only by the cultivation of the intellect, the emotions and the will through prayer and contemplation. No one can know the truth without being the truth. An absolute inward purity demanding self-mastery and self-renunciation is demanded. 'He who has not first turned away from frivolity, who is restless and uncollected, who has not a peaceful mind, cannot through searching reach Him.'[2] The souls forgets its true origin if it fancies itself as part of the drift of events and is swept in its currents and eddies. The Hindu thinkers ask us to abstract from all definite manifestations of life, outward and inward, from

1 'The sun's light, when he unfolds it, depends on the organ that beholds it' (Blake).
2 *Kaṭha Up.*, ii. 24.

our sense-impressions and feelings, thoughts and aspirations, let ourselves sink into the pure silent spirit from which
the turbid stream of our present being wells forth.[1] Such is
the way to get inwardly into touch with the source of universal life. Buddha prescribes the eightfold path of morality
and tells us that men with unpurified minds and unchas-
tened sensibilities cannot rise into the domain of spiritual
experience. The cultivation of the interior life is not a fad of
the oriental mind. Every great religion asks us to retire from
the world and be alone and prescribes a discipline for
assisting the individual to come into vital contact with the
spiritual environment. The Orphics and the Pythagoreans
tried to secure the recovery of the soul to its original condition by means of purifications. By exalting contemplative
life above practical activity, the Greeks suggest that the
most perfect of all objects could be apprehended only by
those whose powers of spiritual apprehension are perfected.[2]

1 Cp. *Katha Up*: 'The self-existent pierced the openings of the senses
   so that they turn outwards. Therefore man looks outward, not
   inward, into himself; some wise man, however, with his eyes
   closed and wishing for immortality, saw the self behind' (iv. I). 'The
   mind which sees the divine essence must be totally and thoroughly
   absolved from all commerce with the corporeal senses, either by
   Death, or some *ecstatical* and *Rapturous Abstraction*' (Norris: *Reason
   and Religion* (1689), quoted in Stewart, *The Myths of Plato* (1905),
   p. 481).
2 Commenting on the text 'About the going down of the sun, a deep
   sleep fell upon Abraham,' Philo says: 'This describes what happens
   to the man who goes into the state of enthusiasm, the state of being
   carried away by God. The sacred scripture bears witness that it is
   to every virtuous man that prophecy belongs, for a prophet utters
   nothing of his own; in all his word there is to be discovered the
   voice of another. It would not be lawful for any not virtuous man
   to become the interpreter of God so that by the fitness of things no
   vicious man is capable of the state of enthusiasm. Such things
   belong to the wise alone, because the wise man alone is the
   sounding instrument of God, struck and played by God after an
   invisible sort'(quoted in Edwin Bevan's *Sybils and Seers* 1928 ,

'Religion is the art and theory of the internal life of man' according to Whitehead, 'so far as it depends on the man himself and on what is permanent in the nature of things'.[1] By doctrine, devotion and worship our life is awakened to the unseen reality. Salvation is attained not so much by placating God as by transforming our being by achieving a certain quality and harmony of the passions through severe self-discipline. The effort is costly. No tricks of absolution or payment by proxy, no greased paths of smooth organs and stained-glass windows can help us much. The spirit has to be stripped bare if it is to attain its goal.

Meditation is the way to self-discovery. By it we turn our mind homeward and establish contact with the creative centre. To know the truth we have to deepen ourselves and not merely widen the surface. Silence and quiet are necessary for the profound alteration of our being and they are not easy in our age. Discipline and restraint will help us to put our consciousness into relation with the Supreme. What is called *tapas* is a persistent endeavour to dwell in the divine and develop a transfigured life. It is the gathering up of all dispersed energies, the intellectual powers, the heart's emotions, the vital desires, nay the very physical being itself, and concentrating them all on the supreme goal.[2] The rapidity of the process depend on the intensity of the aspiration,

p. 188). There is a well-known passage in Plotinus: 'Oftentimes when I awake out of the slumber of the body, and come to a realising sense of myself, and, retiring from the world outside, give myself up to inward contemplation, I behold a wonderful beauty. I believe, then, that I belong to a higher and better world, and I strive to develop within me a glorious life and to become one with the Godhead. And by this means I receive such an energy of life that I rise above the world of things' (quoted in Rufus Jones's *New Studies in Mystical Religion*, pp. 43-44).

1 *Religion in the Making* (1926), p. 6.
2 A true religious culture will train the body also so as to develop rhythm and balance, grace and strength.

the zeal of the mind for God.

No man on earth has ever maintained spiritual poise all through his life. The Jesus who declared that men must not resist evil if they are to become the sons of the Father who makes his sun shine upon good men and bad, and his rain to fall upon the just and the unjust, was the same Jesus who cursed the fig-tree and drove the tradesmen from the temple. There are moments in the life of the best of us as the one in Gethsemane when we shrink from the ordeal before us and pray if possible to escape from it, and it requires some effort before we can bring ourselves to say, 'Thy will be done'. To keep one's balance in the face of an uncomprehending and hostile world is not a light affair. It is possible only if we get back to the depths constantly, and develop a disinterested-ness of mind which no pleasure can entice nor pain over-power.

The mystics emphasize being more than doing. While their lives escape triviality, pettiness and intolerance, it is possible that they may exaggerate a negative self-feeling and non-aggressiveness. They are more inclined to sur-render their rights than fight for them, but their gentleness is born of courage and strength and not fear and cowardice. But in the heart of asceticism there is a flame of spiritual joy which is of the very essence of religion. Withdrawal is not the whole of the religious tradition; there is also participa-tion, enjoyment. The *Īśa Upaniṣad* asks us to enjoy by renouncing. It is a deep and dis-interested acceptance of the world and a joyful recognition that no part of it may be refused. We renounce the world in order to return to it with the knowledge of its oneness to sustain us.

9. *The life of the reborn*

Life is different from the moment of the insight. The vision of the one is the beginning of the process of conversion. The soul hath seen, the mind must control our whole being, the word recognized as true must become flesh. If the new harmony glimpsed in the moments of insight is to be achieved, the old order of habits must be renounced. In the life of Socrates, for example, a change takes place from the time he had the experience in the camp at Potidea (431 B.C.), where he is said to have stood still in a trance for twenty-four hours. Thereafter he became entirely devoted to the teaching of his fellow citizens. In the *Apology*, Plato makes Socrates affirm that his mission was divinely imposed on him and he dared not neglect it even if it led to his death as it actually did. The divine call cannot be accepted by anyone whose soul has not found its anchorage, whose discords have not been resolved. There cannot be any conflict between body, mind and soul. The harmony of the different sides of our nature is the condition of peace and their mutual understanding the means of perfection. The suppression of any one side mars self-fulfilment. Asceticism is an excess indulged in by those who exaggerate the transcendent aspect of reality. If the real is yonder, in another sphere, and this world is only appearance, then the real can be found only by those who turn away from the temporal and the finite. The mystic does not recognize any antithesis between the secular and the sacred. Nothing is to be rejected; everything is to be raised. The perfection aimed at is not the perfection of a void, of a nature whose brain is barren and heart dry. The spiritual is not an essence apart, to be cloistered and protected from the rest of life, but something which pervades and refines the whole life of man. It cleanses all parts of our inward being and brings about a rebirth of the soul, a redemption of our loyalties and a remarking of our personalities. Life puts on immortality and the whole being of man becomes intenser. Feeling the unity of himself and the universe, the man who lives in spirit is no more a separate and self-centred individual but a vehicle of the universal spirit. He does not shut his eyes to the evil in the world so obvious and obtrusive, though nothing can shake his conviction of the soundness of the inward frame. His vision of life is so clear and complete that it lives through days of darkness, beholding the sun with the eye of the soul. He struggles to weave into the fabric of life the vision he sees with his inner spirit. He throws himself on the world and lives for its redemption, assured that it backs his dreams. His life burns out in a blaze of sorrow and suffering. He is able to face crises in life with a mind full of serenity and joy, the joy which is the sign of proper fulfilment of function, nature's seal that life's direction is right and secure.[1] For souls of faith, renunciation becomes easy and natural. They walk over thorns with a tread as light as air and a stillness of mind sure of itself. They are great optimists with unlimited faith in the powers of the soul. Pessimism is for them disloyalty to the highest they know, a betrayal of the light in them.

These rare and precious souls, filled with the spirit of the whole, may be said to be world-conscious. They have the vision of the self in all existences and of all existences in the self. 'The three worlds are my native home,' declares the Hindu sage. 'The poet hath said "Dear City of Athens",'says Marcus Aurelius: 'but will not thou, my soul, say rather, "Dear city of God"?' Those who develop this large impersonality of outlook delight in furthering the plan of the cosmos, in doing the will of the Father. They are filled with love and friendliness

---

1 Wesley tells us: 'By this faith we are saved from all uneasiness of mind, from the anguish of a wounded spirit, from discontent, from fear and sorrow of heart, and from that inexpressible listlessness and weariness, both of the world and of ourselves, which we had so helplessly laboured under for so many years, especially when we were out of the hurry of the world and sunk in calm reflection' (Earnest Appeal to Men of Reason and Religion)

to all humanity. *Ahiṁsā* or love becomes the central virtue.
A well-known Sanskrit verse reads: 'Considerations of mine
and thine weigh only with the little-minded; to the large-
hearted, on the other hand, the whole world is like a single
family.' In the spiritual commonwealth, everyone has a
definite place by reason of his specific mode of being. No
man, whatever be his qualities, has any claim to precedence
over others. Value and significance are judged by the extent
to which meaning and expression attain congruence. Even
our enemies are not objects of contempt and aversion as
they are moral personalities. We are called upon to love our
enemies even as ourselves, a rule more honoured with our
lips than observed in our lives. To those dwelling in the
spirit of God, it is the natural law of their being. They have
an abiding realization of the secret oneness which is the
basis of universal love, the love that is patient and endures
all things, that wears out conceit and cruelty, that constrains
the wicked and converts the sinful. It lasts even when the
night is dark and the stars are hidden and man seems
forsaken of all. It is the love that does not expect any reward,
return on recompense. It is its own excuse for being. The
saints love because they cannot help it. It would be strange
not to love. The universal compassion of Buddha enfolds
even the lowest forms of animal life in its merciful arms.
Plato says in the *Crito*: 'When injured we must not injure in
return as the many imagine; for we must injure no one at all.'
For Jesus, to bear and forbear is the path of virtue. The
Gospel of the Nazarenes reports a saying of Jesus: 'Never be
glad except when ye look upon your brother in love.'[1] Those

1 Marcus Aurelius says: 'In anger let the thought be ever present that
   indignation is not a form of courage, but that meekness and
   gentleness are not only more human, but also more manly, and it
   is he who possesses these that has strength, nerve and bravery,
   not the angry and discontented. For the nearer patience is to
   dispassionateness, by so much is it nearer strength; and as pain is

who dwell in God refuse to shut the door of effort in the face
of any sinner however vile or believe that anywhere in the
universe there is a gate bearing the inscription, 'Who enter
here leave hope behind'. If there is a spirit at the centre of
things, no one can be betrayed.[1] The great sin is the sin of
disbelief in the potential powers of the human soul. To know
oneself and not to be untrue to it is the essence of the good
life. It does not mean that we should impose our views on
our neighbour. Love is non-resistance. Conflicts are to be
overcome not by force but by love. Instead of incessantly
resisting the evil in the name of an ideal, we are to endure it
lovingly on its behalf. Love of neighbour means endurance
of evil.

Those who have had the vision feel that so long as they
are guided by it they can do no wrong. They are *svarāṭs*,
sovereigns over themselves. Their life is a spontaneous
growth and not a routine conformity. It is vital and not
mechanical. The moral sense is not external to them but is
rooted in the depths of the soul. They therefore do things
which respectability is ashamed or afraid to do. They are
not worried about the standardized conceptions of conduct.
As intellectual integrity is impaired when we acquiesce in

---

a characteristic of weakness, so is anger. For their victims have
both received their wounds and both succumbed' (*Meditations* xi.
18f. John Jackson's E. T. (1906); 9-11; 7-70). The same work has the
following: 'It vexes not the gods, though they live for ever, that for
all eternity they must needs bear with the wicked, whose
wickedness is great, and whose numbers legion. Nay, more than
this, they aid them in a thousand ways. Shalt thou then, whose end
is all but here, fall weary of bearing with evil-doers?--And this, too,
when thou art numbered with them.'

1 Augustine says: 'I entered into my inmost soul and beheld even
beyond my light and soul the Light Unchangeable. He who knows
the truth knows what that Light is, and he who knows it knows
eternity. Thou art love! And I beheld that thou makest all things
good, and that to thee is nothing whatever evil' (*Confessions*, vii. 10).

beliefs which we do not accept, so sensibility of conscience is disturbed if we mechanically conform to dictates of societies which our conscience does not approve. Buddha opposed individual truth to dogmatic tradition, the sense of community to class divisions, the inner spirit to external conformity. The same is true of Socrates, of Jesus and of other men of dynamic vision.

Naturally, the seers are free from dogmatism and breathe the spirit of large tolerance. They welcome all who worship God revealed, not once, but everywhere, and always accept the variety of the world with understanding and sympathy. 'All things that have been rightly said by all teachers are ours,' says Aśoka, and Justin and Martyr endorses it.[1] They are members of an all-comprehending church of spirit, including all who have any religion whatsoever, all who believe that there is a right worth fighting for and a wrong fighting against. Religious absolutism which attempts to legislate for the whole universe and believes in an isolated supernatural revelation argues that human souls can be saved only if they accept the one official view of God which is its own. Failure to conform to it is threatened with the torments of hell on the other side, since modern democracies do not permit open persecution on this. It is dualistic philosophy that encourages the spirit of exclusiveness. If God is essentially distinct and separate from the world, man

1 'We have been taught and have proclaimed that Christ is the firstborn of God, as being the Logos (Reason), whereof every race of men partakes. And those who have lived by reason are Christians, even if they were regarded as atheists, as, for instance, among the Greeks, Socrates and Heraclitus, and their like....Not that the doctrines of Plato are alien from Christ , but that they are not altogether similar any more than those of other teachers--Stoics, poets and historians. For each saw in part that which is congruous with the divine seminal Reason and uttered it well. Whatever has been well spoken among them all belongs to us Christians' (*Apology*, II, xiii. 2-4).

is admitted to salvation only through his special favourites. But those who are anchored in the centre of all being know that every religion is a response to divine condescension that has uplifted us. The different traditions are like so many languages in which the simple facts of religion are expressed. Speech may vary but the spirit is the same. There is significance in all forms of worship, however crude and foolish they may seem to us. After all, conceptual expressions are tentative and provisional, not because there is no absolute but because there is one. The intellectual accounts become barriers to further insights if they get hardened into articles of faith and forget that they are constructed theories of experience. The greatest idolatry is the worship of the letter. Besides, we should recognize that by far the greater number of men and women acquire their religion as they do their language as the result of being born in a particular place and at a particular time. They cannot be criticized for not choosing their parents. It is all to the advantage of the individual to have a ready-made faith and established ceremonial matured by age and growth to some dignity of thought and procedure. So long as the tradition is able to awaken the spirit in us, it is valid and valuable. While no tradition coincides with experience, every tradition is essentially unique and valuable. While all traditions are of value none is finally binding. Each tradition, so long as its followers are spiritually alive, is bound to grow. It is a system of notation that usually varies from age to age. The spirit is not tied to any mortal form. Those who quarrel about forms do not see the word of god for its shadows or hear its sound for its echoes. The traditions are accepted as beaten tracks in the wilderness of ignorance. The seers, however, go behind the words and give them a new meaning in the light of their experience. Simply because we substitute new symbols for the old, the reality to which they point is not altered. Different systems use different symbols, and even in the history of any one religion one symbol succeeds another because it is truer than the one which went before. The positive appreciation of other creeds which the seers exhibit is not a mere pose of intellectual liberalism but a conviction born of a spiritual insight.

The seers believe in an individualistic religion and plead for freedom and spontaneity. Science may impose a common standard for all, but in art and literature, philosophy and religion, individualism is more true. Man's search after the infinite is not restricted to any given types. The many-sided call of the divine to its children demands an open and flexible discipline. Religious endeavour which tries to convert recognition into realization, to restore the union of that which has become separated in the process of the universe, into its own true self, may start in the emotional heart, the active will or the understanding mind, but wherever the process may begin it results in a general conversion of the total nature of man. An idea of the mind, an aspiration of the will, a need of the heart may set the whole being in activity. Freedom is the supreme law of spiritual life. The Upaniṣad says: 'As the birds fly in the air, as the fish swim in the sea leaving no traces behind, even so is the pathway to God traversed by the seekers of spirit.' Each man has written in the blood of his own heart his pathway to perfection. Buddha abstained from clear-cut answers to metaphysical riddles, not out of indecision or timidity. No one knew his own mind more surely; no one was less afraid to speak unpleasant truth, but he persistently declined to have a creed for his followers. He insisted that each one will learn the lesson for himself. The mission of the teacher is to inspire the quest; it is for the pupil to discover the treasure. 'There is not, nor shall there ever be, any writing of mine on this subject. It is altogether beyond such means of expression as exist in other departments of knowledge; rather, after long dwelling upon the thing itself and living with it, suddenly, as from a leaping spark, a light is kindled, which, when it has arisen in the soul, thenceforward feeds itself.'[1] Jesus did not announce a creed, a code or a constitution, but left to us in his life and ministry an example of religious life. Each of us has the right to explore the universe for himself. Each individual has to blaze out his own trail into the unknown. And however much others may assist, the achievement is an individual one. Each must tread the weary path up the steep mountain from the top of which alone the vision can be seen in all its splendour. The teacher may put us on the way, speak to us of the hazards and hardships, but grasping the final mystery is an individual achievement.[2]

Since the religious effort is primarily the individual's own he is allowed freedom in his approach to God. Any name, any form, any symbol may set the whole being astir, and the divine in the heart of the seeker lifts him up and accepts the offering. God is sometimes viewed as a personal friend and lover. Many feel the need for a human intermediary, example or incarnation. Some want to feel the divine in something entirely close to humanity, an *avatār* like Kṛṣṇa, Buddha or Jesus. Some find that even this is not quite sufficient and seek for a prophet like Mohammad, and still others are restless without a living teacher, a *guru*, one who does not so much impart instruction as transfer vitality.

1 Plato, Cornford's E. T., quoted in J. Middleton Murry's *Keats and Shakespeare* (1925), p. 223.
2 As with Dante, the hour strikes when Virgil must cease to guide:
'What reason here discovers, I have power
To show thee; that which lies beyond, expect
From Beatrice, faith not reason's task'
(*Purgatory*, xviii, 47-8).

10. *Rebirth*

The way to realization is a slow one. Hindu and Buddhist thought, the Orphic mysteries, Plato and some forms of early Christianity maintain that it takes a long time for realizing the holy longing after the lost heaven. The souls that have fallen from the higher estate and that now dwell on earth as in a prison pass up and down in their wanderings so that the deeds of an earlier life condition the existence of the following one. The Hindu hold that the goal of spiritual perfection is the crown of a long patient effort. Man grows by countless lives into his divine self- existence. Every life, every act, is a step which we may take either backward or forward. By one's thought, will and action, one determines what one is yet to be. According to Plato, the wise man turns away from the world of the senses, and keeps his inward and spiritual eye ever directed to the world of the eternal idea, and if only the pursuit is maintained, the individual becomes freed from the bonds of sensualism, and after death his released spirit slowly mounts up higher and higher until at last it finds its way back to the home of the eternal light.[1] Our feet are set on the path of the higher life, though they wander uncertainly and the path is not seen clearly. There may be the attraction of the ideal but no assent of the whole nature to it. The utter self-giving which alone can achieve the end is not easy. But no effort is wasted. We are still far from realizing the implications of the spiritual dignity

1 Dean Inge writes: 'The disbelief in the pre-existence of the soul, a doctrine which for Greek thought stands or falls with the belief in survival after death, is more important and may be partly attributable to Jewish influence. But pre-existence does not seem to have been believed by the majority of Greeks, and in fact almost disappears from Greek thought between Plato and the Neo-Platonists. It is possible that the Pythagorean and Platonic doctrine may still have a future' (*The Legacy of Greece* (1922), ed. by Livingstone, p. 44).

of man in matters of conduct, individual and social. It requires an agelong effort carried on from life to life and from plane to plane.

11. *Salvation*

It is the aim of religion to lift us from our momentary meaningless provincialism to the significance and status of the eternal, to transform the chaos and confusion of life to that pure and immortal essence which is its ideal possibility. If the human mind so changes itself as to be perpetually in the glory of the divine light, if the human emotions transform themselves into the measure and movement of the divine bliss, if human action partakes of the creativity of the divine life, if the human life shares the purity of the divine essence, if only we can support this higher life, the long labour of the cosmic process will receive its crowning justification and the evolution of centuries unfold its profound significance. The divinizing of the life of man in the individual and the race is the dream of the great religions. It is the *mokṣa* of the Hindus, the *nirvāṇa* of the Buddhists,[1] the kingdom of heaven of the Christians. It is for Plato the life of the untroubled perception of the pure idea. It is the realization of one's native form, the restoration of one's

1 The Udāna states clearly the Buddhist view: 'There is a stage (*āyatana*) where there is neither earth nor water, nor fire nor wind, nor the stage of the infinity of space, nor the stage of the infinity of consciousness, nor the stage of nothingness, nor the stage of neither consciousness, nor non-consciousness. There is not this world nor the other world, not sun nor moon. That I call neither coming nor going nor staying nor passing away nor arising; without support or going on or basis is it. This is the end of pain. There is an unborn, an unbecome, an unmade, an uncompounded; if there were not, there would be no escape from the born, the become, the made and the compounded' (viii. 1-4). For a detailed discussion of the Buddhist view of *nirvāṇa*, see the author's *Indian Philosophy*, vol. i, 2nd ed. (1929).

integrity of being. *Tadā draṣṭuḥ svarūpe avasthānam* as the *Yoga Sūtra* has it. Heaven is not a place where God lives but an order of being, a world of spirit where the ideas of wisdom, love and beauty exist eternally, a kingdom into which we all may enter at once in spirit, which we can realize fully in ourselves and in society though only by long and patient effort. The expectation of the second advent is the expression of the soul's conviction of the reality of the spiritual. The world process reaches its consummation when every man knows himself to be the immortal spirit, the son of God and is it. Till this goal is reached, each individual is the centre of the universal consciousness. He continues to act without the sense of the ego. To be saved is not to be moved from the world. Salvation is not escape from life. The individual works in the cosmic process no longer as an obscure and limited ego, but as a centre of the divine or universal consciousness embracing and transforming into harmony all individual manifestations. It is to live in the world with one's inward being profoundly modified. The soul takes possession of itself and cannot be shaken from its tranquillity by the attractions and attacks of the world. The spiritual illumination does not make the individual life impossible. If the saved individuals escape literally from the cosmic process, the world would be forever unredeemed. It would be condemned to remain for all time the scene of unending strife and darkness. The Hindus assert different degrees of liberation, but the complete and final release of all is the ultimate one. Mahāyāna Buddhism declares that Buddha standing on the threshold of *nirvāṇa* took the vow never to make the irrevocable crossing so long as there was a single undelivered being on earth. The *Bhāgavata Purāṇa* records the following prayer: 'I desire not the supreme state with all its eight perfections nor the release from rebirth; may I assume the sorrow of all creatures who suffer and

enter into them so that they may be made free from grief.'
The self-fulfilment which they aspire to is inconsistent with
the failure to achieve similar results in others. This respect
for the individual as individual is not the discovery of
modern democracy, so far as the religious sphere is concerned. When the cosmic process results in the revelation of
all as the sons of God, when all the Lord's people become
prophets, when this universal incarnation takes place, the
great cosmic rebirth of which nature strives to be delivered
will be consummated.

We may now bring together the several affirmations of
religious experience.

There is a mode of consciousness which is distinct from
the perceptual, imaginative or intellectual, and this carries
with it self-evidence and completeness. Religious men of all
ages have won their certainty of God through this direct
way of approach to the apprehension of reality.

The larger environment is of the nature of one's own self,
with which the individual occasionally comes into contact.
There are differences regarding the interpretation of the
nature of this spiritual environment, while this at any rate
is true, that it offers the only justification for a life of truth
seeking and good realizing.

The intuition of the all-pervading unity of the self and the
universe is emphasized sometimes to the extent of rejecting
a God who can reciprocate our love or a self which has real
independence.

Those who have this consciousness are the saintly souls
whose lives are characterized by an unshakable faith in the
supremacy of spirit, invincible optimism, ethical universalism and religious toleration.

The attainment of steady spiritual insight is the aim of
religious endeavour and the means to it are an ethical life
and the art of meditation.

While it is not possible to deal at length with all the issues these affirmations raise, some general considerations may be offered which may prove somewhat helpful in testing the validity of these dicta.

CHAPTER IV

Intellect and Intuition

IF all knowledge were of the scientific type, the contemporary challenge to religion would seem to be conclusive. The problem thus narrows itself to the reality of intuitive knowledge and the conditions of its validity. Is there or is there not knowledge which by its nature cannot be expressed in propositions and is yet trustworthy?

1. *The eastern emphasis on creative intuition*

The alleged dialogue between Socrates and the Indian philosopher suggests that for the whole Western tradition man is esentially a rational being, one who can think logically and act in a utilitarian manner. The Western mind lays great stress on science, logic and humanism. Hindu thinkers as a class hold with great conviction that we possess a power more interior than intellect by which we become aware of the real in its intimate individuality, and not merely in its superficial or discernible aspects. For the Hindus a system of philosophy is an insight, a *darśana*. It is the vision of truth and not a matter of logical argument and proof. They believe that the mind can be freed by gradual training from the influences of speculative intellect as well as past impressions, and that it can unite itself with the object whose nature is then fully manifested.[1] They contend that we can

---

1 *Vaiśeṣika Sūtra*, ix. 2. 13. Different names are given to this apprehension which is not due to the senses of inference, such as prajñā, pratībhā, ārsajñāna, siddhadarśana, yogipratyakṣa (Jayanta's *Nyāyamañjari*, p. 178; *Bhāṣāpariccheda*, 66).

control destiny by the power of truth. Knowledge means power. The lack of this knowledge is the root of all trouble. *Vidyā* is *mokṣa: avidyā* is *saṁsāra*. Intuitive realization is the means to salvation. He who knows is saved directly and immediately, and by means of that knowledge. Intuitive insight is identical with freedom. 'Whoever knows "I am Brahman" becomes this all.'[1] 'He who knows that supreme Brahman becomes that Brahman itself.'[2] We cannot know Brahman fully and truly unless we partake of its essence, become one with it. To know God is to become divine, free from any outside influence likely to cause fear or sorrow. Brahman, which symbolizes the absolute reality, means also holy knowledge, intuitive wisdom. Intuitive wisdom becomes personified as the first principle of the universe. The acceptance of the authority of the Vedas by the different systems of Hindu thought is an admission that intuitive insight is a greater light in the abstruse problems of philosophy than logical understanding.[3] Śaṁkara, for example, regards *anubhava* or integral experience as the highest kind of apprehension. While it may not be clear and distinct, it is sure and vivid. Buddha emphasizes the importance of *bodhi* or enlightenment. His impatience with metaphysical subtleties is well known. The sophistries of the intellect were, according to him, hindrances to the higher life. Knowledge of reality is to be won by spiritual effort. One cannot think one's way into reality, but only live into it. In early Buddhism, *prajñā* or intuitive insight represents the highest activity of the human mind.[4] The general tendency

1 *Bṛhadāraṇyaka Upaniṣad*, i. 4. 10 and 15.
2 *Muṇḍaka Upaniṣad*, iii. 2. 9.
3 *Manu*, vii.
4 'This *bodhi* amounts to realizing in the spirit and in life the basic unity of existence, the spiritual communion pervading the whole universe.' Anesaki: *History of Japanese Religion* (1930), p. 53. Buddhaghosa makes *prajñā* or intuitive insight superior to *vijñāna*

of Hindu and Buddhist thought is to take hold of the aspiration of the human soul after a higher life, and treat this fact as the key to the interpretation of the universe, and all critical philosophy took this into account.

2. Western emphasis on critical intelligence

While the dominant feature of Eastern thought is its insistence on creative intuition, the Western systems are generally characterized by a greater adherence to critical intelligence. This distinction is not to be pressed too closely. It is relative and not absolute. It describes the chief tendencies, and there are in fact many exceptions. It is only a question of the distribution of emphasis.

If we may trust the Pythagorean tradition, the method and achievements of Greek philosophy were largely affected by the example of mathematics. Socrates is credited by Aristotle with two things, inductive arguments and universal definitions.[1] Whatever is real must have a definable form. Things are in virtue of their forms. The classification of moral concepts is the first step to any improvement in practice. Suggested definitions are tested by Socrates with reference to actual facts. For Plato, geometry was the model science. Even God geometrizes. Aristotle invented the science of logic. For him, man is pre-eminently a rational animal. Logic for the Greeks is not so much a science of discovery as one of proof. The civic life of the ancient Greeks centred round the assembly and the law courts, where intellectual subtlety and mental dexterity are most in demand. The great aim was to secure victory in debate, and the chief means to it was to master the technique of argument. More prominence was given to the expression

or logical knowledge and *samjñā* or perceptual knowledge.
1 See Aristotle: *Metaphysics*, M. 1078, b 27.

and communication of thought than to its discovery and growth. There is an intimate relation between grammar and logic in Aristotle's *Organon*. The tendency to stereotype thought in conventional ways grew up. The canons of formal logic would be of excellent use, when all truths are discovered and nothing more remained to be known, but logic cannot dictate or set limits to the course of nature and progress of discovery.

I have no doubt that this summary description is quite inadequate to the complexity and richness of Greek thought. The non-mathematical side of Plato's teaching is perhaps his most important contribution. For Plato, noesis is the highest kind of knowledge, immediate and supra-intellectual. He believed in what he called dialectic or the conversation of the soul with itself, which is not scientific knowledge. Aristotle speaks of the absolute self-knowledge of God, a pure activity which knows no law and no end outside itself. This is not the place to discuss the alleged influence of Eastern thought on the Orphic mysteries and Pythagoras, and through them on Plato's philosophy. Pythagoras and Plato may owe to Indian thought more than the Hellenists are willing to admit.[1] Speaking generally, however, it is not incorrect to hold that the Greeks attempted to give an explanation of the problem of certainty in terms of logical reason, and failed to justify the logical postulates themselves.

1 The Dean of St Paul's traces this mode of Plato's teaching to Asiatic thought. Professor Muirhead, commenting on Dean Inge's *Platonic Tradition in English Religious Thought* (1926), says: 'Beginning in Asia, this mystical faith swept over Greece and southern Italy in the form of Orphism and Pythagoreanism. It found an intelligent sympathiser in Socrates, and under his inspiration reached its highest expression in the *Dialogues* of Plato' (*The Platonic Tradition in Anglo-Saxon Philosophy* (1931), p. 27).

Plotinus[1] and the Neo-Platonists were convinced that logical knowledge alone was inadequate. Neo-platonism which originated in Alexandria, where Oriental modes of thought were not unknown, presented a more organic view and grounded logical processes on the certainty of immediate experience. But the post-scholastic philosophers[2] fell back upon a purely rationalistic approach to certainty, and the attempt to ground philosophy in science became more popular with the growth of natural sciences, which were actually engaged in pushing back the frontiers of knowledge through observation and experimental verification. Though the methodology of the sciences studied the processes by which beliefs grew and thoughts evolved, its actual interest was more in the grammar of discovery than the life of it. The latter by its very nature sets limits to logical exposition.

For Descartes, with whom modern European philcsophy takes a new direction, truth means clearness and distinctness. Whatever can be expressed in mathematical form is clear and distinct. Descartes sets forth a system of universal concepts of reason which are derived from a consideration of certain fundamental, logical and mathematical relationships. In a famous sentence he observes, 'I was especially delighted with mathematics. I was astonished that foundations so strong and solid should have had no loftier superstructure raised on them.'[3] His conception of universal

---

1 Plotinus accompanied Gordian's army in order that he might have an opportunity of studying Indian and Persian Philosophy. Though Gordian's death in Mesopotamia stopped him half-way, his enthusiasm for it is evident.
2 Look at the order of studies in the mediaeval trivium, grammar, rhetoric and dialectic.
3 *The Philosophical Works of Descartes*, E. T. by Haldane and Ross (1911), vol: i, p. 85. Cp. 'In our search for the direct road towards truth, we should busy ourselves with no object about which we cannot attain a certitude equal to that of demonstrations of arithmetic and geometry' (*Discourse of Method*).

mathematics and faith that all things are mutually related as the objects of geometry[1] imply a strictly mechanical world. For Spinoza, even Ethics should be treated by the geometrical method. For Leibniz, again, the monads or perceiving minds differ in nothing other than the *form* of perception, for each monad resembles the others as regards the content of its perception. Each reflects the total universe from its own special angle. But the lowest monads, the plant and the animal ones, have dim and confused modes of perception. Divine cognition consists in completely distinct and adequate ideas. We, human beings, are in between. Our ideas of sense qualities are confused, those of logic and mathematics distinct. We attempt to transform the former into the latter kind, factual presentations into notions conceived by reason. The accomplishment of this ideal means for Leibniz the setting forth of a general system of the possible forms of thought and the universal laws of connection which these laws obey. Such a plan was outlined by Leibniz and became the foundation, in a sense, of symbolic logic which reached its great development in the works of Boole and Peano, Frege, Russell and others.

Kant's fundamental aim was to lead philosophy into the safe road of science, and he inquired into the possibility of philosophy as a science with the intention of formulating its conditions. The 'nature' with which we deal in science and everyday life is due to the work of the understanding which arranges the multiplicity of sense in an orderly world according to a logic which Kant distinguished as synthetic from the traditional formal or analytical logic. His successors took over this logic of synthesis and utilized it for the purpose of resolving the imperfections of Kant's system. The tendency in Kant to postulate an intelligible world as the

1 *The Philosophical Works of Descartes*, p. 92.

foundation of ethics is dismissed as irrelevant, and the world of things in themselves declared a poetic fiction. In Hegel, logic ceases to be a mere theory of thought, but becomes an account of reality. It is an abstract representation of an actual process by which the absolute spirit reveals itself as the universe in the different forms which the universe assumes to human consciousness, nature, history, society, art and religion. 'What is rational is real and what is real is rational.' [1] Hegel's view of history as the manifestation of spirit in the threefold moments of thesis, antithesis and synthesis is an intellectual scheme which largely forced the facts into conformity with an *a priori* formula. Hegel's influence is continued in the later idealists. 'No fact,' says Edward Caird, 'which is in its nature incapable of being explained or reduced to law can be admitted to exist in the intelligible universe.'[2] For the Hegelians, reality is essentially knowable in the logical way. While Bosanquet is more Hegelian in his outlook, Bradley is more Kantian. For Bradley, thought moves within the realm of relationships and can never grasp or positively determine the ultimate reality. The realists are the worshippers of logic and the scientific method. Faith in the logical intellect as the supreme instrument of knowledge has led the realistic thinkers to devote their major energies to the precise formulation of specialized problems. The Behaviourists insist on the close relation between thinking and talking, and reduce thinking to a matter of language or expression. In the words of Max Müller, 'To think is to speak low. To speak is to think aloud.'

From the Socratic insistence on the concept to Russell's mathematical logic, the history of Western thought has been

1 Hegel: *The Philosophy of Right*, E. T. by Dyde (1896), p. xxvii.
2 *Hegel*, p. 141; see also Ritchie: *Philosophical Studies*, p. 226; Watson: *The Interpretation of Religious Experience* (1912), vol. i, pp. 74 and 294.

a supreme illustration of the primacy of the logical. Rationalism is deep in our bones, and we feel secure about scientific knowledge and sceptical about religious faith. If 'there is no higher faculty than those involved in ordinary knowledge', if 'the truth of religion' or the validity of religious experience is to be established, 'as reasonable inference from discursive knowledge about the world, human history, the soul with its faculties and capacities; and above all from knowledge of the inter-connections between such items of knowledge',[1] then it will be difficult for us to be certain about God. But the tradition of religion holds that those who have known God by acquaintance and not by hearsay have known him not as a valid conclusion from logical reasoning but by the constraining authority of experience. But is the authority of the latter valid, trustworthy?

3. *Different ways of knowing*

While all varieties of cognitive experience result in a knowledge of the real, it is produced in three ways, which are sense experience, discursive reasoning and intuitive apprehension. Sense experience helps us to know the outer characters of the external world. By means of it we obtain an acquaintance with the sensible qualities of the objects. Its data are the subject-matter of natural science which builds up a conceptual structure to describe them.

Logical knowledge is obtained by the processes of analysis and synthesis. The data supplied to us by perception are analysed and the results of the analysis yield a more systematic knowledge of the object perceived. This logical or conceptual knowledge is indirect and symbolic in its character. It helps us to handle and control the object and its workings. Conceptual explanations alter with the growth

1 Tennant: *Philosophical Theology,* vol. i (1928), ch. xii, pp. 325 ff.

of experience and analysis. They are dependent on our perceptions, our interests, and our capacities. Both sense knowledge and logical knowledge are the means by which we acquire for practical purposes a control over our environment.

Both these kinds of knowledge are recognized as inadequate to the real which they attempt to apprehend. Plato contrasts the world of eternal forms with the transitory forms of sense impressions. The former is real, and the latter unreal. Knowledge is of the former, while the latter belongs to the realm of opinion. It is clear, however, that the objects revealed by logical knowledge are not those which we perceive. From the same position, it is sometimes argued that the perceived object is more real than the conceived one. The immediacy of the objects we perceive in sense experience is lost when the intellectual activities supervene. No amount of conceptual synthesis can restore the original integrity of the perceived object. Bradley and Bergson insist on the symbolic character of logical knowledge. Whatever be the object, physical or non-physical, intellect goes about it and about, but does not take us to the heart of it. He who speaks about sleep and discusses its nature and conditions knows all about sleep except sleep itself. All intellectual analysis is, for Bradley, a falsification of the real, in that it breaks up its unity into a sytem of separate terms and relations. Thought lives in the distinction between the reality of *that* and the abstract character of *what*. However wide the 'what' may extend, it can never embrace the whole of existing reality.[1] Intellectual symbols are no substitutes for perceived realities. Besides, the whole life of feeling and emotion, 'the delights and pains of the flesh, the agonies and raptures of the soul' remain outside of thought. If thought is

1 See, *Appearance and Reality*, 8th impression (1925), ch. xv.

to be equal to the comprehension of these sides of life, then it is 'different from thought, discursive and relational. It must have been absorbed in a fuller experience.'[1]Bradley's insistence on the separation in judgment of existence from character, as well as the assertion of the unity which is the basis of its separation, brings out the reality of a higher mode of apprehension than discursive reason. The unified structure of reality is revealed more in feeling than in thought, in what Bradley calls the higher unity, in which 'thought, feeling and volition are blended into a whole'. It is the creative effort of the whole man as distinct from mere intellectual effort that can comprehend the nature of reality. Bradley says: 'We can form the general idea of an absolute experience in which phenomenal distinctions are merged, a whole become immediate at a higher stage without losing any richness.'[2]

4. Bergson on conceptual knowledge

According to Bergson, conceptual analysis yields not the component parts of the object, but its varied expressions. It does not give us a split sunset which has its own beauty, but a conceptual notation that it has qualities of gold, light, etc. A set of qualities is not a sunset.[3] Partial notations are not real

1 See, *Appearance and Reality*, 8th impression (1925), ch. xv., pp. 70-71.
2 *Ibid.*, p. 160.
3 'We really persuade ourselves,' he says. 'that by setting concept beside concept we are reconstructing the whole of the object with its parts, thus obtaining, so to speak, its intellectual equivalent. In this way we believe that we can form a faithful representation of duration by setting in line the concepts of unity, multiplicity, continuity, finite or infinite divisibility, etc. There precisely is the illusion. There also is the danger. Just in so far as abstract ideas can render service to analysis, that is, to the scientific study of the object in its relation to other objects, so far are they incapable of replacing intuition, that is, the metaphysical investigation of what is essential and unique in the object. For, on the one hand, these

parts. If the conceptual analysis gave us real parts, then perhaps we might try to fit them together so as to obtain the original object, but such a procedure is impossible with a mere notation. Intellect finds it easy to distinguish and separate, but when it synthesizes it is artificial in its methods and results. It gives us a patchwork and not a harmony. Science, according to Bergson, is essentially utilitarian in its origin, and therefore vitiated in its method. Being practical and directed toward action, it is incapable of grasping change in its mobility. We cannot construct movement by putting together immobilities. Reality is life, movement, duration, concrete continuity, and logic gives us concepts which are timeless, immobile, dead. If all knowledge were of this conceptual kind, truth lies not only beyond the grasp of the human mind, but beyond the grasp of omniscience itself. Bergson substitutes intuition for intellect as the proper organ of absolute knowledge.

5. *Croce*

Croce is of the opinion that logical knowledge takes us

concepts, laid side by side, never actually give us more than an artificial reconstruction of the object, of which they can only symbolize certain general, and in a way, impersonal aspects; it is therefore useless to believe that with them we can seize a reality of which they present to us the shadow alone. And, on the other hand, besides the illusion there is also a very serious danger. For the concept generalizes at the same time as it abstracts. The concepts can only symbolize a particular property by making it common to an infinity of things. It therefore always more or less deforms the property by the extension it gives to it. Replaced in the metaphysical object to which it belongs, a property coincides with the object, or at least moulds itself on it, and adopts the same outline. Extracted from the metaphysical object and presented in a concept, it grows indefinitely larger and goes beyond the object itself, since henceforth it has to contain it along with a number of other objects' (*An Introduction to Metaphysics* (1913), E. T., pp. 15-17).

away from the individual and the actual into a world of
abstractions, while intuitive knowledge gives us an insight
into the individual. 'Knowledge has two forms; it is either
intuitive knowledge or logical knowledge; knowledge we
acquire by imagination or knowledge we acquire by intellect; knowledge of individual or knowledge of the universal;
knowledge is, in short, either productive of images or productive of concepts.'[1] By imagination we give shape to individual things; by thought we relate images in universal
concepts. Artistic activity apprehends the living, palpitat-
ing reality, though the artist does not know that he is apprehending. Art cannot err, but it cannot know that it cannot.
No intellectual distractions disturb it. Bradley, Bergson and
Croce urge in different ways that intellect succeeds in stif-
fening life and binding it in concepts.

6. *Intuitive knowing*

There is a knowledge which is different from the conceptual, a knowledge by which we see things as they are, as
unique individuals and not as members of a class or units
in a crowd. It is non-sensuous, immediate knowledge. Sense
knowledge is not the only kind of immediate knowledge. As
distinct from sense knowledge or *pratyakṣa* (literally presented to a sense), the Hindu thinkers use the term *aparokṣa*
for the non-sensuous immediate knowledge. This intuitive
knowledge arises from an intimate fusion of mind with
reality. It is knowledge by being and not by senses or by
symbols. It is awareness of the truth of things by identity.
We become one with the truth, one with the object of knowledge. The object known is seen not as an object outside the
self, but as a part of the self. What intuition reveals is not so
much a doctrine as a consciousness; it is a state of mind and

1 Wildon Carr: *The Philosophy of Croce* (1917), p. 59.

not a definition of the object. Logic and language are a lower form, a diminution of this kind of knowledge. Thought is a means of partially manifesting and presenting what is concealed in this greater self-existent knowledge. Knowledge is an intense and close communion between the knower and the known.[1] In logical knowledge there is always the duality, the distinction between the knowledge of a thing and its being. Thought is able to reveal reality, because they are one in essence; but they are different in existence at the empirical level. Knowing a thing and being it are different. So thought needs verification.

There are aspects of reality where only this kind of knowledge is efficient. Take, e.g., the emotion of anger. Sense knowledge of it is not possible in regard to its superficial manifestations. Intellectual knowledge is not possible until the data are supplied from somewhere else, and sense cannot supply them. Before the intellect can analyse the mood of anger, it must get at it, and it cannot get at it by itself. We know what it is to be angry by being angry. No one can understand fully the force of human love or parental affection who has not himself been through them. Imagined emotions are quite different from felt ones.

The great illustration of intuitive knowledge given by Hindu thinkers is the knowledge of self. We become aware of our own self, as we become aware of love or anger, directly by a sort of identity with it. Self-knowledge is inseparable from self-existence. It seems to be the only true and direct knowledge we have: all else is inferential. Śaṁkara says that self-knowledge which is neither logical nor sensuous is the presupposition of every other kind of knowledge. It alone is beyond doubt for 'it is of the

1 'A man only considers discursively that which he does not yet possess . . . perfect reason no longer seeks, it rests upon the evidence of that with which he is filled' (*Enneads*, viii. 2-5).

essential nature of him who denies it.'[1] It is the object of the
notion of self (*asmatpratyayaviṣaya*), and it is known to exist
on account of its immediate presentation.[2] It cannot be
proved, since it is the basis of all proof.[3] It is the light which
is not nature, which is not man, but which made them both.
all experience--cognition, affection, or conation--is always
an experience to an 'I'. An 'I' is implicit in all awareness. This
'I' is not the body, however intimate the connection of the
body with the 'I' may be. The body is something which can
be perceived by the senses. We do not say 'I am the body',
but only 'I have a body'. As part of the empirical consciousness, the reality of the body is that of the empirical world.
We say 'I see or hear,' and not the eye sees or the ear hears.
The 'I' implicit in all knowledge is not something inferred
from experience, but something lived and known by experience. It is experienced as a fundamentally simple existent, and is not to be confused with the self as conceived.
What is immediately apprehended is different from what is
conceptually constructed. The self immediately known in
experience is known as a 'that' and not a 'what'. We have in
this immediate apprehension a knowledge of acquaintance
with being, and not knowledge about its essence or nature.
What is immediately apprehended is known as unique, as
subject of all experience while everything else is object.
There is no real but only a logical distinction between subject
and object in the immediate intuitive awareness of the self
as real being. 'That which knows and that which is known
(reason and the world of reason) are really the same thing.'[4]

Many Western thinkers confirm this view of Śaṁkara.
The scepticism of Descartes reaches its limits and breaks

1 Śaṁkara's commentary on *Brahma Sūtra* ii. 3. 7; i. I. 4.
2 *Ibid.*, i. I. I.
3 *Indian Philosophy*, vol ii, 2nd ed. (1931), pp. 476 ff.
4 Aristotle: *de An.*, iii. 4-12.

against the intuitive certainty of self-consciousness: *Cogito ergo sum*. Unfortunately, Descartes' expression is misleading. Self-knowledge is far too primitive and simple to admit of an *ergo*. If the 'I am' depends on an 'I think,' the 'I think' must also depend on another '*ergo*,' and so on, and it will land us in infinite regress. 'The man who calls this syllogism,' says Hegel, 'must know little more about a syllogism, save that the word "*ergo*" occurs in it. Where shall we look for the middle term? It was as a self-evident or immediate truth that the *cogito ergo sum*, the maxim on which the whole history of modern philosophy was built, was started by its author.'[1] It is not an inference, but the expression of a unique fact. In self-consciousness, thought and existence are indissolubly united. The self is the first absolute certainty, the foundation of all logical proofs. Descartes' 'I am' is akin to the 'I am' with which the ancient seer sought to convey to his people the ultimate authoritativeness of his Yahweh. Even Locke, who waged a vigorous polemic against innate ideas, concedes the reality of intuitions. 'As for our own existence,' says he, 'we perceive it so plainly and so certainly that it neither needs nor is capable of proof.'[2] In Kant, the 'I think'

1 *Logic of Hegel*, Wallace's E. T. (1874), sec. 64.
2 *Essay on the Human Understanding.* Pascal observes: 'We know that we are awake; however, we may be unable to prove this by reason, this inability of our only shows that weakness of our reason not (as the sceptics assert) the uncertainty of all our knowledge. For the knowledge of first principles, such as the existence of Space, Time, Motion, Number is as secure as any knowledge obtained by reasoning. And it is on such knowledge, acquired by the heart and by instinct, that reason relies, and takes it for the foundation of all its indirect inferences' (see Webb: *Pascal's Philosophy of Religion* (1929), p. 45).
    Cp. Newman: 'I am a Catholic by virtue of my believing in God; and if I am asked why I believe in a God, I answer that it is because I believe in myself, for I feel it impossible to believe in my own existence (and of that fact I am quite sure) without belief in the existence of Him who lives as a personal, All Seeing, All-Judging

accompanies all representations. It is the vehicle of all concepts in general. All knowledge and logic start with this first principle of self-certainty. For Fichte, the knowledge of self is due to intuition. Schopenhauer contends that we become aware of something that is more than phenomenal in our inner experience. It is will, and all phenomena are its manifestations. Not through intellect, but through the immediate consciousness we have of our own volition, we attain to awareness of reality. Bergson holds a somewhat similar view. For him the true self is not the growing self which goes on gathering its past experience through memory and pressing forward to its future ends. It is to be defined by reference to pure duration which knows not past history or future progress. It is the undivided present to which the categories of time are irrelevant.[1] We are or get near to pure duration only in those rare moments of real freedom. We cannot intuit pure duration if we do not get rid of our tendency to misinterpret what we see by applying to it the categories of the intellect. In other words, we can intuit pure duration only if we make ourselves into it. Ordinarily our life is not pure duration, for it is partly mechanized. This is Bergson's way of expressing the truth that intellect working with distinctions of the knower, the knowledge and the known cannot attain to self-knowledge where these three are not different. Intellect ignores the fundamental oneness of the movement which is indivisible and not distributed in its forms. Intuitive self-knowledge knows itself as a single indivisible act of knowledge, an act which is one with its self-existence. It is through intuitive understanding or sympathetic interpretation that we know other minds.[2]

Being in my conscience' (*Apologia*).

1 *Creative Evolution*. E. T., p. 210.

2 Cp. Alexander: 'That a mind is there is assurance. It is not invented by inference or analogy, but is an act of faith forced on us by a

The deepest things of life are known only through intuitive apprehension. We recognize their truth but do not reason about them. In the sphere of values we depend a good deal on this kind of knowledge. Both the recognition and creation of values are due to intuitive thinking. Judgments of fact require dispassionateness; judgment of value depend on vital experience. Whether a plan of action is right or wrong, whether an object presented is beautiful or ugly can be decided only by men whose conscience is educated and whose sensibility is trained. Judgments of fact can be easily verified while value-judgments cannot. Sensitiveness to quality is a function of life, and is not achieved by mere learning. It is dependent on the degree of development of the self.

Besides, what we normally notice through the senses or infer through the intellect can also be known by intuition. We can see objects without the medium of the senses and discern relations spontaneously without building them up laboriously. In other words, we can discern every kind of reality directly. In normal circumstances we seem to be incapable of knowing what is going on in another's mind except through the expression of that mind through speech or gestures. The facts of telepathy prove that one mind can communicate with another directly.

7. Intuition and imagination

The reality of the object is what distinguishes intuitive

peculiar sort of experience'(*Space, Time and Deity* (1920), vol ii, p. 37). 'It may very well be held that a *complete* knowledge of anything in the whole infinity of its relations (including that to our sensitive nature) would mean the making of that thing. Can we really think of omniscience apart from omnipotence? If I knew another individual through and through, I should be that person' (Ritchie: *Mind*, vol. xiii, p. 260).

knowledge from mere imagination. Just as in the common perception of finite things we become directly and inevitably aware of something which has its own definite nature which we cannot alter by our desires or imagination, even so intuitive consciousness apprehends real things which are not open to the senses. Even as there is something which is not imagined by us in our simplest perceptions and yet makes our knowledge possible, even so we have in our intuitions a real which controls our apprehension. It is not fancy or make-believe, but a *bona-fide* discovery of reality. We can see not only with the eyes of the body but with those of our souls. Things unseen become as evident to the light in the soul as things seen to the physical eye. Intuition is the extension of perception to regions beyond sense.

8. *Intuition and Intellect*

According to Bergson, the life force evolves intellect as an instrument for the practical control of the environment. Intellect is useful for action. It is the toolmaking faculty by means of which life fashions inanimate matter into instruments for the extension of its own powers. If we wish to know the inner nature of reality, we must resort to the whole personality of which intellect is only a part. Logic is successful only to the extent that it displaces the living flux of reality by a system of static concepts. Thought is useful but not true, but intuition is true though not useful. Intellectual consciousness is practical. When a man points a pistol at me, I do not care to ascertain its colour and make, but simply react to it by running away from it. Its dangerous character alone is of practical interest to me; all else is irrelevant. Scientific knowledge is an extension of the workings of practical consciousness. It abstracts from the real certain aspects which are practically useful, and which happen to be repeated in others. Action is impossible without abstraction, and thought, in so far as it is logical, is abstraction.

As we do not get at the real, we await confirmation of our theories. We test the truth of our views by the power of prediction. But symbols and relations do not have the flavour of immediate experience, however much they may enable us to predict. A physicist says that he knows the laws of electricity, though he is ignorant of what electricity is in itself. His knowledge of electricity, which is indirect, grows from more to more. Direct knowledge is incapable of growth, for it is individual and therefore incommunicable. We cannot verify it and therefore cannot dispute it. It transcends the partial truths of the divided mind, the intellectual or the sensuous. Intuitive knowledge is proved on our pulses. It is the only kind of absolute knowledge. It is possible only when the individual is fully alive and balanced. We can see truly only when our inner being is harmonized. Intuition is the ultimate vision of our profoundest being.

It is expressed and transmitted not by means of precise scientific statements, but by myth and image, literature and art. Ideas expressive of intuitions are vital in character since they are expressive of life and not mere logical analysis. They are free, flexible and fluid, and bear on their faces the breath of the spirit.

If the term 'knowledge' is restricted to what is communicable, what can be expressed in formulas and propositions, then intuitive insight as ineffable and non-propositional is not knowledge. But certainty and not communicability is the truest test of knowledge, and intuitive experience has this sense of assurance or certainty, and therefore is a species of knowledge.

If all our knowledge were of an intuitive character, if reality bore immediate witness to itself, there would be no need for logical tests. The unity between the knower and the known would be perfect and our knowledge complete. In it there is no reference to external objects, no correspondence of an idea with something other than itself. Knowledge and being, the idea and the reality, the reference and the identification, are both there. It does not stand in need of proof. It is existence aware of itself. It is knowledge which is neither superficial, nor symbolic, nor second-hand.

Actual knowledge, however, falls short of completeness as there is a distinction between subject and object. The object reaches the subject through an intermediate mode. Thought and sense-perception become necessary as means of objective knowledge. Here there is always the duality. The knowledge of a thing and its being are distinct. Existence refuses to become incorporated in thought. Thought therefore demands verification. Within the world of knowledge we can distinguish facts from fancies by standards of empirical reality. We are said to know a thing when we are able to place it in definite relations to other objects of experience. Empirical reality means necessary connection within the logical universe. As our information derived from the senses increases, as new phenomena are assigned definite places within the framework of knowledge, our knowledge itself grows. New sense-facts are accepted as true if they can be fitted into our scheme. Their validity is derived and not immanent.

Intuitive truths as simple acts of mental vision are free from doubt.[1] They do not carry conviction on the ground of their logical validity. We cannot help assenting to them as soon as we intuit them. Doubts occur when reflection supervenes. Strictly speaking, logical knowledge is non-knowledge, *avidyā*, valid only till intuition arises. The latter

---

[1] Cp. Locke: 'The mind is at no pains of provoking or examining, but perceives the truth as the eye does light, only by being directed towards it' (*Essay on the Human Understanding*, iv. II. I.).

is reached when we break down the shell of our private, egoistic existence, and get back to the primaeval spirit in us from which our intellect and our senses are derived. If intuitive knowledge is knowledge by coincidence or identity, the possession of the intuitive knowledge of reality means that it is possible for us to coincide or be one with reality. If our nature is spirit, so is the real. The fact of the spiritual character of both subject and object is lost in our conventional life where we mistake our true self for the superficial one. The deeper we penetrate, the more unique we become, and the most unique is the most universal.

Both intellectual and intuitive kinds of knowledge are justified and have their own rights. Each is useful for its own specific purposes. Logical knowledge enables us to know the conditions of the world in which we live and to control them for our ends. We cannot act successfully without knowing properly. But if we want to know things in their uniqueness, in their indefeasible reality, we must transcend discursive thinking. Direct perception or simple and steady looking upon an object is intuition. It is not a mystic process, but the most direct and penetrating examination possible to the human mind. Intuition stands to intellect in somewhat the same relation as intellect stands to sense. Though intuition lies beyond intellect, it is not contrary to it. It is called *samyagjñāna*, or perfect knowledge. Reflective knowledge is a preparation for this integral experience. Śaṁkara observes that the fruit of knowledge is manifest to intuition.[1] He is in agreement with Plato, for whom the dialectic is a progressive rational inquiry which helps the mind to a direct vision of reality.[2] In his *Symposium* the prophetess Diotima instructs Socrates in the pursuits preparatory to the

1 Commentary on *Brahma Sūtra*, iii, 4-15. See also *Kaṭha Up.*, iii. 12.
2 *Symposium*, 211; *Republic*, 515, 532-535; see also Spinoza, *Ethics*, v. 28.

apprehension of the form of beauty. We survey a variety of beautiful objects, then recognize the common quality of beauty shared by them all, appreciate the abstract beauty in laws and morals, and at last we attain to a knowledge of the form itself. The *Republic* makes out that the apprehension of form is not possible except for those minds who have been prepared for it by the preliminary training in the exact sciences of measuring, weighing and counting, and hard and strenuous exercise in abstract studies.[1] Intuition is not a-logical but supra-logical. It is the wisdom gained by the whole spirit which is above any mere fragment thereof, be it feeling or intellect. The whole life of mind is more concrete than that of any specialized mode of it. It follows that the great intuitions bear the stamp of personality. Any two men may hit on the same law of science, as Darwin and Wallace actually did, but no two men can ever produce the same work of art, for art is the expression of the whole self, while science in its ordinary usage is the expression of a fragment of the self.

9. *Hegel on intuition*

It is necessary to insist on this integral nature of intuitive knowledge, for the criticism that a thinker like Hegel makes against it is due to a misapprehension that the intuitive power is something cut off from the rest of mental life, and the reality which it apprehends is equally abstract and isolated from the rest of existence. Immediate knowledge which excludes meditation cannot, for Hegel, possess a content which is true. He regards intuition as something unrelated to intellect and incapable of giving us anything else than simple being. Even as the bare category of being requires to be filled with the wealth of the concrete world,

Republic, 525-528.

so is the intuition to be sustained by the other parts of mental activity. As a warning against views which oppose intuition to intellect and identify it with crude fancy or mere feeling, Hegel's criticism is justified.

There is a tendency in Bergson to oppose intuition to intellect, though this does not represent his main intention. Bergson has profited by the teaching of Plato that the vision of the Good is possible only for those who are prepared for it, by intellectual discipline and hard thinking.[1] Intellect, he urges repeatedly, prepares the ground for intuition. He says: 'We do not obtain an intuition from reality--that is an intellectual sympathy with the most intimate part of it--unless we have won its confidence by a long fellowship with its superficial manifestations.'[2] He illustrates his view by a reference to literary compositions which assumes a patient study of the materials, a painful effort to place oneself in the heart of the subject and a constant brooding over it till the happy idea occurs to us which we try to analyse and develop into a thousand details. Genius in one sense of the term is a gift of the gods, in another it is an infinite capacity for learning in patience and humility. By defining intuition as intellectual sympathy, Bergson suggests that intuition is not to to confused with a primitive, abstract, sub-intellectual immediacy, but is to be understood as indicating a higher immediacy which supervenes on intellectual analysis. This latter is gained by a concentration of our whole nature, moral and intellectual, on a single effort. While Bradley is right in his contention that genuine immediacy gives truth and reality, we have to distinguish between the immediacy which appears at the sub-intellectual level before practical necessities and intellectual analysis break up the unity and the immediacy which appears at the supra-intellectual

1 *Republic*, vii.
2 *An Introduction to Metaphysics*, E. T. (1913), p. 77.

level, at the end, and to some extent as the result of discursive thinking. The former or the primitive immediacy remains with us through the process, though at the second stage it is purified of its primitivity and seizes the real in a direct act. The immediacy of intuition as distinct from that of feeling is of the latter kind. Plato and Śaṁkara agree that this kind of intuitive certainty is reached after a long process of discursive analysis. When once the intuition is reached, it is prolonged into an intellectual ordering of images and concepts. All dynamic acts of thinking, whether in a game of chess or a mathematical problem, are controlled by an intuitive grasp of the situation as a whole.

If intuitions are so intellectual in their nature, why call them intuitions at all? Is not the distinction between intellect and intuition analogous to that between understanding and reason as Hegel employs it? Understanding which is concerned with bare self-identities is abstract thought, while reason is concrete thought, finding the universal in the particulars and forming with them an inseparable unity. While the bare identity of understanding leaves all difference outside itself, to the identity of reason difference is organic and essential. The opposite s which understanding breaks reality into are opposed to each other but not to the whole. Being and non-being are aspects of one concrete movement seen from two points of view. At one end there is being; at the other non-being, but the real is neither pure being nor pure non-being, but a concrete becoming. Mere being and mere non-being as understanding takes them are meaningless. The opposites are mutually dependent though antagonistic movements of the real becoming, and their unending strife constitutes the genius of creation. For Hegel the whole life process is a strife of opposites and a labouring to overcome the opposition. The conflict and the transitoriness of all things proceed from the attempt to overcome the opposition and effect a reconciliation. If the reconciliation were complete there would be no world order. The process of becoming is either being in the act of overcoming non-being or non-being in the act of overcoming being. This overcoming is never at an end, for were it ever complete, were there not a non-being for being to overcome or a being for non-being to overcome, there would result either pure being or pure non-being, which are both meaningless abstractions. The world process is a strife of the two, and can be truly conceived only by thinking out completely the mutual indispensability of the concepts whose seeming negation of each other expresses the aspect of strife in the real.

What is the point of dispute between the Hegelian view of reason and understanding and the distinction between intuition and intellect? The question resolves itself into whether we *see* becoming or only *think* it, whether we conceive reality by thought or only intuit it by an altogether peculiar power of direct insight. Hegel, by the exaggerated importance he attaches to conceptual thinking, is inclined to make reason organic to reality, if not to elevate reality to the rank of a concept. He makes logical opposition the prime condition of all being. Dialectic becomes for Hegel not merely a method of philosophical discovery and exposition, but also a description of the way in which things habitually come into being and grow. While it may be true to say that Hegel reduces the rich life of concrete nature to a bloodless dialectic of categories, some of his followers, such as T. H. Green, make thought not merely revelatory but constitutive of reality.[1] In Hegel logic rules, turning life itself into an argument, converting the living truth into an abstract formula. If life could only be expressed in a logical system, it

1 Cp. Green: Thought is things and things are thought'(*Works*, iii. p. 144).

would cease to be life. Hegel's dialectic does not start from the whole in which the opposite terms manifest themselves, but stands with one side which takes us over into its opposite and later builds a unity that holds them together. While the indivisible unity is for intuition the primary reality, it is for Hegel something which is built up out of opposite parts which are logically prior to the whole. The unity appears as the result of a synthesis, the members of which are apprehended prior to the whole. The essential nature of Hegel's dialectic is an immanent transcendence by which a limited and finite something passes over into its opposite so that the former cancels itself and together with its opposite is taken over into a higher and more comprehensive concept. The insight into the whole is obtained by a synthesis. It is perhaps the heritage from Kant, who does not believe in any unity prior to reflective thought. It is the synthesis of a manifold (whether given empirically or *a priori*) which first gives rise to knowledge.[1]

Besides, by reducing reality to a set of relations which can be dialectically understood, Hegel ignores the elements of feeling and will and psychical inwardness; at any rate, he assigns a privileged position to the merely rational. Though man is a thinking being, his being does not consist solely in thinking. For some Hegelians, if not for Hegel, thought alone, in and by itself, is creative of all existence. Reality becomes thought incarnate, the idea made flesh. It is an all-inclusive rational experience or mind. The world process is a fragment of a rational process, an unfinished syllogism, The whole future is in a sense contained in the present. There is no room for novelty or unpredictability in the cosmic process.

If life is history, if reality is genuine becoming, a perpetual

---

1 *Critique of Pure Reason*, Norman Kemp Smith's E. T., sec. 10.

renewal, and not mere repetition, then its apprehension cannot be merely dialectical. Absolute knowledge in its concreteness is more in the form of effortless insight or intuition. It is more immediate than mediate, perceptual than conceptual. Philosophy is not so much a conceptual reconstruction as an exhibition of insights. The truest account of reality which is of the nature of life, a concrete becoming or a growth, partakes of the character of a historical narrative rather than dialectical development. That which reduces real growth to a logical scheme is pseudo-history. The ancient tradition of a geometrical world with its reversible and recurrent order is not only the rationalist view but also the Platonic. If the real is a genuine becoming, then knowledge can only be an insight. Philosophy as conceptual knowing is a preparation for intuitive insight, and an exposition of it when it arises. There is a need for logic and language; for the expression of all knowledge perceptual, conceptual, or intuitional requires the use of concepts. Only we have to remember that the rationalization of experience is not its whole truth. The great truths of philosophy are not proved but seen. The philosophers convey to others visions by the machinery of logical proof. All that the critics of philosophy do is to find out whether the views are partial or total, pure or impure.

There is no break of continuity between intuition and intellect. In moving from intellect to intuition, we are not moving in the direction of unreason, but are getting into the deepest rationality of which human nature is capable. In it, we think more profoundly, feel more deeply, and see more truly. We see, feel and become in obedience to our whole nature, and not simply measure things by the fragmentary standards of intellect. We think with a certain totality or wholeness. Both intellect and intuition belong to the self. While the former involves a specialized part, the latter employs the whole self. The two are synthesized in the self, and their activities are interdependent.

Intuitive knowledge is not non-rational; it is only non-conceptual. It is rational intuition in which both immediacy and mediacy are comprehended. As a matter of fact, we have throughout life the intuitive and the intellectual sides at work. Even in pure mathematics where the conclusion is not evident, until the data are brought together and set forth in logical sequence, there is an element of intuition. In other cases we arrive at convictions without deliberate reasoning as in judgments of value. While the two are not exclusive, intellectual processes are more useful in the observation and description of things and their quantitative relations. Intuition gives us an idea of the whole and intellect analysis of parts. The union of apparent opposites which intellect effects is itself inspired by the drive of intuition. Intuition gives us the object in itself, while intellect details its relations. The former gives us the unique in the object, the latter tells us of the qualities which it has in common with others. Every intuition has an intellectual content, and by making it more intellectual we deepen the content. Even if intuitive truths cannot be *proved* to reason, they can be shown to be not contrary to reason, but consistent with it. Intuition is neither abstract thought and analysis nor formless darkness and primitive sentience. It is wisdom, the *nous* of which Aristotle speaks, the all-pervading intelligence of Dante.

10. *The need for intuition in philosophy*

The deepest convictions by which we live and think, the root principles of all thought and life are not derived from perceptual experience or logical knowledge. How do we know that the universe is in its last essence sound and consistent? Hindu thinkers affirm that the sovereign concepts

which control the enterprise of life are profound truths of
intuition born of the deepest experiences of the soul. For our
senses and intellect the world is a multiplicity or more or
less connected items external to themselves, and yet logic
believes that this confused multiplicity is not final, and the
world is an ordered whole. The synthetic activity of
knowledge becomes impossible and unmeaning if we do not
assume the rationality of the world. It is not arrived at by
way of speculative construction; we have not searched the
outermost bounds of nature or the innermost recesses of the
soul to be able to say that the systematic unity of the world
is a logical conclusion. While thought cannot stir without
faith in the consistency of the world, for thought itself it is
only a postulate, a matter of faith. Our logical impulse is a
power of the self, and therefore possesses in its own being
the vision of the law that governs the universe. The order of
nature is a dependable unity because the self is itself a unity.
So long as I remain myself, everything is capable of being
thought as unity. Thought is guided by the spirit in man, the
divine in us. The orderedness of the universe is a conviction
of life which is beyond mere logic. It will not do to be merely
logical. It is necessary to be reasonable. We have to start
with right premises if logic is to yield fruitful results. Intuition is as strong as life itself from whose soul it springs. It
tells us that the world is part of a spiritual order, though we
may not have clear and consistently logical evidence for it.
Through intuition we become aware of the harmony which
critical intelligence attempts to achieve. In spite of so much
obvious arbitrariness we assume the trustworthiness of
nature. Scientific experience increasingly confirms the venture of faith, but at no stage does the act of faith become a
logically demonstrated proposition. Our whole logical life
grows on the foundations of a deeper insight, which proves
to be wisdom and not error, because it is workable.

Again, how do we know that it is good to be alive in the universe? Theories of ethics which attempt to answer this question assume that it is worth while to live, and the universe will not disappoint us. There is ultimate decency in things. Even as scientific understanding starts with the assumption that our powers are trustworthy, and will lead to a system of truth which will make the universe intelligible, ethical endeavour assumes that life is worth living and will yield to the vision of the good, and we can compel the world to consent to its transformation. We assume a spiritual imperative which urges us to seek not the safe and the expedient but the good, which is not to be confused with the temporal well-being. Logic and ethics take for granted the meaningfulness of life, which they require but cannot establish.

Simply because we require the world to be good, is that any argument why it should be so? Can we be sure that the universe will respond to and implement the demands of the human spirit, that the world of facts will accord with the claims of spirit? From the point of view of empirical understanding it is a mere hypothesis that the realms of nature and spirit, existence and value are not alien to one another, but for intuition it is a fact. There is nothing in the structure of reality when viewed from the logical point of view to contradict this assumption, though logic by itself cannot offer any demonstration of it. It is not a question of believing the world to be what we want it to be. It is the fundamental affirmation of the spirit of man, the ground of all values and the governing principle of all life. It asserts that the ground of the moral order is the source of the universe in time. It is life that imposes on us the obligations to be true and good. Our very vices are the false steps of something which aims not at vice but at virtue. Nature in its ultimate being abhors evil and strives for goodness. This is the first principle of all ethics.

Similarly, the heart of man craves for happiness. The rejection of pain is a sovereign instinct in our nature. Life is opposed to death. There is a persistent endeavour to eliminate pain, error and ugliness, which are opposed to the profounder possibilities of our being, our true self. All intuitions are involved in self-knowledge. All growth in knowledge is an elaboration of this instinct, an increasing assimilation of the mind of man to the spirit in him. All experience issues forth from it and rests in it. It is beyond the reach of the mind and the senses, though the mind and the senses are thought by it, as the Upaniṣad says.

If intuitive knowledge does not supply us with universal major premises, which we can neither question nor establish, our life will come to an end. The ethical soundness, the logical consistency and aesthetic beauty of the universe are assumptions for science and logic, art and morality, but are not irrational assumptions. They are the apprehensions of the soul, intuitions of the self quite as rational as faith in the physical world or the intellectual schemes, though not grasped in the same way. Disbelief in them means complete scepticism. If all knowledge were of the type of perception or conception, disbelief would become inevitable. The proof of the validity of intuitive principles is somewhat similar to Kant's proof of a priori elements. We cannot think them away. Their opposites are inconceivable. We cannot disbelieve them and remain intellectual. They belong to the very structure of our mind. They are native to the soul. They are not data received by the senses or inferred by logic, and yet there can be no perception or conception if we do not employ them. If we deny self-knowledge, if we make nothing evident of itself into man's self, we deny the possibility of all knowledge and life. It is a great saying of Theophrastus, They who seek a reason for all things do utterly overthrow reason.' If all knowledge depends for its validity on external criteria, then no knowledge is valid at all. One thing depends on another, and we slide into infinite regress, and we can escape it only by assuming knowledge which is valid in itself. Self-knowledge is self-valid knowledge. It is not possible for thought to think what is not true. It is were, then no external criterion or standard of truth could ever be substituted for that which thought in itself would lack, since the apprehension of such external standards would itself be an act of thought. 'It is *prima facie* the nature of a thinking being to frame true or adequate thoughts.' Commenting on this statement from Spinoza, Bosanquet writes: 'Truth is normal to mind and error is the exception.' 'If you can get the mind's thought pure--that is, as it is in its own nature, and free from certain definite defects--you must possess in it a true characterization of reality. For this is the nature of thought, to characterize reality. Its doing so is not exceptional, it is inherent. It is what we mean by thinking.'[1] The belief in the validity of human thought is implicit in every thinking being. Error is non-thought. We do not think it. It is due to the passions and interests of men which cloud our thought. Our logical knowledge is a mixture of truth and error, for practical motives interfere with the unclouded thought. Unless the mind is set free and casts away all desire and anxiety, all interest and regret, it cannot enter the world of pure being and reveal it. It is prior to the distinction of subject and object, of truth and error, which arise at the reflective level. No logical knowledge is possible of that which underlies all logical knowledge. The living self is the final ground of all thought, and as independent of any further ground is free and absolute. Similarly, ethical certainty requires a highest end from which all other ends are

---

1 *Meeting of Extremes in Contemporary Philosophy* (1921), 82.

derived, an end which flows from the very self and gives meaning and significance to the less general ethical ends. The ultimate assumption of all is the spirit in us, the divine in man. Life is God, and the proof of it is life itself. If somewhere in ourselves we did not know with absolute certainty that God *is*, we could not live. Even the sun and the moon would go out if they began to doubt. Our lives are not lived within their own limits. We are not ourselves alone; we are God-men.

11. *Plato*

The great philosophers admit that the major convictions of life are born of intuition. Socrates, for example, preferred to rest his case not on inductive evidence from observed facts but on arguments based on axioms and intuitions. The voice of the inner demon counted for him more than external perception or logical reasoning. Plato's theory of recollection points out that the adventure of human life in all its aspects requires certain truths which are not supplied by the traffic of the senses with outward things or intellect with relations. 'Recollection' is Plato's name for that concentrated endeavour of the whole man by which the essential principles of life and logic are apprehended. The immortal soul learned all truth long ago, and it is reminded by sense experience of truths it once knew and has forgotten. Recollection is the basis of the logical process which consists in the discovery of ideas in which the particulars participate. The universal mind, according to Plato, consists of different essences which are reproduced in the world and act as vital controlling forces in its evolution. To the mind of man they appear as 'ideas' and are the supreme efficient causes of his thoughts. However much reason may help us to apprehend them, we do not owe them to reason. It is by the memory of a direct vision we had before birth that we apprehend them. When Plato tells us that 'that which imparts truth to the known and the power of knowing to the knower, is what I would have you term the Idea of Good, and this you will deem to be the cause of science',[1] he is asking us to admit the reality of good which is made known to us by recollection. No knowledge can become our own if it does not conform to the experience of the self. When Plato says that all learning is a process akir. to remembering, he is making out that ali truth is at once new and old, mysterious and familiar, cognition as well as recognition. The 'good' which is the principle at once of existence and value cannot be logically expounded, and Plato uses an analogy. The 'good' is to the system of forms what the sun is to the system of visible things, the source at once of their existence and the light by which they are apprehended. It is an unproved first principle. If Plato presents this foundational idea in a mythical form, it is because it is not a matter of logical knowledge. It is an object of faith or belief as distinct from demonstration or knowledge. From the logical point of view it is a great hypothesis or a glorious venture. It is felt and affirmed, and not derived or explained. We know it to be true not through logic but through our whole nature, impulses and emotions included. Plato's doctrine of recollection is taken from the Orphics. His distinction between discursive and intuitive thought has remained with us in one form or another.

Aristotle's *nous* represents the intuitive apprehension of the first principles which all reasoning assumes to start with. They are incapable of proof or disproof. 'How,' he asks, 'can there be a *science* of first principles?'[2] Their truth is evident to everyone. We become aware of them by *nous*, by direct intuition and not by demonstrative science.

1 *Republic*, vi. 508.
2 *Metaphysics*, 997a.

12. *Descartes*

Descartes insists on the clear evidence of God's existence
yielded by the nature of our thought itself. It belongs to the
same region of intuitive certainty to which the foundations
of mathematical sciences belong. The truth of these ideas is
their clear intelligibility. No other evidence is necessary, as
all experience testifies to it. Descartes unnecessarily com-
plicates the situation by making the veracity of God the
ground of our belief in the truth of clear and distinct ideas.
Even God cannot make clear and distinct ideas false. They
are essentially true, and their clear intelligibility is sufficient
warrant of their truth. Cudworth rightly remarks with reference to Descartes' criterion of clear and distinct ideas:
'Truth is not factitious; it is a thing which cannot be arbitrarily *made*, but *is*. The very essence of truth is this clear percep-
tibility or intelligibility.'[1] Descartes admits that intuitive
knowledge, that which springs from what he calls the light
of reason, is a knowledge different from the fluctuating
testimony of the sense or the misleading judgments that
proceed from the blundering constructions of imagination.
It is the intuition which an unclouded and attentive mind
gives us so clearly and distinctly that we are wholly freed
from doubt about that which we understand.

13. *Spinoza*

Spinoza distinguishes imagination and reason from intuition (*scientia intuitiva*). The first gives us opinions, inadequate and confused ideas. By reason we attain the
systematic knowledge of the man of science. But the breath
of life has escaped from the world of science and only
intuition can restore it. 'We delight in whatever we understand by the third kind of knowledge, and our delight is

1 *Intellectual System*, iv. pp. 31-38.

accompanied with the idea of God as its cause.'[1] 'To know the essences of things, i.e. to understand them not in their general aspect, as the scientist does, but so to say, as God does, from within, we need the higher grade of knowledge to which the scientific is said to point.'[2] In the *Short Treatise* intuitive knowledge is said 'not to consist in being convinced by reasons but in an immediate union with the thing itself.' 'It does not result from something else but from a direct revelation of the object itself to the understanding.'[3] From intuitive vision arises the highest possible peace of mind.[4]

14. *Leibniz*

Leibniz in his *New Essays* tells us that there is something like 'pure reason' which can be tested by self-observation. His faith that there is nothing innate in the intellect except the intellect itself does not favour the view that all knowledge is either perceptual or conceptual.

15. *Pascal*

Pascal's saying that the heart has its reasons which reason knows not is well known. The knowledge of first principles, like the existence of space, time, movement and number, is as certain as any of the principles given to us by our reasoning. Reason itself concedes that there is an infinite region beyond reason. According to Pascal, the mind thinks in two ways, the mathematical way (*l'esprit géométrique*) and the finer, subtler way (*esprit de finesse*). In the latter case we see and feel the truth.

1 *Ethics*, V. xxxii.
2 II. 47 Sch. Roth: *Spinoza*, p. 123.
3 Roth: *Spinoza*, pp. 146-147.
4 *Ethics*, V. xxvii.

16. Kant

Kant's chief contribution to the philosophy of religion is his insistence on the logical indemonstrability of God. In the *Critique of Pure Reason* he shows that the arguments employed for proving the existence of God are defective and lead to contradictions. Our capacities of knowledge are limited to the phenomenal world, and if we extend the principles of space and time experience to regions beyond it, we are betrayed into what he calls 'the illusions of the understanding'. For our categories are useless until the material is furnished by sense, and sense can never supply material adequate to the requirements of the principles of speculative reason. God is not an object of perception or of inference, and if he exists, his being must be apprehended in some way other than that which holds for the finite world. But unfortunately Kant did not discuss the question of the possibility of a different mode of apprehension for the world in its non-spatial and temporal character, though there are valuable suggestions especially in his treatment of the Ideas of Reason, the moral problem and the teleological judgment.

The categories of the understanding, like causality and substance, give us only partial unities, but the mind of man is haunted by the ideas of a completely integrated whole of experience. It seeks to bring the whole that is experienced. Whether as subject or object, or as a union of both, into a form in which it could be grasped as one. Kant called the ideas, after Plato, Ideas of Reason. There are three ideas of reason--Soul, World in its entirety, and God. They cannot be construed as objects of experience, though they have a *regulative* use. They prescribe the problems which the understanding is called upon to solve in its search for knowledge. They are at the same time limiting concepts. They do not represent the nature of reality; for the Ideas cannot receive empirical verification, for everything empirical is conditioned and relative, and the Ideas are unconditioned and absolute. If we ask how such ideas arise at all, since they are in conflict with the content of experience, Kant answers that the understanding forms these ideas by removing the conditions under which objects are known in experience. The Ideas express the demands of the understanding, the subjective interests which inspire the work of understanding in organizing the contingent facts of experience into a unified system. Their sole function is to regulate the work of understanding, and they have no metaphysical significance. They help us to organize our experience and estimate its worth. Science in the last analysis rests on a faith and a hope, the faith of reason in its own supremacy, and the hope in the rationality of the world.

Kant conceives of reason as the faculty by which we learn about ultimate or unconditioned principles. In the matter of cognitive experience, these principles do not give us valid knowledge, since one has to depend on sense for the matter of knowledge, and the matter actually supplied is not adequate to the requirements of the principles of reason. But reason in its practical capacity is in a better position. A command can be valid, even though it is not actualized in the world of space and time. So there is no inherent defect in the unconditional validity of the principles of practical reason. A deeper meaning to the Ideas of Reason is given by moral life. The fact of duty is an illustration of the kind of reality to which the Ideas of Reason point, a reality which, although it has a definite content, is in no sense an object in the context of experience. We have an intuitive recognition of moral law as good in itself, not because it is commanded by a superior or is felt to be conducive to our happiness. The unconditioned principles are admitted to be valid in the sphere of practical reason, even though they have not received any fulfilment in the world of space-time. Kant is fully alive to the fact that the kind of apprehension we have in the mathematical and physical sciences is not all. The moral consciousness is the point where we touch absolute reality. Conscience is the call of reality within the individual mind. The intuitive apprehension of the moral law is quite different from the logical apprehension of any object in the space-time scheme.

It is interesting to find that Kant actually assigns to reason in its practical aspect not merely the abstract principle of all morality, orderliness, or regulation, but also the more concrete principles of conduct. In the sphere of pure reason, Kant always insisted that the matter of experience was no less necessary to knowledge than form. But he believed that in the sphere of practical reason, the bare, abstract formula of reason, the categorical imperative is sufficient by itself to determine the whole duty of man without any reference to the specific desires of human beings. We know our duty, according to Kant, by means of rational intuition and not by an intellectual calculation of results. But as a matter of fact, Kant is not quite consistent. The mere criterion of self-consistency, which is all that the categorical imperative amounts to in practice, is incapable of guiding us in life. There is nothing theoretically inconsistent in willing universal destruction. If Kant thinks suicide to be wrong, it is not because of its violation of the formal principle of the categorical imperative, but because of its incompatibility with certain ends with which the will is identified. These ends are not the casual desires of the individuals, which are contingent in character, but the supreme ends of humanity. Clearly, then, Kant admits that not merely general principles of morality but the specific duties are known by rational intuition.

One would have expected Kant to have developed the

implications of this mode of apprehension and applied it to the knowledge of God, but he did not do so. God is left in a precarious position, as a postulate of the moral consciousness. God remains an ideal to be used instead of a reality to be apprehended, or a person to be worshipped. God is a regulative conception and not an object of scientific understanding, or of possible experience. Our knowledge of reality does not give us religious truth. Moral consciousness tells us of the practical indispensableness of certain values, and we have no means of knowing whether there is any real object possessing these values. If we assume God to be real, it is only a case of wish-fulfilment, however much belief may be justified in view of the contingency of phenomena, the appearance of design in nature and the consciousness of the moral law.

In the *Critique of Judgment*, Kant urges that beliefs are sometimes grounded in the necessities of feeling. Our feelings also involve knowledge or discernment to some extent. Our feeling of the fit and the worthful in nature is a dim recognition of some ultimate background which we might term God. But he suggests that a higher type of mind might possess an intuitive knowledge which would render the teleological judgment superfluous.[1] These three lines of reflection in Kant, Ideas of Reason, the forms of moral life, and the notion of adaptation, confirm the view that reason is in Kant another name for the deeper rationality or intuition. Kant is convinced of the reality of God, for we have besides theoretical reason working through categories another source of apprehension which Kant traces to moral consciousness. We have not only an *a priori* consciousness of good and evil, but also that of the unconditioned. They

1 Schelling used the Kantian suggestion that our aesthetic sense may contain a perception of the ultimate truth of things, and art may be the organ of philosophy.

issue from the soul's own deepest source of knowledge. Reason, theoretical and practical, our whole nature, constrains us. If we do not believe in God, we will be proving false to the deepest in us. Kant proves that God is the reality with which the mind of man at its deepest is in communion, though no object is present in phenomenal experience adequate to it. The self-evidencing and underivative character of intuitions is the lesson of Kant's philosophy, though he was himself not conscious of it. Kant thinks that intuitive understanding is a prerogative of God and not a possession of the human spirit. Such a misconception is traceable to the arbitrary limits he imposed on human knowledge. For him it is always conditioned by the senses apart from which we have no faculty of intuition or direct perception. Our perceptions are always sensible, and our understanding deals with general notions and is not therefore intuitive. Kant conceives that possibility of an intuitive understanding. In his *Dissertation* he says, 'The intuitive power of our mind is always passive; and is only possible so far as some object can affect our senses; but the intuitive power of God, which is not the effect of objects but their cause, since it is independent of them, is their archetype, and hence is completely intellectual.'[1] If Kant denied this privilege of intuitive understanding to man, it is due to his intellectualism, which is a sheer misfortune. Though he draws a distinction between theoretical and practical reason, even the latter is for him intellectual. Virtue is not virtue if it is accompanied by a thrill for the act. He arbitrarily separated thought from feeling and the other side of man's psychical nature, and would not realize that the mind as a whole can know things which are beyond the ken of mere intellect. If we follow the spirit of Kant's work we will see that it is quite friendly to

1 Webb: *Kant's Philosophy of Religion* (1926), p. 44.

the hypothesis of intuition as the primary source of our highest knowledge. If we depend on sense data and logical proof we cannot account for the laws of substance and causation, for experience itself is based on these and has no meaning if they are not presupposed. The method of proof is of no avail since first principles are unprovable.[1] By a criticism of reason Kant shows that we possess independent of all experience, i.e. *a priori*, a knowledge of certain first principles. The certainty of mathematics and natural science is due to the contributions made by pure reason. The categories themselves are various forms of the one fundamental idea of the reasoning mind, the idea of universal unity and necessity. They are individual determinations of the fundamental knowledge of the necessity and unity of all that is. This knowledge is something most immediate and most profound. It is this that is the real basis of Kant's criticism, and not what is exhibited as the proof in the transcendental deduction of the categories. The categories are only the extensions of the one fundamental idea of the unity and interconnection of things in the universe. It is because Hume denied any other kind of knowledge than that derived from perception or proof that his system ended in scepticism, whilst Kant assumes that independent of all experience, from ourselves alone, we know the fundamental condition of all being.

Unfortunately, Kant believes that since this knowledge is altogether *a priori* it is true only of objects as known and not of objects as they are. Things in themselves are known by us only in so far as they 'affect' us. The picture of the universe shaped by the categories has no claim to objectivity. Kant is inconsistent on this point, for the 'ideal' category of causality is applied to the thing in itself where it is conceived

1 *Critique of Pure Reason*, 2nd ed., Introduction.

as causing our perceptions. He overlooks the natural self-confidence of reason that it knows things as they are in sense perceptions. Unity and interconnection are true of the objective world itself. No scepticism can really shake this conviction. What we know is not an illusion arising from our own subjectivity. It is the appearance for us of things themselves. Only we see them under limitations. Our knowledge is valid, though within limits. Unless we become aware of the limitations we cannot correct them.

Again, while Kant tells us that nature is a construction of our minds in the sense that the categories synthesize the multiplicity of sense, he did not ask how our *a priori* forms happen to suit sense-material. Unless both the self with its categories and the non-self or nature have a common source, unless there is unity between our thought and the nature of things, this adaptation is inexplicable.

Kant's view of the Ideas of Reason is somewhat inadequate and defective. While the categories of the understanding are certain *a priori* conceptions, without which there could be no experience or knowledge of sensible phenomena, the Ideas of Reason guide and inspire human thought by prescribing to it the goal to which experience must approximate, if it is true to itself. The effort of intellect to systematize knowledge is guided by the Ideas of Reason. There are no objects in the empirical world answering to them; they therefore remain unaccomplished. Yet we are called upon to act as if there were such objects; otherwise our life would come to naught. While the categories of the understanding are necessary, if we are to have any knowledge at all, the Ideas of Reason are necessary if our knowledge is to attain a completely systematic character. The Ideas are for Kant not central truths but future possibilities. The difficulties of Kant's system are due to his inadequate perception of the power of human mind to pass beyond the distinctions of the understanding to the unity that underlies them. The forms of understanding with the abstractions they involve may fail to give us the truth of things, but it is possible to interpret these 'Ideas' not as Kant does, as regulative principles bereft of any substantiality, but as Plato did as the underlying basis of the whole structure of knowledge, not only constitutive, but also productive. The concepts of the understanding may be abstract and partial; but the Ideas may be the reality. We do not derive the Idea of the unconditioned from the conditioned by the elimination of the conditions as Kant often suggests, but we start with the unconditioned. All consciousness is consciousness of a whole which precedes and conditions its parts. We cannot be conscious of limit unless we are conscious of what is beyond the limit. That which is altogether limited or finite cannot know itself as limited or finite. The Idea of the unconditioned is distinct in nature from all other concepts, and so cannot be derived from them. It is a pure *a priori* idea of reason. If Kant regards the world of experience as limited and phenomenal, it is because it falls short of the ideal demands of pure reason. Besides, the Ideas of Reason are to some extent realized in the world of experience. The beauty and sublimity of nature and the purposiveness exhibited in living organisms suggest the conformity of nature as a whole to the ends of reason. We are able to judge empirical truth by the standards of reason. If these Ideas help us to organize experience and test the value of concepts, if they control and regulate our thought about the world, surely they possess the highest kind of reality, and the world of experience which never realizes it falls short of it.[1] If inclusiveness and coherence are sub-

1 On this view, Kant is in agreement with Plato's theory of Ideas. As he himself expresses it: '(For Plato) Ideas are the archetypes of the things themselves, and not, like the categories, merely keys to

stituted for correspondence with an external given object as the test of truth, it is to no small extent due to the understanding of the implications of Kant's theory of the Ideas of Reason. These Ideas of Reason may be greater realities than the facts obvious to the outer senses and the intellect. Instead of assuming that Ideas are only pale reflections of the forms which they so much exceed, we may take the facts as partial representations of the reality which they reveal. Reason is, for Kant, the faculty by which we become conscious of the ultimate or unconditioned principles. It is different from understanding in the empirical sense. For the empirical understanding the Ideas of Reason are only ideas, demands for an unconditioned which in Kant's view can never be given, though there is an unceasing effort on the part of thought to reach a fuller comprehension of conditions. But reason is not a faculty co-ordinate with others. It is the whole mind in action, the indivisible root from which all other faculties arise. To say that the Idea of God is a product of reason is to say that it is the outcome of the deepest life in man, the reaction of the whole nature of personality to the nature of the real. God is the answer which the full being of man utters when it presses against the whole nature of things. If the faculty of reason gives us the notion of a world higher than the phenomenal, some-

possible experiences. In his view they issued from the Supreme Reason and from that source have come to be shared in by human Reason . . . . He very well realized that our faculty of knowledge feels a much higher need than merely to spell out appearances according to a synthetic unity, in order to read them as experience. He knew that our Reason naturally exalts itself to forms of knowledge which so far transcend the bounds of experience that no given empirical object can ever coincide with them, but which must nonetheless be recognized as having their own reality, and which are by no means mere fictions of the brain' (Norman Kemp Smith: *A Commentary to Kant's 'Critique of Pure Reason,'* 2nd ed. (1923), p. 447).

thing that is not the effect of any cause but the ultimate cause of all effects, and if it shapes this notion into the ideas of God, freedom and immortality, it means that these ideas are worked into the very structure of the mind. They are not subjective fancies, or even ethical postulates, but the necessary fruits of the mind issuing from its most vital springs. They are not objects of logical knowledge, but are intuited certainties. Kant's successors realize that the true or the objective is what thought is compelled to think by its own nature. Whatever we are constrained to think is real. When Hegel said the real is the rational, he is stating this important truth. Only his Reason is not what Kant meant by it, the faculty which gives the unconditioned principles both theoretical and practical. God is not real, if the real is identified with the actual in space and time, but He is real if the real means that which thought is obliged to assume as the operative principle in all existents, mind as well as its objects, drawing them together into a satisfying universe. Both God and the moral laws belong to the same region of certainty, though they are not observed facts. When Kant urges against the proofs of God that the existence of a thing cannot be got from its idea (ontological argument), the necessary can never be derived from the accidental (cosmological argument), that the physico-theological proof retreats on the other two, he means that we cannot *prove* the reality of God. The highest idea is not derived from sense, or proved by logic, but is founded in the secret places of the soul, and its validity is self-established by reason of the soul's trust in itself.

17. *Hegel*

Hegel thinks that he makes little use of intuition. As a matter of fact he attacks Jacobi's view of intuition for the obvious reason that he views it as an abstraction unrelated to the rest of mental life. For Jacobi, metaphysical truth can be reached not by the mediate knowledge of ideas, but by immediate insight or direct knowledge which he called faith. Hegel, who professed to be a foe of all abstractions, protested against Jacobi's view of faith.

Hegel believes in a monistic view of the universe. For him all reality is a single spiritual organism. The one ultimate being is Absolute Spirit, which in attaining its self-realization appears in forms which seem other than itself, though they are in reality necessary forms through which the ultimate self-expression is obtained. Nature is the process by which the infinite spirit attains its fullest concreteness. But how does Hegel arrive at this unity? It is not a discovery of the dialectic. Hegel's philosophy is one long dialetical exposition of the concrete unity, but dialectic is not the way by which the mind of man arrives at the idea of the One. When once the idea is there, dialectic expounds its implications. But we cannot explain the sense of the One by a compounding of concepts. We must put the One in the premises if the dialectic is to deduce it in the conclusion. It is clear that the sense of the One is just realized in mind before it is conceptually determined. With Kant we may say that no legitimate concept is possible without a previous intuition. This sense of the One which is the central feature of Hegel's system is an announcement of an intuition and not the result of a demonstration. When intuition gives us the idea of something real behind and beyond all that we know and seem to be, our dialectic strives to express the sense of the unity by the concepts of God, eternity, immortality, heaven and the like. William James makes a profound observation about Hegel, when he asks, 'What reader of Hegel can doubt that that sense of a perfected being with all the otherness soaked up into itself, which dominates his whole philosophy, must have come from the prominence in his consciousness of mystic moods?'[1] Hegel admits as much in some places.[2] Only he is inclined to treat religious intuitions as imaginative representations. While both religion and philosophy deal with an identical object, viz. ultimate reality, religion gives us imaginative representations (Vorstellungen) of it, while philosophy gives us clear concepts or notions (Begriffe). The former precede the latter. 'In point of time the mind makes general *images* of objects long before it makes *notions* of them'.[3] Philosophical knowledge is said to be more adequate to the object known. We need not deny that religious experience is not exclusively intellectual. It has mixed up with it elements of feeling and imagination. We may also admit that the real is represented through symbols and pictures. But all this does not make religious knowledge less true than the philosophical. It gives us the truth which philosophy analyses and clarifies. If intuition is to be identified with emotional feeling and not integral knowing, then it does not give us the truth; but if it is, as Hegel himself in some passages suggests, creative insight, which cannot be adequately represented by exact concepts and is obliged to

1 *Varieties of Religious Experience* (1906), p. 389.
2 Comparing religion with philosophy, Hegel writes: 'It is not the concern of philosophy to produce religion in any individual. Its existence is, on the contrary, presupposed as forming what is fundamental in everyone. So far as man's essential nature is concerned, nothing new is to be introduced into him. To try to do this would be as absurd as give a dog printed writings to chew, under the idea that in this way you could put mind into it. He who has not extended his spiritual interests beyond the hurry and bustle of this finite world, nor succeeded in lifting himself above this life through aspiration, through the anticipation, through the feeling of the Eternal, and who has not yet gazed upon the pure ether of the soul, does not possess in himself that element which it is our object here to comprehend' (*Philosophy of Religion*, E. T. (1895), vol i, p. 4).
3 *Varieties of Religious Experience* (1906), p. 389.

employ images and symbols which suggest it, then it follows that the universal spirit is apprehended concretely in
religion, and not abstractly in philosophy. The function of
philosophy is interpretative rather than creative. If popular
religion substitutes symbolic for literal forms, it is false, and
if philosophy assumes that it provides the final goal of the
spiritual quest, it is also false. The form in which philosophy
grasps reality is less adequate to the true nature of reality
than is the form under which religious intuition grasps it. It
is in integral knowing that the spirit of man reaches its
highest development. Again, Hegel argues that the idea that
only philosophy can give us assurance of Gods reality
'would find its parallel if we said that eating was impossible
before we had acquired a knowledge of the chemical,
botanical, and zoological qualities of our food, and that we
must delay digestion till we had finished the study of anatomy and physiology'.[1] It is clear that we have to turn to
religious experience for the living substance of our knowledge
of God and all that dialectic and philosophy do is to clarify
our intuitions.

It is fairly obvious that the great philosophers admit that
the root principles are articles of faith, and not attained by
argument. They are not arrived at through the senses, or by
the ordinary processes of logical reasoning. Conviction arises
only through our realizing them as the common ground of all
our knowledge. The archetypal Ideas of Plato, the *a priori* of Kant,
are the contents of intuitive wisdom and the conditions of human
knowledge. They point to the working of a Universal Spirit in us,
the eternal subject without whose presence in the mind of man
sensations would be blind and concepts barren. Intuition, faith,
spiritual experience, or the testimony of scriptures in theological
language is necessary for knowledge and life.

1 *Ibid*, pp. 3-4.

CHAPTER V

The Spirit in Man

I. *Intuition and genius in science*

The roots of all great thinking and noble living lie deep in life itself and not in the dry light of mere reasoning. All creative work in science and philosophy, in art and life, is inspired by intuitive experience. While we all possess intuitive perception, and exercise it to some extent, in exceptional minds it is well developed. Intuitive life, spiritual wisdom at its highest, is a type of achievement which belongs only to the highest range of mental life. The great scientific discoveries are due to the inventive genius of the creative thinkers and not the plodding processes of the intellect. The latter might give us more precise measurements, more detailed demonstrations of well-established theories, but they cannot by themselves yield the great discoveries which have made science so wonderful. Creative work is not blind imitation or mechanical repetition. I is synthetic insight which advances by leaps. A new truth altogether unknown, startling in its strangeness, comes into being suddenly and spontaneously owing to the intense and concentrated interest in the problem. When we light upon the controlling idea, a wealth of unco-ordinated detail falls into proper order and becomes a perfect whole. Genius is extreme sensibility to truth. Scientific discovery is more like artistic creation in its reaching out after new truth. Tyndall says of Faraday's electro-magnetic speculations: 'Amid much that is entangled and dark, we have flashes of wondrous insight which appear less the product of reasoning than of revelation.' A new law in mathematics is just as much a bit of spontaneous intuition as is a composition in music by Mozart. In his work on *Science and Method*, Henri Poincaré has a chapter on Mathematical Invention where he contends that his own mathematical discoveries were more or less artistic intuitions. 'It may appear surprising,' he says, 'that sensibility should be introduced in connection with mathematical demonstrations, which, it would seem, can only interest the intellect. But not if we bear in mind the feeling of mathematical beauty of the harmony of numbers and forms of geometric elegance. It is a real aesthetic feeling, that all true mathematicians recognize. . . . The useful combinations are precisely the most beautiful.'[1]

When a region of blurred facts becomes suddenly lit up, illuminated, as it were, to what do we owe this enlightenment? It is due not so much to a patient collection of facts as to a sudden discovery of new meaning in facts that are already well known. Apples had been falling to the ground a long time before Newton worked out the law of gravitation. The genius discovers the meaning which binds the facts which remain distinct and separate for the ordinary

1 P. 58, E. T., Mr Needham says: 'The fact that the scientific investigator works 50 per cent. of his time by non-rational means is, it seems, quite insufficiently recognised. There is without the least doubt an instinct for research, and often the most successful investigators of nature are quite unable to give an account of their reason for doing such and such an experiment, or for placing side by side two apparently unrelated facts. Again, one of the most salient traits in the character of the successful scientific worker is the capacity for knowing that a point is proved when it would not appear to be proved to an outside intelligence functioning in a purely rational manner; thus the investigator feels that some proposition is true, and proceeds at once to the next set of experiments without waiting and wasting time in the elaboration of the formal proof of the point which heavier minds would need' (*The Sceptical Biologist*, 1929, p. 80). Again, 'The scientific worker operates to a high degree unconsciously, as it were, like the builders of coral reefs.' (*ibid.*, p. 81).

understating. It is the intuitive grasp of the dynamic principle which enable one to organize the facts successfully.
Bergson has dealt with this problem in a suggestive way. It
is generally supposed that scientific discovery is reached
by conceptual synthesis, that is, by putting side by side or
externally attaching to each other concepts arrived at by
abstract analysis. The support for this view arises in two
ways. No one unfamiliar with abstract analysis can hit on
the rational insight. The insight does not arise if we are not
familiar with the facts of the case, the contradictions and
the half views which intellect throws up. The successful
practice of intuition requires previous study and assimilation of a multitude of facts and laws. We may take it that
great intuitions arise out of a matrix of rationality. Secondly,
when the discovery is made, we find that it has room for the
partial concepts which preceded the discovery, if only they
submit to a little readjustment and reinterpretation. The
readjustment is so easy that, when the insight is attained it
escapes notice and we imagine that the process of discovery
is only rational synthesis. Thirdly, for purposes of communication, the insight has to be set forth as a rational
synthesis. It is logical reason that consolidates the position
and renders it easy for others to follow the intuitions of
minds of more than average sensitiveness. Knowledge
when acquired must be thrown into logical form and we are
obliged to adopt the language of logic, since only logic has
communicable language. When the formal logical presentation is set forth, a confusion arises between discovery and
proof. As proof takes the form of conceptua' synthesis,
discovery is supposed to be of the same kind. The art of
discovery is confused with the logic of proof and an artificial
simplification of the deeper movements of thought results.
We forget that we invent by intuition though we prove by
logic. The art of explanation is an adventure of the mind.

When the intuition arises, thought gives it a form and makes it possible for it to be communicated to others. If the process of discovery were mere synthesis, any mechanical manipulator of prior partial concepts would have reached the insight and it would not have required a genius to arrive at it. By an external intellectual synthesis, we may reach a wider reading of facts, a more comprehensive law, a more complete notation, but the creative idea is not seized by the studious pursuits of intellect. The creative insight is not the final link in a chain of reasoning. If it were that, it would not strike us as 'inspired' in its origin.[1] It is the spark of genius that lights the fire and makes it burn. Intellect supplies the necessary tools. They are quite valuable, but they are not knowledge. An intuition is not a construction. There is a difference between external synthesis and inner development, between the raw material and the finished product, between what is given and what supervenes. When the insight occurs to the discoverer's mind, it is found to contain in living unity the properties previously isolated in dead notation and many others previously unnoticed. The idea goes beyond all formulation and schematism. It arises out of profound experience.

The function of discovery is sometimes attributed to imagination.[2] Through the exercise of imagination we hit upon hypotheses which help us to combine the discrete data into synthetic wholes. Hypothesis is the principle of growth in knowledge. In farming a hypothesis we seem to contemplate a situation which does not necessarily exist. We contemplate the non-existent and review a number of alternatives.

1 Cp. Sir Leslie Stephen: 'Genius begins where intellect ends; or takes by storm where intellect has to make elaborate approaches according to the rules of scientific strategy. One sees truth where the other demonstrates' (Hours in a Library, vol. iii).
2 Professor Whitehead uses insight and imaginative experiment as synonymous (Process and Reality 1929., pp. 5-6).

Such an attitude of mind where the activity of assertion is suspended, and possible alternative situations are supposed seems to be obviously one of imagination. Croce identifies the activity responsible for hypothesis with artistic imagination. But an illuminating hypothesis is not the work of mere uncontrolled imagination. Imagination unvivified by intuition, imagination which is day dreaming, fancy, reverie or guess work, will not help us to light upon the truth except by accident. There is a difference between a mere guess which is the work of imagination and integral knowing or intuition. Those who attribute the framing of hypothesis to imagination assign it, not to the analytical intellect, but to the appreciative part of our mind. The insight does not arise so much as the solution of a problem but as the perception of something true.

The intuition which is an activity of the whole being cannot be gained by mere intellectual effort, though it is equally true that it cannot be gained without it. Intellectual inaction seems to be the prelude to the intuitive flash. To allow the non-intellectual and yet rational part of our mind to play on the object, relaxation is necessary. Creative work is due as much to relaxation as to concentration. When we effectually concentrate on the object and think attentively about its many details, we do not seem to move far from the point at which we started. We must allow the intellect to lie fallow, let the object soak into the subsoil of our mental life and elicit its reaction to it. In addition to reflection on the facts with our conscious powers, we should commune with them with the whole energy of our body and mind, for it is the whole mind that will reach the whole object. The essence of things cannot resist the concentrated attack of the whole mind. The mind moves on to something new when it is relaxing indolently or trifling with futilities. Intuitive ideas spring in those deep silences which interrupt our busy lives.

In them the mind is brought under the grasp of the spirit. It is then that our deeper consciousness grows and becomes intensely aware of the nature of the object. The truth shapes itself from within and leaps forth as a spark from fire. The relaxation of intellect means the activity of the whole mind, the awaking of the whole being for the crucial act to arise. When the flash occurs, we feel it to be true and find that it lifts up the puzzles and paradoxes into a luminous atmosphere. There is no more helpless fumbling over trifles or distraction in details. The truth is not so much produced as achieved. Though inexplicable in its origin, it is quite simple when it arises. It seems to be as direct and as effortless as ordinary perception when it occurs, though a multitude of details have to be overcome before it arises. The latter requires concentration and the former demands relaxation. Archimedes solved his problem in his bath and not in his study. 'Happy ideas come unexpectedly without effort like an inspiration, so far as I am concerned,' says Helmholtz. 'They have never come to me when my mind was fatigued or when I was at my working table'. [1] A sort of intellectual passivity is demanded of us. When the religious scriptures require us to keep the mind still in a perfect purity and peace, so that we might hear the silence from which all words are born, they are only insisting on the passivity which is the preparation for the highest knowledge.

Intuitions are convictions arising out of a fulness of life in a spontaneous way, more akin to sense than to imagination or intellect and more inevitable than either. There is no control over them. The upward urges are a creation of the

1 Rignano: *The Psychology of Reasoning*, E. T. (1923), pp. 267-268. 'What is generally meant by genius,' writes Galton 'is the automatic activity of the mind, as distinguished from the effort of the will. In a man of genius, the ideas come as by inspiration; he is driven rather than drives himself' (*English Men of Science, Their Nature and Nurture* (1874), p. 233).

unconscious and the unwilled. 'The spirit bloweth where it listeth and thou canst not tell whence it cometh and whither it goeth.' Genius is not made by effort. It is a gift of the gods. Plato, himself a genius, suggests that creative thought is a kind of madness sent upon men by the gods in accordance with some purpose of which they and not we are conscious.'We Greeks,' says Plato, 'owe our greatest blessings to heaven-sent madness. For the prophetess at Delphi and the priestesses at Dodona have in their moments of madness done great and glorious service to the men and cities of Greece, but little or none in their sober mood.'[1] The plodding intellectual, the man without intuition, is a useful worker quite necessary for the world of thought, but the genius is at a different and higher level. His messages take shape in the secret depths of the soul.

Genius or inspiration is not something which first deprives us of our reason and then takes possession of us. As the findings of our whole consciousness, they are not non-rational. When they arise they can and should be logically demonstrated. Intuitions are not substitutes for thought. They are challenges to intelligence. Mere intuitions are blind while intellectual work is empty. All processes are partly intuitive and partly intellectual. There is no gulf between the two. The strictest scientist who believes that he does not go beyond the facts is also intuitive without knowing it. Intuition is the basis of all thinking. Though inarticulate in itself, it gives rise to all discourse. In every logical proof there is a grasping of the intellectual togetherness as a whole, an intuition of the whole as sustained by the different steps. Not only creative insight but ordinary understanding of anything implies this process. All active thinking is more than a mere linking together of images and

1 *Phaedrus*, 244.

conceptions. The intuited idea is operative throughout the whole process of the collection of facts, the brooding over them, the gradual heightening of the tension, the sudden release and the slow and steady mastery of the detail by the elaboration of the conceptions and judgments. In any concrete act of thinking mind's active experience is both intuitive and intellectual.[1]

We now see the justification for the ancient view of philosophy as an insight (darśana) of the whole experience. To mistake it for an intellectual discipline which deals with highly abstract concepts is to make it irrelevant to life. While it is necessary to insist that a philosopher should not allow his thinking to be disturbed by his passions, no one can be a philosopher whose non-logical sides are not well developed. If the philosophers today are not so influential as they used to be, it is to no small extent due to the fact that they are specializing in abstruse problems which are beyond the comprehension of the layman. They manipulate abstract concepts with the weapons of logical analysis. Philosophy which was once the pursuit of wisdom has become the possession of a technique. Though philosophy is a system of thought, the experience of organizes must be both rich and comprehensive. The vision of the philosopher is the reaction of his whole personality to the nature of the experienced world. The great systems of the past had an adequate sense of the vastness of the universe and the

1 Cp. Henri Poincaré: 'It never happens that unconscious work supplies ready made the result of a lengthy calculation in which we have only to apply fixed rules . . . . All that we can hope from these inspirations, which are the fruit of unconscious work, is to obtain points of departure for such calculations. As for the calculations themselves, they must be made in the second period of conscious work, which follows the inspiration, and in which the results of the inspiration are verified and the consequences deduced'(Science and Method, E. T. (1913), pp. 62-63).

mysteries of the soul. It is a mistake to think that the only qualifications for elucidating truth in the sphere of philosophy are purely intellectual. Only those whose lives are deep and rich light on the really vital syntheses significant for mankind.

2. *Intuition and artistic achievement*

All art is the expression of experience in some medium. The experience is clothed in forms which appeal to our emotions through the senses. Sculpture has for its medium stone and marble, painting colours, music sounds and poetry words. The relation between the experience and the medium is closer in some than in others, in poetry than in music, in painting than in sculpture. By means of the work of art, the experience is released afresh, in the spectator or the auditor. The enjoyer becomes a secret sharer of the creator's mind.

Attempts are sometimes made to treat artistic experience as an illusion or trace it to the causes which intellect is able to discover. We may confine ourselves to the great art with which we are all familiar, poetry, and look at the suggestions of the new sciences. Anthropology makes poetry rhythmic song. Rhythm helps breathing. So poetry and music employ it. If we turn excited speech into rhythmical utterance, we get music. Psychoanalysis argues that art is the unconscious and symbolic expression of the sensuous instinct.[1] Poetry it is sometimes said, is but a reaction to environment. Historical factors can easily account for it. A statement of origins is not, however, an explanation of the phenomenon. Origins may help us to understand the pathology of art, its failures, but not its normal creativity. If we trace all art to rhythm, sex or environment, we shall not be

1 See Roger Fry: *The Artist and Psychoanalysis* (1924).

able to discriminate between Beethoven and a brass-voiced beggar, Shakespeare and a clever undergraduate versifier. When all is said and done, art is an accident, which depends on what we make of the conditions and not what they make of us. The genius of the artist is the determining factor. The nature of the experience he has and the ability with which he communicates it to others through his work, require to be explained and all these ingenious theories which confuse origins and conditions with results do not touch the central issue.

3. *Poetry*

The experience or the vision is the artist's counterpart to the scientific discovery of a principle or law. To what is this creative experience or vision due, fancy, imagination, sensibility or thought or something else which, including them all, yet transcends them? In poetic experience we have knowledge by being as distinct from knowledge by knowing. The mind grasps the object in its wholeness, clasps it to its bosom, suffuses it with its own spirit, and become one with it. 'If a sparrow came before my window,' Keats wrote, 'I take part in its existence and pick about the gravel.' There is a deliberate suspension of individuality, an utter submission to the real, a complete absorption in the object as it is, so as to breathe its life and enjoy its form. When in the words of Byron 'the heart and soul and sense in concert move', the individual is absorbed by the object, lives in its rhythm and hears its inward harmony. In that heightened consciousness subject and object become interchangeable and, as Blake said, 'we become what we behold.' In a note to the *Ode on the Intimations of Immortality*, Wordsworth writes: 'I was often unable to think of external things as having external existence and I communed with all that I saw as something not apart from, but inherent in my own immaterial nature.' The object becomes clothed, as it were, with a strange light, revealing itself as the specific form, the concrete picture of an idea, 'a faultless essence of God's will'.[1] The endless variety of the sensible world becomes the symbol of an invisible ideal world which is behind and within it, sustaining both it and the mind which perceives it. Browning in his *Essay on Shelley* speaks of the poet's aim thus: 'Not what man sees but what God sees, the Ideas of Plato, seeds of Creation, lying burningly in the Divine Hand--it is towards these he struggles.' The actual world is reborn and reveals its truest self. It is the old world and yet new. We apply our powers of sense to note the outward semblance of things; we use the skill of intellect to understand their logical relations. But the powers of the soul are needed to know the soul of things. The spirit in man is as profound and true as the reality that answers to it in the constitution of things. So long as we are lost in the details of sense and intellect our soul is inactive. But when we are

> laid asleep
> In body and become a living soul
> While with an eye made quiet by the power
> Of harmony, and the deep power of joy
> We see into the life of things.

It is then that one passes into the object, flings oneself on it, lives in its rhythm and sees into it. Whatever be the object to which our energies are directed, a physical thing or a metaphysical idea, a passing mood or a particular person, the poet puts his whole being in the centre of the object contemplated and construes its nature from that centre outwards. Poetry, then is a form of life, a realization of the meaning of common life by living it more intensely. It is a

1 Bridges: *The Testament of Beauty* (1929), ii. 32.

ripe nature as organic as life itself. It is life come to utterance. It is utterly spontaneous. Keats says of the poet, 'if
poetry comes not as naturally to him as the leaves to a tree,
it had better not come at all'. The work of art is the crystal-
lization of a life-process. It is creative contemplation which
is a process of travail of the spirit. The mind is in labour and
derives sustenance from the whole being. The intellectual
facilities are there operative but suffused by the creative
life. True poetry which is rich with a world of suffering and
experience, has the fulness and mystery, and depth and
authority of life itself. It is because the poet sees so intensely
that he is able to communicate to us his feeling and judgment.[1]

The creative spirit and its activity are so unlike the conscious mind that the latter feels itself to be inspired and
raised above its normal power by the breath of spirit. The
inspired souls speak from a centre of consciousness that has
transcended the limits of its finitude and so claim an
authoritativeness which is not within the power of the normal individual to bestow. They do not think so much as
thoughts come to them. The poet believes that his work is
due not to his intellectual skill or imaginative boldness but
to what he calls his inspiration. Since it comes into the poet's
life and fades out of it regardless of his inclination, he traces
it to a power more unconscious than conscious.[2] To the

1 'Poetic creation,' Carlyle asks, 'what is this too, but seeing the thing
  sufficiently?' and adds, 'the word that will describe the thing
  follows of itself from such clear intense sight of the thing' (*On
  Heroes*, iii).
2 'They remember moments when a new light or a reviving force
  appeared to stream upon them coming whence it would, from the
  presence or the thoughts of the living or the dead, from intercourse
  with nature, from the heights of personal joy or the obscure deeps
  of pain; and they think of these moments as inspired' (A. C. Bradley:
  A Miscellany (1929), p. 226).

ancient Hindus and the Greeks, the poetic exercise is a religious act, and the poet invokes his muse and begins with prayer. It is always a dialogue between the daimon and the psyche. The authors of the Vedic hymns regarded themselves as channels of something greater than they knew, instruments of a higher soul beyond themselves. They do not so much create the contents as contemplate them in their moments of deepest insight. Plato in his *Symposium* suggest a similar view. Aristotle says that the poet is either 'happily gifted by nature' or 'a bit of a maniac'. 'The words which I speak unto you are not mine but the Father's who sent me.' Dante says: 'I am one who, when love inspires, take note and as he dictates within me I express myself.'[1] 'Sing heavenly muse', is the sublime opening of *Paradise Lost*. Milton speaks of the 'celestial patroness' who

> deigns
> Her nightly visitations, unimplored
> And dictates to me slumbering; or inspires
> Easy my unpremeditated verse.[2]

The poetic experience is but momentary for the veil is redrawn and the mood of exaltation passes. The poet attempts a translation of the ineffable experience into words. While poetry is in the soul, the poem is a pale reflection of the original, an attempt to register in words an impression which has become an image in memory. There is something incommensurable, eluding expression in words. The poetic temper is in all of us though only a few develop it. The poet

1 *Purgatario*, Canto xiv, quoted in Graham Wallas: *The Art of Thought* (1926). George Eliot declared 'that in all she considered her best writing there was a "not herself" which took possession of her, and that she felt her own personality to be merely the instrument through which this spirit, as it were, were acting' (Cross: *Life of George Eliot*).
2 *Paradise Lost*, Book ix. II. 21-24.

has the gift, which fewer still have, of communicating the experience by words of immediate power which compel the wandering mind to respond to his appeal. It is difficult to translate states of soul into words and images. The success of art is measured by the extent to which it is able to render experiences of one dimension into terms of another. An adequate control of technique is essential. Even in the act of composition the poet is in a state in which the reflective elements are subordinated to the intuitive. The vision, however, is not operative for so long as it continues, its very stress acts as a check on expression. The experience is recollected but not in tranquillity. Poetry is the language of excitement. For in recollecting the exciting experience, the poet recreates the conditions of its happening and identifies himself with it. The spell of the experience is still on the poet and under its influence he employs intuitive words and images which possess emotional value more than logical meaning. While poetry is not the vision itself, but only the image of it, still its quality depends on the degree with which it calls up the vision.

Such an account of poetic experience and expression seems to be opposed to Croce's view of the identity of intuition and expression. He says that it 'is a principle of ordinary common sense, which laughs at people who claim to have thoughts they cannot express or to have imagined a great picture which they cannot paint.' [1] While we cannot divide intuition from expression, Croce's view does not seem to take into account the fact that inarticulateness stands between experience and expression for the average man. The moment the poet has the intuition or the experience, i.e. the experience is vividly felt, the intuition unmistakably known, its expression or embodiment is also implicitly present. For the purely formless cannot be known or conceived.

1 'Aesthetics,' *Encyclopædia Britannica*, 14th ed. (1929), vol i. p. 266.

The form is present in the experience itself, but the great poet is he whose nature it is to represent experience through words winged with magic, capable of evoking the experience. The experience has its full shape in the words and phrases which clothe it. In the experience itself the expression is only implicit. To the extent to which the poet is perfectly aware of the experience, we may say that his expression is in sense also complete but certainly its verbal equivalent is not developed in it. Croce seems to ignore the problem of artistic communication.

The difference between a poet and a non-poet is that the experience of the former is larger and his verbal control greater. There are some who speak of poetry even as a mechanic talks about his engine. If we do certain things, certain things will result. There is no more mystery in poetry than there is in engineering. If we observe a few tricks of the trade, we will get poetry. It is reduced to technical power. But technique without inspiration is barren. Intellectual powers, sense facts and imaginative fancies may result in clever verses, repetition of old themes, but they are only manufactured poetry. Those who depend on them are designers of verses and not poets. They may please us by their pretty fancies, but the seer who gives us the inner quality thrills us. It is not merely a difference of degree in the quality but a difference of kind in the source itself, of the plane in which the poet moves. True poetry has that maturity of experience, that magnificence of mind, that touch of the soul which escapes one who lives on the surface. We measure the value of poetry by the depths of its roots in reality. Only poems that come from the soul trailing clouds of glory make the heart beat and the eye brighten. Plato distinguishes the man of genius, the madman inspired by the muses, from the industrious apprentice to the art of Letters and maintains that the latter has no chance against the former. 'He who has no touch of the muses' madness in his soul comes of the door and thinks that he will get into the temple by the help of the art, he, I say, and his poetry are not admitted; the sane man is nowhere at all when he enters into rivalry with the madman.'[1] Coleridge in the opening section of his *Table Talk* brings out the vital difference between an artist and a craftsman. To produce an impression of terror Schiller sets a whole town on fire, throws infants into the flames and locks up old men in old towers. Shakespeare drops a handkerchief and freezes our blood. But unless the poet speaks from the depths, he cannot engage the depths in others. When Carlyle gave the finished manuscript of the French Revolution to his wife, he said, 'I know not whether this book is worth anything, not what the world will do with it, or misdo, or entirely forbear to do, as is likeliest; but this I could tell the world; you have not had for a hundred years any book that comes more direct and flamingly from the heart of a living man.'[2]

It is often asked whether the power of poetry is due to the music of words, or the images they suggest or the ideas they express. Each view counts powerful support. 'The best words expressed in the best order' is poetry according to some. There is no doubt that rhythmical words exert an enchanting influence on the mind. We respond to music even when we fail to seize the sense. Again, it is true that we do not go to poetry to gain information. The function of art is to stir the spirit in us, humanize our nature, refine life and produce profoundly satisfying states of mind which gradually become fashioned into more persistent attitudes. The light of knowledge commends itself by its own sweetness. The harmony which an educated sensibility feels in the appreciation of inner reality is also valid knowledge.

1 *Phaedrus*, 245.
2 *Carlyle'sLife*, vol. i. p. 89.

Verbal music and logical meaning are present in poetry, but they are not all. Its essential quality is that emotional fervour, that strength of passion, that intensity of life, which bursts out in ecstatic utterance. Mere passion unaccompanied by thought is sentimentality. But unless the passion is present the poet cannot induce in the reader an acceptance of his experience. The experience is a unique event and cannot be repeated. The poem is only a recollection or record of it. But the poet's words must establish a natural sympathy with the reader and induce in him the mood of exaltation favourable to the implicit apprehension of the idea. The reader must insinuate himself into the mood of the poet, see with his eyes, feel with his heart and judge with his mind. What matters is not the massiveness of thought or the importance of the subject but the purity and profundity of the experience. The poet's mind is finer, his heart more sensitive to the remotest murmurs of things. It hardly matters on what subject he speaks, a night wind or a love fancy, a flower or a fleeting memory. He mediates between the Divine Logos and the things of the world that pass away. But this does not mean that all themes are equally good for poetry. Form and content are closely bound up and only great themes can give great poetry. Prose which is meant for discussion and communication is not competent to deal with the highest themes. Poetry is the language of the soul, while prose is the language of science. The former is the language of mystery, of devotion, of religion. Prose lays bare its whole meaning to the intelligence while poetry plunges us in the *mysterium tremendum* of life and suggests the truths that cannot be stated. An atmosphere of the numinous envelops all poetry. In the last analysis, the essentially poetical character is derived from the creative intuition which holds sound, suggestion and sense in organic solution.[1]

Modern literature is essentially trivial. Even our greatest masters like Bernard Shaw and H.G. Wells do not touch the height of genius. They have not given us one epic which brings out the full meaning of life, which leaves us throbbing with wild hopes and dazzled by new vistas, not a single drama of a profoundly moving nature which devastates us by its grandeur, burns into us unforgettable visions of men at grips with fate, which shakes, exhausts, cleanses us. It is because they deal with the tumult of the soul and not with its depth. They are predominantly intellectual. We are a generation of intellectuals, keen in analysis, patient in observation, but no great art was ever made of observation and analysis. We are acutely conscious of the present disorder and are anxious to remould society to a better plan. We burn with indignation against wrong and preach ways of overcoming it. But our sufferings are only mental, torments of mind, not agonies of spirit. The true artists undergo profound experience, intense suffering. They have no time to preach. They live and love. When they translate their experiences into words, we see in them that incalculable quality of mind, the creative passion, which is not a mere skilful arrangement of dead flowers, a work of passion and not mere cleverness. They give us things of beauty and not mere decorations. A true work of art is an unanalysable one comparable to a lightning flash flung from heaven, which strikes the earth and lifts it into a blaze. Robert Bridges' *The Testament of Beauty* is a case in point. It seems to be an

1 See Herbert Read: *Phases of English Poetry* (1928), v. Speaking of art, Robert Bridges says:
'Where of all excellence upspringeth of itself,
Like a rare fruit upon some gifted stock ripening
On its arch-personality of inborn faculty
Without which gift creative Reason is barren.'
(*The Testament of Beauty* , 1929, ii. 738-741).

elaborate exposition of a philosophic thesis in language which is more often abstract than poetic. Judged by the cosmic range of its knowledge, the nobility of its faith and the plentitude of its spirit, it is undoubtedly a great work. There are passages in it of extreme loveliness, of lyrical beauty, but for a poetic masterpiece we need emotional intensity and sustained inspiration. It is for the critic to say whether *The Testament of Beauty*, which is certainly a great work, is also great poetry, whether it has the poetic energy which is genius, the poetic quality which is magic.

4. *Artistic knowledge*

Art as the disclosure of the deeper reality of things is a form of knowledge. It is imitation, as Aristotle said, but not of outward nature but of inner reality. Poetic objectivity is not photographic realism. Even the so-called imitative art is not mere imitation. The artist's mind is at work in it, aiming at a definite purpose. He discerns within the visible world something more real than its outward appearance, some idea or form of the true, the good or the beautiful, which is more akin to the spirit itself than to the visible things. Yet this idea or form, this meaning or value is not an added grace or refinement, but the very heart of the object itself, and we cannot tear it away from it. Poetic truth is a discovery, not a creation.

Croce denies that poetry reveals the nature of reality. It is an expression of a personal mood and the poet deceives himself if he claims that in his receptive mood he knows and in his creative mood he expresses the nature of reality. Poetry is essentially self-expression. On this view it is difficult to explain why the expression of one man's self should be valid or at least significant for other men. Again, even Croce admits that art is intuition and intuition is always of the real or the individual. It follows that poetic intuition also gives us a kind of knowledge. Besides, art can be said to give us subjective impressions, only if the real is interpreted as what exists utterly independent of our knowledge of it. In that case even science and common sense do not give us knowledge. The sensible is not the real. The man with sight knows more than the blind man. Even if we had nearly a thousand senses as Voltaire's imagination conceived, we cannot be sure that our apprehension of reality is knowledge of reality. The sensible is not independent of the observer. The colour of the rose exists only for one who has the human sense of sight. The scientific picture of the universe again depends on our ways of knowing. Vibration as much as colours are relative to the observer. All knowledge, perceptual or conceptual, is the meeting ground of subject and object. The knowledge we gain in art is not peculiar in this respect. We have in it the reaction of delicate sensibili'.ies to qualities of the real. Poetic truth is different from scientific truth since it reveals the real in its qualitative uniqueness and not quantitative universality. It does not speak of material qualities that can be measured but inward graces than can only be felt. The truths of poetry cannot be set out in elaborate arguments but are conveyed more subtly. To behold the vision is to be convinced of the truth.

Even if art is self-expression, the self that is expressed is not the narrow particular one. In the *Critique of Judgment*, Kant argues that the pleasure we experience as the enjoyment of beauty is individual and in that sense subjective; it is also disinterested, and our our judgment concerning it is universal. Deepest poetry has the widest appeal.

What the scientist does when he discovers a law is to give a new ordering to observed facts. The artist is engaged in a similar task. He gives a new meaning to our experience and organizes it in a different way due to his perception of

subtler qualities in reality. He increases our understanding
of life and gives us a heightened sense of reality. He bestows
comprehension by bringing things into deeper accord. 'What
is holiest?' asks Goethe, and answers, 'That which, now and
always, as it is deeplier felt, brings into deeper accord.'

The greatest gifts of art are peace and reconciliation. In
those rare moments when we are moved by some beautiful
poem or a great work of art, we are not only absorbed by it
but our mind is raised to a higher altitude when it beholds
the vision of things far above sense knowledge or discursive
reasoning. Every beautiful statue has a certain air of repose,
every great poem conveys a sense of peace. It is no use
discussing a work of art by the standards of intellect and
dismissing its characters and events as purely imaginary.
The particular persons and events in a play may not be
existent and yet the play may have a meaning and a value
which have a higher and more abiding reality than the
existent things. The imagined persons and events may be
such stuff as dreams are made on' and yet they help us to
understand the reality or the significance. Fanciful forms
may reveal a quality of life. After all, 'the play's the thing', the
rest are shadows. It is the function of the artist to induce in
us a sense of the significance of life. As Kant puts it, art gives
us the form of purposiveness in general 'without the representation of any special purpose'. It is not the function of art
to give a detailed justification of particular events. It only
gives us a sense of the meaningfulness of life, evokes in us
ideas of the larger beauty, justice and charity of the
universe. The artist does not turn his back on the realities of
the world. He knows its sorrows and sufferings as well as
its virtues and victories. The wrongs and cruelties are there
but there is no need for alarm. The universe is sound at the
core. The darkness of the world is painted but it does not
depress us. When we read a great play like *Hamlet* or *King*

Lear, we seem to be somewhere near a clue to the world's secret. The poet shares with us the knowledge which he has gained of the foundations of life. The outward results may be calamitous but the mind is left restful. Juliet dies but only after establishing the greatness of love. If Othello had killed himself the instant he had struck the blow, he would have died with a grievance against the world. But he sees the innocence of Desdemona and dies; for then death is trivial. Outward defeats and failure do not touch the inner meaning of life. We get a general impression of an ultimate decency in things. Like the God of Genesis, when we look upon all creation, we find that its total impression is good. We not only accept the universe but feel at home in it. It does not stand for an immutable perfection. We see in it growth, continuance, endurance, growing pains, tragic accidents and yet it is our duty to share in the general movement and push it along. Art restores the isolated individual into fellowship with the world. It results in a catharsis, an emotional cleansing, a sense of fulfilment. Without the quickening of vital forces which art produces, life is an unlovely business. The author of the *Bhagavadgītā* tells us that the superior soul is he who experiences the intensest pain and pleasure without being affected by them. Only such seasoned souls who not only test life but are tested by it can see life always as we sometimes do when we are under their spell. Our sweetest songs are of our saddest moods. We give in song what we learn in suffering.

Aesthetic appreciation demands the exercise of the whole mind and not merely of the logical understanding. We cannot truly appreciate if we are not aided by a higher insight. We must share the world which the artist presents to us. The reader of poetry is one of a similar heart and temperament (*sa hṛdaya* or *samānahṛdaya*). Schopenhauer suggests that the artists lend us their eyes and we see with hem. Appreciation requires sympathy and understanding hough not belief and agreement. We must for the moment)ecome disinterested and severely contemplative. Goethe ;aid that Schlegel, if he was to criticize Euripides, ought to lo it on his knees. He should first give himself away, for hat is the only way to understand. Aesthetic creation and :njoyment are both non-intellectual actions.

. Intuition and ethical life

In our ethical life also, intuitive insight is essential for the ιighest reaches. The hero who carves out an adventurous •ath is akin to the discoverer who brings order into the cattered elements of a science or the artist who composes piece of music or designs a building. Mere mechanical bservance of rules or imitation of models will not take us ır. The art of life is not a barren rehearsal of stale parts. 'The ιan that is not an artist', cried Blake in one of his most rresting paradoxes, 'is not a Christian.' Life is a game which nds only when one retires. It calls for the exercise of skill nd adventure. The player of mettle is a master of technique. Vhen he grasps the position, with a sure insight he moves)rward. In the chessboard of life, the different pieces have owers which vary with the context and the possibilities of ιeir combination are numerous and predictable. The sound layer has a sense of the right and feels that, if he does not)llow it, he will be false to himself. In any critical situation ιe forward move is a creative act. It springs from the self y the laws of its nature. There is a secret, organic, in-ʌitable fatality about it.

The moral hero follows an inner rhythm which goads him ι and he has the satisfaction of obeying his destiny, fulfill-g his self. By following his deeper nature, he may seem to : either unwise or unmoral to those of us who adopt the

conventional standards. But for him the spiritual obligatio
is of more consequence than social tradition. The inwar
constraint is more important than the law imposed fror
without. He craves for inward truthfulness, utter sincerit
and not conventional propriety. He is fighting for th
reshaping of his society on sounder lines. His behaviou
might offend the sense of decorum of the cautious conver
tionalist and it is sad to feel that men of vision and creativ
ness have suffered at the hands of social leaders, thoug
not always without justification. They illustrate the tragi
truth that when any one grows better than his fellow me
he incurs their hatred. Crucifixion is the way in which w
honour our supreme guides and teachers. The cold calcula
ing men who are careful of appearances will never fa
grievously low, though they will not soar high. Only th
deeply sincere can make fools of themselves. The gospel
Jesus is antinomian as compared with pharisaism. 'Love an
do what you like.' Love takes us to the deeper secrets of li
and gives us a more integrated view than intellectual su
tlety and a few plain moral rules can do. Through morali
commands conformity, all moral progress is due to nonco
formists.

Society judges all acts according to well-known commo
standards. It assumes that everything is susceptible
scientific or impersonal treatment. It regards men
machines and reduces every personal problem to gener
terms and decides the moral worth of individual acts in th
light of typical situations and moral formulas. We are slav
of a mechanical system of ideas. Rationalist codes
morality sacrifice flexibility and richness to correctness a
consistency. Professing to act on principles, our intellectua
are cut off from the deeper sources of vitality and their sou
are at strife with their minds. Life, love and suffering cann
be so easily handled. No two events or conjunctions

events are alike. We must look at each of them as a unique situation, as an absolutely free and living adjustment to the circumstances and not a mechanical adaptation to a preconceived end. Only men with a delicate conscience and deep love, who have found themselves on a higher level, whose minds are guided by a deep sense of realities, and who have developed a sense for the right and the true can understand other people's feelings and problems. They are the souls who are able to endure the evil even though they do not succeed in removing it. They have a knowledge of the foundations; they have seen into the seeds of time.

It is only in moments of supreme freedom that we are or get near to the deepest self in us. In daily life we act on useful conventions devised for the normal situations, and even in great crises most of us are incapable of grasping the opportunity to respond with our whole self. But there is not work, however lowly, no drudgery, however toilsome, no passion, however vile, that cannot engage the self in us and yield this serene content if only the individual is spiritually alive. Virtue, said Socrates, is knowledge; only it is not intellectual knowledge which is teachable. It is knowledge which springs from the deeper level of man's being. It is acquired by the raising of one's mind, the growth of one's consciousness. The deeper a man is rooted in spirit, the more he knows directly. To one of ethical sensitiveness, the path of duty is as clear as any knowledge we possess. In its perception we come as near to absolute certainty as it is possible for us to do. We have in it a case of intuitive apprehension, though later reflection may discover reasons for its truth.[1] He whose life is directed by insight expresses his deeper consciousness not in poems and pictures as the artist does but

1 Cp. Bradley: 'We know what is right in a particular case by what we may call an immediate judgment or an intuitive subsumption' (*Ethical Studies*, 22nd ed. 1927 , p. 124).

in a superior type of life. He leaves behind the world of claims and counter-claims. He is indifferent to the morality which is a matter of checks and balances, for the highest morality which is not law but love is a necessity of his being. The lives of heroes like Buddha and Christ are not merely truthful and austere but beautiful beyond all dream.

6. *Religious consciousness and the other values*

Religious consciousness is not reducible to either intellectual or ethical or aesthetic activity or a sum of these. If it is an autonomous form of spiritual life which, while including these elements, yet transcends them, the object of religion is not either the true or the good or the beautiful or a mere unity of them, but God the universal consciousness who includes these values and yet transcends them. The human mind is value-seeking. It strives for unity and coherence, for harmony and beauty, for worth and goodness. Each of the values of truth, beauty and goodness has its own specific characters. We cannot arrange them in as hierarchy or subsume one under the others. We have clear testimony that these values are absolute and this means faith in God. They are the thoughts of God and we think after him. Truth, beauty and goodness and not existent objects like the things that are true, beautiful and good, and yet they are more real than the persons, things and relations to which they are ascribed. Though not known by the senses or reason, they are apprehended by intuition or faith as the theologians would put it.[1] Truth, beauty and goodness cease to be the

_____

1 It is unfortunate that we are obliged to employ the single term 'intuition' to represent scientific genius, poetic insight, ethical conscience, as well as religious faith. Though these diverse movements represent the integrated activity of the mind, the activity is oriented towards knowing in some cases, enjoyment or creation in others. In Hindu Philosophy, *pratibhā* denotes the

supreme realities and become a part of the being and essence of God. From the external values we pass to a supporting mind in which they dwell. They thus acquire an objectivity and are not simply dependent on our individual minds. As possessed by a divine consciousness they cease to be static ideals but become dynamic forces. Religious consciousness would then be the *amor dei intellectualis* of Spinoza. It is *amor* because it is vivid and warm; joyous and hearty; *amor intellectualis* because it depends on a quickened perception and understanding; *amor dei* because all values are referred to the being of God.

The cognitive, the aesthetic and the ethical sides of our life are only sides, however vital and significant. The religious includes them all. While science strives to comprehend the law that sustains the universe, while art yearns to reveal the beauty that is worked into the world, while morality struggles to realize the goodness the universe is labouring to achieve, while in their perfection these different aspirations merge into one another, in the process itself, each seems to be incomplete, though it is true that true art or philosophy or morality cannot be had without all of them in some degree. The nature of man is not built of parts which are independent of one another. Our instinct for truth, our moral sense and artistic craving are all organically bound up. But so long as they are inorganic or unwhole, thought is futile, feeling petty and action crude. The harmony which art reveals may be fleeting and transitory, a dream, not a desire, much less a dedication. The artist--not the greatest, however--may be intellectually feeble and morally depraved. The heroes of history are not noted for their aesthetic sense; nor are the artists as a class patterns

creative intuition of the genius, and *ārṣajñāna* is the name given to the religious intuitions of the sages (see *Indian Philosophy*, vol. ii, 2nd ed. (1931), p. 68) of morality. Strictly speaking, an art independent of morality, which has no roots in our deepest ethical instincts, which does not draw towards the divine in things is not true art. The insight into philosophy may not be a steady and assured possession. The truths of philosophy any more than the ideas of art may not incite to life. We require the three together, cognitive illumination, emotional stability and practical power, inward light, ineffable beauty and strong fire, a life in which the three become closely bound up with one another, where what we see, adore and live are one. Here we find the essence of religion, which is a synthetic realization of life. The religious man has the knowledge that everything is significant, the feeling that there is harmony underneath the conflicts and the power to realize the significance and the harmony. He traces the values of truth, goodness and beauty to a common background, God, the holy, who is both without and within us. The truth we discern, the beauty we feel and the good we strive after is the God we apprehend as believers. While art or beauty or goodness in isolation may not generate religious insight, in their intimate fusion they lead us to something greater than themselves. The religious man lives in a new world which fills his mind with light, his heart with joy and his soul with love. God is seen as light, love and life.

The religious intuition is an all-comprehending one, covering the whole of life. While the spirit in man fulfils itself in many ways, it is most completely fulfilled in the religious life. Here is consciousness at its full and simultaneous realization. While every genius is in his own way a pioneer of the evolution of spirit, in the religious genius we have a simultaneous exaltation of the different powers of the inward life. He combines most or all of the superiorities and intensities, imaginative vision, intellectual strength, emotional fervour and practical power. An integral life entirely free from error and perversion will be pure disinterestedness, impersonality incarnate. Some men are so vividly constructive that they are able to organize anew the society in which they live according to their vision.

These souls are men transfigured, rendered new, whose every power is raised to its highest extent. In them the universal finds its expression, God manifests himself more than in others. The contours of their God-intoxicated faces possess the radiance of such as have seen eternity (*brahmatejas*). They are men apart, free from the magic of this world. They stand to the commonalty somewhat in the same relation as the great creators of art stand to the large body of appreciators. When an artistic genius creates work of beauty, it is not an esoteric mystery but a common possession prized by the whole race. When the prophets reveal in symbols the truths they discover, we try to rediscover them for ourselves slowly and patiently. The gifted spirits who win forward steps for the race or add grace to daily life seek to extend these values to others, and that is, in the language of religion, to live to the glory of God.

Even as there is a difference between the scientific genius and the plodding intellect, poetic energy and versifying talent, moral heroism and conventional good form, spiritual insight differs from religious intellectualism. While the latter believes that interest in religion is promoted by the adducing of proofs for the existence of God, the forr er asks us to train our consciousness to the level where it can see God. The intuitive seers shrink from precise statements and clear-cut definitions.[1] They speak in picture and allegory,

1 Cp. Erasmus: 'We have been disputing for ages whether the grace by which God loves man and the grace by which we love God are one and the same grace. We dispute how the Father differs from the Son, and both differ from the Holy Ghost...and how there can be one when neither of the three is the other . . . Entire lives have been wasted on these speculations, and men quarrel, and curse

parable and miracle. It is a law of the human mind that the letter grows at the expense of the spirit, the material at the cost of the meaning. Intuitions are not dogmas. The two differ not only in degree but in kind. It is the difference between feeling after God and knowing Him. We cannot get the intuition of God unless we strive for it with our whole being. The experience has to be earned with costing effort, passion and suffering, faith and struggle, but the intellectuals wish to acquire it cheaply. The great body of believers in any religion wish to enjoy the consolations of religion without undergoing the labour of being religious. They are religious not with their whole beings or their souls, but with their brains, more frequently with their spinal cords. The priests feed on the weakness of human nature and tell us that it is necessary to believe to be saved. They are well versed in mechanical theology and dull formalism and are quite competent in their own range but they are not enough in critical times. The prophets with the creative spirit find themselves in conflict with the priests with their respect for exaggerated repetition. They contend that the spirit can leap into life only if the moulds in which it is cast are broken. They are more dissenters than conformists. They are considered to be irreligious and antisocial forces and are often faced with isolation and death, but all progress in religion is due to these persecuted spirits. They deepen and enrich the life of God in the world, and when the priests fail to satisfy the honest and hungry minds, the prophets attract them.

Dogmatism is the danger of an intellectual religion which

and come to blows about them . . . The schoolmen have been arguing for generations whether the proposition that Christ exists from eternity is correctly stated; whether He is *compounded* of two natures, or *consists* of two natures . . . and all this stuff of which we know nothing and are not required to know anything, they treat as the citadel of our faith' (Note on I *Timothy* i. 6).

is so attractive to a world in which standardization and quantity are superseding individuality and quality. When the dogmatisms are breaking down we are disturbed that religion may disappear. If we regard the forms as final, we are rightly sceptical when they are shaken. We may be encouraged when we find that the great seers of religion do not prescribe definite systems of dogma or ritual. They invite the soul to its lonely pilgrimage and give it absolute freedom in the faith that a free adaptation of the divine into oneself is the essential condition of spiritual life. The nature of man is a life demanding to grow and not 'clay waiting to be moulded'. The examples of the great religious geniuses are there as broad directions of effort and attainment and even when they belong to organizations, they attempt to keep up the spirit of life in them. They are not in a hurry to turn a great life into a rigid formula, a mystery into a metaphysics which can be learnt by heart by everybody. If our temples, mosques and churches understand that their primary function is to awaken the spirit in us and not impart sacred wisdom, they will convert themselves into houses of God which will have the courage to be comprehensive and welcome believers of varied views and tastes into their spiritual atmosphere. They will prepare for an invisible church which will embrace all souls of good will. A life or an atmosphere is opposed to a creed or a code. It is some-thing incalculable in its possibilities and offers full scope for variations to suit different minds. If we believe that man needs a framework for the tendrils of his mind, we may provide symbols and examples and leave the rest to the God in man. The true teacher, like Socrates, plays the part of a midwife. The lack of definiteness in a religion like that of the Hindus seems to me to stand for a higher form of definite-ness. Religion means conscious union with the Divine in the universe, with love as its chief means.

7. Creative intuition

Creativity in cognitive, aesthetic, ethical or religious activity springs from thought which is intuitive or spiritually quickened. There is no greatness, no sublimity, no perfection whatever be the line, without the touch of this creative energy of life. The heroes of humanity, its Buddhas and Christs, its Platos and Pauls, are all shaped after the same pattern and are inspired from the same elemental source of life. They have touched the deeps of spirit and speak from that undivided impersonal root from which our personal thoughts, emotions and strivings arise. The thinkers, the artists and the heroes, though they may not use, though they may often quarrel with the language of religion, are still religious in a true sense. For they have broken down the barriers between the individual and the universal. They have the sweet dignity, the quiet resignation, the patient faith of those who dwell in another world, the world of spirit. They are lonely, self-centred, not by choice, but by necessity. Genius has no place for team-work. Poets and prophets do not go into committees.

8. The spirit in man

If we are asked to define what the spirit in man is, it would be difficult to give a definite answer. We know it, but we cannot explain it. It is felt everywhere though seen nowhere. It is not the physical body or the vital organism, the mind or the will, but something which underlies them all and sustains them. It is the basis and background of our being, the universality that cannot be reduced to this or to that formula. 'That which one thinks not with the mind, that by which the mind is thought, know that indeed to be the supreme, not this which men follow after here.'[1] There is a

1 Kena Up. i 5.

parable in the Upaniṣads which speaks of two birds sitting on the same bough, one of which feeds and the other looks on. The spirit looks on disinterestedly, its delight is pure and free; the empirical self is concerned with the business of life. The former is vaster, profounder, truer, but it is ordinarily hidden from our knowledge. When the supreme light in us inspires the intellect we have genius, when it stirs the will we have heroism, when it flows through the heart we have love, and when it transforms our being, the son of man becomes the son of God. Put the fire of spirit on any altar, it blazes up to heaven. Its powers are infinite, its dreams angelic, its apprehensions godlike. There is no natural limit to its expression, it is potentially all-embracing. Wherever there is genius, ardour, heroism, there is the creative spirit at work in however nebulous and untried a way it may be. Completeness of achievement is always satisfying. It is glimpse of the divine. Inspiration in every one of its forms is a manifestation of the universal spirit in us; only the religious man is conscious of this fact.[1] He knows that his true self is something universal which influences his normal ego in its highest activities and is therefore moved by feelings of gratitude and devotion to it.

In the rush and clamour of our conscious life, we do not pay attention to this mystery of our being. We do not realize that we have sensibilities strange to our normal life, ways of apprehending reality which are not strictly logical. We

1 'The Greek sculptor who wrought his stature, and when it was finished fell on his knees before it, felt that its beauty was no mere creation of his own, but something heavenly. Milton's passionate prayer to the celestial muse was not a poetic convention. And to Wordsworth what in literary phrase is named the consciousness of genius was in truth the consciousness of dependence upon, union with and devotion to, the spirit of thought and love which manifests itself in nature, and is more fully revealed in the thought and love of humanity' (Bradley: *A Miscellany* (1929), pp. 235-236).

do not have an adequate consciousness of what we really are, of what invisible threads link us to the universe. Worse still, we sometimes confuse the spirit in us, responsible for the flashes of insight, for the sudden intuitions, for the unexpected emotions, with a primitive and elementary state of our being. The psychoanalyst explains the moments of our heightened consciousness in terms of his 'complexes', instead of regarding them as suggestions of an undeveloped power in us. The genius is not one with exceptional access to the primitive elements of our being, but one who gives us a foretaste of the spiritual man to be. He has become aware not of the suppressed primitive desires but of the greatness of spirit which lifts him into a higher state of being than the normal.

Our analysis of intuitive consciousness tells us that we ourselves are that one indivisible spirit and the empirical world we are familiar with is the arrangement produced by the limited part of ourselves active in walking consciousness. If we learn to live within, we shall respond to the presence within us, which is our more real self, profound, calm and joyous, that which supports and sustains all manifestations.

We cannot attain to this greatness of soul unless we are reborn. Those who have reached the heights are literally reborn, made new. While this quality or reborness manifests itself in the lives of the lords of mankind, it is not absent in any of us. Though we may not have developed this greatness, we are ready to pay our homage to those who have reached it. The thoughts, the raptures and the deeds of the great induce in us an attitude of adoration. If the spirit were not in us, we would not have thrilled with joy when face to face with the great works of art, science of life. We claim their intensities of significance, their splendours of heroism, their visions of rapture as our own. The rhythms of the poet find correspondence in the conditions of our soul; their words an authentic echo in our speech. The gleam haunting our whole life, the undiscovered spirit in us is suddenly recollected in Plato's sense. Any voice which speaks from the depths of one's heart liberates at the same time thousands of silent voices. The poet's words are claimed by us as our native speech; the philosopher's ideas are accepted by us as our highest thoughts. The saint's perfection is felt as something to which we aspire and may attain. We understand an object only when there is something in us akin to it. When any picture, poem or life produces in us a wonderful effect, we may be sure that there is an interior responding wonder that meets it. We cannot understand Plato if we have not the spirit of Plato. To understand Christ we must have the mind of Christ.

Croce's view, that aesthetic experience is active creation, expresses an important truth, though he exaggerates it. Even when we enjoy poetry, our mind is actively creating an intuition and finding its expression though we may not be conscious of it all. The meaning of the poet must become meaning to me, the image he suggests must be found in my mind, and his ideas must be thought by me. I cannot see in a work of art another's thought unless it becomes my own thought. We cannot understand great poetry unless we bring to it some fragment of a like experience. We cannot have a knowledge of God or of the invisible world unless its voice is heard in our own selves. In none of us is the spark of spirit wholly extinct; in none is the image of God wholly effaced. Only the seers in whom the spirit is not merely a presence but an achievement lend us their eyes, in Schopenhauer's phrase, and we begin to see with them. They give us the power to know, love and appreciate the world in a new way. We share their vision of life, splendid and sublime, to the best of our capacity. Even as those who appreciate beauty are artists in a degree, so also those who recognize the prophets are prophets of a kind.

All true greatness has this power to illumine us, to transform us, emancipate us, from the low and the petty, the temporary and the expedient. They do not simply please our senses or interest our mind, but touch our souls and change our being. We acquire through their aid a heightened awareness of the meaning of life. There is no more conclusive proof of the reality of the spiritual world than acquaintance with the saints of God. They shake us out of our scepticism. Their lives reveal the truth and they cannot be refuted. Their influence is compulsive for they do not speak as the scribes but as those having authority.[1]

These geniuses from whose quivering lips ecstatic utterances leap up give us a foretaste of what all human beings are destined to be. They are the heralds of the infinite, the first-fruits of the future man. They and the moods of exaltation they rouse in us are a promise of mankind's future achievement in spiritual understanding. They are the new emergents, the beginnings of a new human species, the 'sports' in the biological expression, in whom a qualitatively

---

1 There is a striking phrase in Plato's *Republic* (382 F), where Adeimantus is represented as assenting to Socrates' statement about God's essential goodness. It seems to become evident to him the moment Socrates asserts it. 'So I myself think, now you say so.' We have in John i. 43-51 an illustration of this personal influence. Nathaniel was unconvinced when his brother Philip told him of a new teacher who, he believed, was likely to prove Israel's promised Messiah. But when he met Jesus and heard him speak, his doubts were silenced, and he became convinced of his divine mission and authority. When the pagan philosopher who was converted to Christianity by an illiterate rustic was asked how it happened, he replied that there was such a power of sanctity in the old man that he could not resist it, though he could answer all learned arguments. Such is the responsive assent of ordinary mankind to the great prophets.

new type is awakened. We have all to be reborn, reveal our potential sonship,[1] share in all the fulness of divine nature,[2] though a long process of development and illumination separates us from that goal. In Buddha and Jesus, the new vision of life, the new unification of nature, inner and outer, has become flesh.

If we remember the wonders achieved in the course of evolution, the hope is not unreasonable that we may all attain to the greatness these have reached. It would not have been possible for the Darwinian ape living its instinctive life in the forest to imagine that one day he would himself grow into an animal using a new power of reasoning and dominating the earth and its conditions mental and material, handling natural forces, sailing the seas, and riding the air, and, more than all, controlling its own life by codes of conduct, in domestic, national and international life. Man today finds it equally difficult to imagine that he might himself grow into the divine status, possessing knowledge without a taint of error, bliss without a shadow of suffering, power without its denial of weakness, purity and plentitude of being without their opposites of defect and limitation. Such an ideal transfiguration of humanity is man's dream of heaven, of the reign of God. Of the creative process and man we may say that 'it doth not yet appear what they shall be'. Our intellect tells us that all that is possible is a relative knowledge, a precarious happiness, conditioned power, limited good, but the moments of insight inspire us with the vision of the kingdom of God and the hope that even as the anthropoid ape became the human being the human may become the divine. If we look at the progress we have achieved in the space of fifty centuries, which in the process of ages is but as the turning of an

1 Romans viii. 17.
2 Ephesians iii. 19.

hour-glass, there is no cause for impatience. The glass has to be turned again and again till the shout of victory comes exultingly from all along the line. A passage such as that in the eighth chapter of St Paul's Epistle to the Romans must hearten us. 'For I reckon that the sufferings of this present time are not worthy to be compared with the glory which shall be revealed in us, for the creation with outstretched hand awaits the revelation of the Sons of God.'

Till that revelation arises, no one individual will be able to organize his life completely. For organization is not only internal but external. We have to organize our own processes and powers with all the best in that which environs us. This full realization of the interactive union is 'life more abundant' and it is possible only with the perfection of the world, its growth into the higher state of being. No one can stand in proud isolation with contempt for the common herd. We can rise in the scale of being only by drawing all into ourselves. While the individual has to cultivate his own garden and integrate his own self, the self is not sharply marked off from the world, the garden is not fenced off from the rest of the universe. The world is our garden and we cannot become self-sufficient until the world is so.

9. Self-integration

Intuitive insight, whatever be the line, is a whole-view where the mind in its totality strains forward to know the truth. The realization of this undivided unitary life from which intellect and emotion, imagination and interest arise is the essence of the spiritual life. Ordinarily we are not whole men, real individuals. Our responses are formal and our actions imitative. We are not souls but human automata. So our lives lack grace, depth and power. To change oneself into a whole and balanced nature, instinct and intellect, emotion and will which have no being apart from the evolving personality require to be integrated. This process is not mere change of creed. We want discernment, not cleverness, purity of spirit, not training of the intellect, an intimate acquaintance with and living closer to the nature of reality. No amount of sense training can make the senses perceive thought; even so no amount of intellectual skill can lead us to intuitive experience. We must reach a new level of consciousness to which the highest truths are revealed even as concepts are given to thought and colours to sense. The life of spirit is essentially creative in its character. We cannot create through the exercise of intellect any more than a flower can evolve in obedience to a formula. Creation is the result of the growth of self, the expansion of consciousness. For this we want religion as an uplifting power and not as a confession of belief or a demonstration of God. Religion is not science nor is church an academy. It is the perception of the eternal in the finite.

Psychoanalysis tells us that the human mind is an arena of conflicting forces which require to be subordinated to some unity. The control of primary instincts takes place according to it in three ways: (1) *Defence reaction*: The conscious mind takes up an attitude of direct opposition to the subconscious instinct. (2) *Substitution*: Instead of repressing the instinct, the mind diverts it into other channels, as when the sex instinct finds its outlet in the cultivation of art. (3) *Sublimation*: Here the instinct is neither repressed nor diverted but is transformed into a higher form. Sexual love is sublimated into spiritual devotion. Dante's spiritualized passion is an instance of this kind. In all these cases the unity the mind acquires is only superficial. The repressed instincts remain in the background with all their energy, waiting for expression on a suitable opportunity. Old maids who have led honourable lives of abnegation suddenly manifest uncontrollable obsessions and erotic impulses. The unused elements of their nature shut down in the cellars of the subconscious clamour for satisfaction. Eager for love and friendship, they squander their affections on pet cats and tame dogs. Dissatisfied with such a substitution, they turn out neurotic and unbalanced. Through these methods, the mind does not acquire the power of balance of a tranquil soul absolutely at peace with itself. The method of Yoga tries to change the very stuff of our nature, which is not possible by the mere conscious control of the individual will.

The Hindu system of Yoga sets forth the discipline by which all parts of our nature, the body and the senses, life and mind are controlled and integrated so as to allow the free and creative working of the spirit of which all these are the developments. Disease obstructs the harmony of the physical self and its environment. Error and ignorance injure the harmony of the rational mind with the universe of reason. Vice obscures the harmony of the will of man with the will of the universe. When the different powers of the self attempt to function in self-supporting isolation, there is disharmony between the self and the universe. We look at things through the refractory medium of our private passions and selfish interests. It is when we free ourselves from their bondage that the scales fall from our eyes and we see things as they are in themselves. Religion as Yoga enables us to attain a mastery over the different forces of our nature. When we are called upon to sink from our surface consciousness into the depths by controlling our activities, it is to let the spirit, large, powerful and luminous, assert its nature. Meditation is the method by which our convictions soak into our bones, become our breath and grow without needless conscious interference.

10. *Instinct and intuition*

Spiritual life is not to be confused with the instinctive or the unconscious. It is true that religious teachers tell us that we cannot enter the kingdom of heaven unless we become as little children. Those who speak of intuition refer to certain qualities which it shares in common with instinct such as directness, spontaneity and a closer contact with life. Instinct is the source of vitality and the bond and unites the individual with the race. The feeling of being one with the world is the reflection in consciousness of that instinctive unity which is the foundation or our conscious life. In the lower stages of evolution, our way to knowledge is through instinct. Primitive man had marvellous knowledge of the ways of nature which we do not possess. Animals know instinctively what we acquire after laborious reasoning. When we are in nature's embrace, our lives are simple and certain. But the scope of instinct as unconscious is limited. While the beings guided by instinct act with unhesitating precision, they are helpless in unfamiliar surroundings. For they act without knowing why they do so. They cannot express themselves. Besides, the unconscious unity of life which made instinctive knowledge possible is sundered by the rise of intellect which helps us to know ourselves and control the forces of nature. Since the primaeval unity is broken, man is uncertain and wavering. We seem to be alienated from nature, leading sceptical, artificial and self-centred lives. If intellect is to be brought closer to life, it must combine with instinctive knowledge. Such a combination is what we possess in intuition. It has the directness and unity of instinctive knowledge as well as the consciousness of the intellectual. It is not confused irrationalism or irresponsible mysticism.

When the prophets refer to the virgin outlook of a child,

they have in view the second innocence which comes after
knowledge and not the first which precedes it. The spontaneity of the child is not a substitute for insight. The spirit
which is the unconscious beginning must become the conscious ending of our life. Children enjoy an innocence, a
sincerity, an integrity, born of harmony between themselves
and their lives. They live in peace; they tell no lies; they do
no wrong. They surrender themselves to spontaneity. Their
behaviour is a perfect expression of their being. Our intellectual consciousness has driven us out of that wholeness
of being. To regain that integrity, to attain to a life where
knowledge and being are not divorced from each other is
the essence of human evolution. To recover the lost unity is
to be reborn. It is the secret of spiritual life, the mystery of
the kingdom of God.

The 'ecstatic' moods induced by drugs, anaesthesia and
such other aids are quite different from the spiritual attitude
of those who have won integrity or wholeness of life. They
are not altogether useless since they point to the feeling of
unity with the universe which is latent in all of us. This
feeling of the unity with the universe is not confined to the
great moments of our life. The Upaniṣads tell us that the life
of man has affinity with the planetary and the physical, the
plant and the animal. This generic feeling of indistinctness
from the world is impressed on us in the condition of sound
sleep. Our oneness with the world always remains with us
whether in our simplest state or highest activity, though it
is lost in divisions and conflicts in our ordinary life. We may
sink or swoon into the bosom of the infinite in a thousand
ways. Such a kind of quieting down into instinctive life or
unconsciousness is different from the raising of the whole
self, its reintegration into the universal spirit. Spiritual life
is not inertia or indifference but is light and freedom, peace
and power; spiritual realization is not hysterical trance or

drug intoxication, for the life of the seer takes on a new depth, a marked increase in coherence and character. There is a general enrichment of personality. It is more life and not less.

The psychoanalysts hold that the fundamental insights of art, religion and philosophy are not due to conscious mind but have their roots in the unconscious, which is the deeper and more vital mind of which the conscious is only a specialization. The relation between the conscious and the unconscious is compared to that between the waves on the surface of the sea and the depth beneath. The great insights which surprise us by their strangeness and significance are born not of the unconscious but of the spirit in us, the self in its entirety which includes both the conscious and the unconscious. Since they are spiritually produced and not simply consciously originated, they are sounder in their content even as the spirit is superior in wisdom to the conscious self. The unconscious is not the condition in which desires stimulated by our nature but rejected by our normal consciousness exist in all their potency waiting for opportunities to overthrow the censor. It is not the asylum of outlawed desires but is the essential unique nature (*svabhāva*) of each individual creature--which is by its nature unanalysable. What we do or think arises out of what we are and not simply what we think we are.

Psychoanalysis throws light on the way in which our interior stresses bear on our conscious attitudes. Many events of the world unnoticed by our waking consciousness leave their marks on the mind and influence behaviour. If intuitive knowledge is the witness of the whole experiencing mind to the whole object, it is necessary to discover our whole mind and keep it trim. The impressions registered in the unconscious mind must be controlled. The buried life that lies concealed in each one of us must be dragged into the light of day and made part of conscious life.

Behaviourist psychology also insists on the potencies of the non-intellectual mind. It contends that when one is thinking, the whole of one's bodily organism is at work implicitly. All thinking is organic thinking, the focussing of the whole organism on the object. The body and the mind join together and the whole of our nature becomes strung up and raised into an intensity, when its life embraces the object. This integrated gathering together of the whole self, the nervous character of severe contemplation has in it something comparable to an erotic ecstasy which has been exploited in inferior cults. We are not called upon to eliminate the body or the senses but only to get rid of their independence and effect an integral self-fulfilment, where the body ceases to be an obstacle and becomes an organ of the self.

The psychoanalysts contend that the truths of religion are the expression of the repressed fears and wishes in the unconscious. They are right in so far as they admit that they are not due to conscious reasoning of the type with which we are familiar in science. They are wrong in their assumption that what scientific reasoning deals with is reality and all else is phantasm. When the psychoanalyst declares that the religious person is deceiving himself, he is passing beyond his limits of psychology and stepping into metaphysics. Religious ideas are certainly due to psychological processes which are different from those at work in self-conscious reasoning, but, as we have seen, even science cannot proceed with its work if it does not assume principles from beyond itself. Reality need not be reduced to what appears to the unimaginative, non-aesthetic, naturalistic vision. Psychoanalysis clearly makes out that living experience is more extensive than logical reasoning. The roots of life are in the unconscious depths of the soul. The term 'libido' which the psychoanalysts employ to denote the deeper centre of one's being is unfortunate. Religious faith emerges from the total nature of man. It is not something uncanny, confined to children, neurotics and savages.

While we have increased immensely our scientific knowledge of the world and human nature, there is not much justification for assuming that we know more about the mysteries of the human soul than our forefathers centuries ago did. In the realm of spirit our ignorance does not seem to be less abysmal. It is a foolish complacency that shuts itself away from the true knowledge that is contained in the great literatures, philosophies and religions of the world, which have a good deal in them which is of immense importance to our lives. They are, perhaps, more important than the other achievements of the human spirit, including psychoanalysis, since they tell us about the development of the soul and insist on the deeper integration of being which alone can result in the right vision of the significance of things.

The powers of the soul can be atrophied or destroyed as much as limbs of the body for lack of use or wrong use. The exercise prescribed in all the great systems for the development of the spiritual in man is the worship of God and the development of love and sympathy. Worship and meditation, prayer and devotion are acts which the soul in its completeness, and not merely the body or the mind, is in exercise. We do not worship by mind or body but in spirit and in truth. Our mind apprehends, our body participates, but worship goes beyond these. It is the communion of the soul of man with the soul of the universe, a direct and ineffable contact with the light divine, more inward and complete than even the relation between the knower and the known, which can only be weakly expressed by acts of mind or of body.

Religion provides us with forms and institutions which

have an emotional appeal. Only in many religions it happens that these forms are morbid and irrational. Even the dying Socrates said: 'I owe a cock to Aesculapius.' A rational faith has little to do with anti-human forms and practices which divide man from man and exalt what is harsh and cruel at the expense of the genial play of life, the tender affections and the quiet pleasures. The codes which invent virtues which are sterile and sins which are imaginary throw out of gear the healthy movement of life and a true religion has nothing in common with this spirit of negation.

Science and criticism have nothing to say against a religion which proclaims an invisible church of spirit which will be a brotherhood of men and women of good will, who find nothing hateful but hypocrisy, nothing immoral except hardheartedness. But religion as it is practised today has a long distance to travel before it can reach this goal. We have seen that a lack of understanding between man and nature is the source of the fear which gives rise to religion. In primitive religion this fear is lulled by the invention of other worlds, of spirits and totems, of magic and propitiation. Science which deals with discoverable facts and religion which revels in unverifiable hypotheses become opposed to each other. Religion, originally invented as an aid to man's normal and healthy life, becomes an encumberance, arresting rational thought, degrading life and perpetuating unhappiness. Even today popular religion is mixed up with wizards and witches, magic cures and incantations, ghostly apparitions and priestly frauds. The mass of men still cling to superstition in the name of religion and believe in priests who affirm that they know the nature of life beyond the grave, the complexion of God and his followers, why precisely the stars are hung in the sky and why they are kept there and what exactly their influence is on the destiny of man. A highly instructive study of mankind might be written under the title of 'A History of Human Stupidity', in which it would become apparent how our religious experiments and adventures since we began to leave records is an account of one crusade after another on behalf of some illusion or other. Loyalty to ourselves, to our intellect and conscience, requires us to withold our assent from propositions which do not commend themselves to our conscience and judgment. We become more religious in proportion to our readiness to doubt and not our willingness to believe. We must respect our own dignity as rational beings and thus diminish the power of fraud. It is better to be free than to be a slave, better to know than to be ignorant. It is reason that helps us to reject what is falsely taught and believed about God, that he is a detective officer or a capricious despot or a glorified schoolmaster. It is essential that we should subject religious beliefs to the scrutiny of reason.

11. *The argument from religious experience*

Human arguments are not at their best logical proofs and the most valuable part of our heritage comes from the prophetic souls who announce their deepest convictions, not as their discoveries or inventions but as the self-revelation of God in their own souls.[1] The value of the Ontological

1 Simmias in the *Phaedo* says: 'I will tell you my difficulty, I think, Socrates, and I daresay you think so too, that it is very difficult, and perhaps impossible, to obtain clear knowledge about these matters in this life. Yet I should hold him to be a very poor creature who did not test what is said about them in every way, and persevere until he had examined the question from every side, and could do no more. It is our duty to do one of two things. We must learn, or we must discover for ourselves, the truth of these matters; or, if that be impossible, we must take the best and most irrefragable of human doctrines, and embarking on that, as on a raft, risk the voyage of life, unless a stronger vessel, some divine word, could be found, on which we might take our journey more safely and more securely' (Church's E. T. in the *Trial and Death of*

argument as well as the moral proof lies in this fact that our
deepest convictions give us trustworthy knowledge of ultimate reality, perhaps the only knowledge possible. The
validity of divine existence is not founded on anything external or accidental but is felt by the spirit in us. The Ontological argument is a report of experience. We cannot
have certain ideas without having had the experience of the
objects of which they are the ideas. In such cases it is not
illegitimate to pass from the ideas to the objects referred to
by them. We should not have had an idea of absolute reality
if we had never been in immediate cognitive relation with
it, if we had not been intuitively conscious of it. The proof of
the existence is founded on the experience. The Ontological
argument is defective if it is treated as a logical inference.
To have the idea of a most perfect being is certainly different
from affirming the existence of such a being. The meaning
which the Ontological argument seeks to convey is that the
idea of God is an underived and self-evident one. Since it is
difficult to express this conviction in precise logical forms,
we find variety and indefiniteness. Anselm argues that the
idea of a perfect being necessarily involves the existence of
that being. If we think of the most perfect being as an idea
or a fancy, we contradict ourselves. We must think of it as
existing. Anselm thought that it was 'a single argument
which would require no other for its proof than itself alone,
and alone would suffice to demonstrate that God truly
exists'.[1] Aquinas rejects it as an 'unsupportable sophism'.
Descartes' reformulation of it came in for Kant's criticism and
Hegel thinks that there is a deeper significance in it than
Kant was able to discover. The only way to establish the
validity of this argument is to trace how the idea arises. If

Socrates 1910 , pp. 156-157).
1 *Proslogium*, Preface. See Baillie: *The Interpretation of Religion* (1929),
p. 79.

the question is put as to how we know that we are alive or awake, we can only exhibit the sources of the belief in the mind. This exhibition is what we attempted to outline. It may seem that the Ontological argument gives semblance to the criticism that the religious objects are the projections of our instincts. But it is all a question of the nature of the compulsion whether it is a mere subjective fancy that the individual is projecting on the screen of the beyond or the deepest needs of his nature.

If God is the whole reality which intuitive knowledge affirms, still, as Aristotle told us in his *Poetics*, no object is a whole which is not logically coherent. Discovery becomes proof when what is revealed by intuition is confirmed by the slower processes of consecutive thinking. We have now to show that the general character of the universe as known is quite consistent with this intuited certainty of God. It is the only way by which religious truths can be recommended to the large majority of people for whom religion is a matter of trust and inference. It is the only way to defend ourselves from uncriticized intuitions and dogmatisms which are prepared to find whatever they want.

CHAPTER VI

Matter, Life and Mind

1. *Belief and certainty*

Intuition is one of the ways in which beliefs arise. We believe because of the immediate certainty which the belief inspires. Often we rely on the testimony of others and such testimony is ultimately traceable to individual belief. We believe when a particular view is shown to be consistent with what we know in other realms or when the results accruing from the assumption of the belief justify our confidence. 'If any man will do his will he shall know of the doctrine, whether if be of God, or whether ᵗ speak of myself'.[1] If the belief works in the realm of mind or knowledge, of life or conduct, it is true; otherwise it is spurious. We reach absolute logical certainty, if what we find to be true is supported by others, if it is coherent with knowledge and works in life. The religious intuition requires to be reconciled with the scientific account of the universe.

2. *Science and philosophy*

There, is, however, a difference between science and philosophy. Their motives and methods vary. While science studies the different facts of experience, philosophy develops the meaning and implications of experience as a whole. It has two sides to it, an explanatory and a descriptive, a metaphysical and an empirical. Science is purely descriptive. It is perfectly satisfied if it relates a fact to its class, a plant to its species, or if it assigns a place to it in an evolutionary scale,

1 John vii. 17.

or if it traces a phenomenon to certain mediating conditions, as when sound is traced to waves, or if it brings certain events under well-known laws, as when Newton brought Kepler's discoveries under the law of gravitation. Science gives us a general history of what happens without raising the further question why things are what they are. Again, matter, life, consciousness and value are facts of experience studied in their abstract isolation by science, while for philosophy they are all interconnected as in human personality. We are one, and therefore the world is one. The experience which philosophy studies is concrete and whole, while the subject-matter of science is abstract and partial. Philosophy does not reveal anything wholly beyond experience, but presents to us the order and being of experience itself.

3. *Limitations of scientific knowledge*

It is necessary to know the limitations of scientific knowledge. It gives us quantitative measurements of events in the world we live in. It is controlled by the maxim, 'nothing can be known completely except quantities or by quantities'. Science is at home in the processes that can be repeated, in systems that can be reproduced. 'Everything is itself and not something else' is the principle of nature; everything is an example of a class is the principle of science.

Again, the objects studied by science are selected from experience. The data of perceived experience are studied as if they were independent of the world of perception, Physical science, for example, believes that the special aspects which events assume in relation to human observers are irrelevant to their intrinsic constitution as physically determined. We select phases of events for study in science. We can look upon man as either a physico-chemical being with certain weight and measurement, or a biological unit of the human species, or as a psychological, ethical or religious being. The subject-matter of science is abstractions from the real, plane diagrams from the solid object. It is a true enough representation of certain aspects of experience, and useful for certain specific purposes. The useful is not necessarily the true. It is now agreed that science gives us only readings, notations, a system of symbols. The laws of science express average and probable results. Given such and such conditions, such and such events happen. These laws express no opinion about the activity by which they happen. The ultimate structure of the universe is not known to science. It may be very different from the scientific model of it. Newton's mechanical conception as much as Einstein's is only an ideal picture, a conceptual model. The practical success of these is no guarantee that they are faithful representations of the actual structure. We can use the wireless, even though we do not understand its mechanism.

There is a tendency on the part of thought to make relative truths into absolute ones, provisional hypotheses into final statements. The success of the scientific hypothesis is tested by the applicability of its results in fields from which it did not originate. If a theory which arises from a restricted field finds additional relevance and cogency in new contexts, the validity of the theory receives an impressive verification. This tendency to generalization requires to be carried out with great caution. What is true of the mindless forces with which physical investigations deal is not true of human beings. Science becomes superstition if it insists on forcing facts into conformity with theories which do not suit them. A theory of physics or biology is not a philosophy of nature. When we pass to the scientific view of reality, we have to bear in mind the dependence of the scientific method on induction, the essentially abstract character of its subject-matter, its constant employment of statistical processes, its inevitable intellectual analysis for practical ends.

4. *Saṁsāra*

Hindu thought is generally associated with the theory that the world is *saṁsāra*, a perpetual procession of events, an incessant flow of occurrences. Expressions like 'the wheel of time', 'the cycle of birth and death', 'the ever-rolling stream', '*saṁsāra*', '*pravāha*', '*jagat*' are employed to indicate the non-substantial or unstable character of the universe. Everything that exists suffers change. Every actuality is a becoming, has in it the principle of unrest. Nothing empirical is eternally conserved. All life is a constant birth or becoming, and all birth entails a constant death, a dissolution of that which becomes in order that it may change into a new becoming. The world is movement (*jagat*), and it would be dissolved by the cessation of movement. The illusion is not in the movement, but in the stationariness. Buddhism took over this conception of *saṁsāra* from Hindu thought and put it at the centre of its scheme. For it, being is only process, a continuous alternation of birth and death, a perpetual transition from one thing to another. The doctrine of *pratītyasamutpāda* refers to the dependent or caused character of the universe. It is always dependent on causes (*hetupratyayāpekṣam*). Incessant change is true of the infinitely small as of the infinitely great. With both the Hindus and the Buddhists, the notion of world-becoming is more a speculative category than a scientific truth, at any rate in regard to the physical world.

If the world is a process, it cannot be divided into parts but only phases. We do not have realms or spheres of being, but only modes or phases of activity. The process of nature is one, supple and continuous, and not a consecutive series of static entities with fixed attributes. There are no sharp divisions of reality.

5. *Matter*

The most obvious way of treating experience is to regard it as a world of events. Of these events the physical ones seems to exist in their own right without any relation to a perceiving mind. In the early stages of cosmic evolution there were no minds to perceive the physical world or reflect on its nature. If the world is *saṁsāra*, movement, we must find in physical nature also transition and gradation.

While the mental world was admitted to be one of continuous movement, perpetually superseding itself, and not much suspicion was felt with regard to the mobile character of the world of life, matter at least was held to be immutable. The familiar conception of matter was that of an enduring substance moving through a static space in a uniformly flowing time. According to the old atomic theory, matter consists of atoms or tiny particles that cannot be divided. Material things are due to the varying combinations of the atoms or the indivisible particles. The changes visible in material things are traced to changes in the arrangements of the atoms, and not in their internal constitution, for the atoms were regarded as unchanging in character.

The solid atom has melted away in the recent developments of physics. J. J. Thomson resolved atoms into more minute corpuscles which were in turn reduced to electrical units, the mass of which was only one factor in electromagnetic momentum. Rutherford explained radioactivity as being due to atomic disintegration. Radioactivity involves the transmutation of elements, which is quite inconsistent with the immutability of atoms. Rutherford pictures the atom as a positive nucleus with negative electrons circling round it. Matter is not any more close, densely packed stuff but is an open structure with large empty spaces and scattered electric charges. Every atom is a structure which consists of electrons and protons of varying degrees of complexity.[1] The chemical properties of an element depend on the number of revolving electrons, and they yield the atomic number of the element. Protons and electrons themselves are sources of radiation or wave groups, a set of events which proceed outward from a centre. As a matter of fact the electron, which is the ultimate constituent of matter, is only a hypothetical centre of a group of radiations. The latter are all that we detect. As to what exists in the centre and the nature of the medium which carries the waves, if we can at all speak of a medium, we know next to nothing. The electrons seem to be mere wave forms. If we suppose that they are more than associated groups of radiations, we are drawing upon our imagination. An electron is the region from which energy may radiate. For Bohr it is little spherical particle, a 'disembodied charge of electricity'. Eddington calls it a 'something' whose mathematical specification can be given. It works, though we do not know why.

If electrons swing round the nucleus of an atom as planets circle round the sun, they should give out radiation of all wave-lengths, the energy increasing in a calculable way as the wave-length shortens. Since this does not happen, Max Planck suggested that radiation is emitted and absorbed in finite packets or definite quanta. The quantum changes which occur in an atom when it absorbs or radiates energy are discontinuous.[2] The electron is in one place and then in another without having passed the intermediate ones. It jumps regularly but discontinuously from one definite orbit to quite another definite but different orbit. At the moment, the physicists are obliged to use the quantum theory for

The atomic theories outlined in this section have naturally been modified to some extent by more recent discoveries. (Ed.).
Schrödinger does not admit this view. See Russell: *An Outline of Philosophy* (1927), p. 112.

certain purposes, and the classical undulatory theory for others, though the two are mutually exclusive. The quantum theory is unable to explain as the classical theory does the fact of diffraction.[1]

Again, we are told that the atomic models have no physical significance. It is perhaps more accurate to look upon the atom as a doubly infinite number of numbers arranged in an infinite matrix, and all that we really know about the atom is contained in this matrix. Strictly speaking we must be content with the equations which express relations between observable phenomena, and we know little about the meaning of the equations.

Matter is a structure of energy-units revolving with immense velocities in space-time, and the various elements arise from the number and arrangement of these units in an atom. Since these can be varied, transmutation of elements becomes possible as in radioactivity. Atomic weights and numbers relate to the number of units and their architectural or patternal grouping in the atoms. Matter is a form of energy or action. Physical objects are events, happenings, occurrences. They are not self-contained, changeless, eternal entities, but only moving points in a continuous passage. Nature is a complex of events, a structure of processes. Events are the stuff of concrete existence. They exist not in space separated by time, but in space-time, in which the relations between space and time are altering so constantly that the universe as it changes is characterized by an

---

1 'There are parts of physics,' says Max Planck, the author of the quantum hypothesis, 'among them the wide region of the phenomena of interference, where the classical theory has proved its validity in every detail, even when subjected to the most delicate measurements; while the quantum theory, at least in it present from, is in these respects completely useless' (Max Planck *The Universe in the Light of Modern Physics*, English Translatio (1931), p. 95; see pp. 30 ff.).

infinitely varying space-time system. Space is not a box in which solid bits of matter move about, nor is matter something extended in space and persistent through time. There is no such thing as a cosmic space or a cosmic time any more than persistent matter. Space, time and material are abstractions from the concrete fact which is a set of events. They exist together in concrete reality. According to Einstein, events are elements in an absolute four-dimensional continuum whose geometrical structure constitutes its intrinsic nature. This continuum is conceived by Einstein as 'finite, but unbounded'.

The theory of relativity follows from the substitution of space-time for the two independent entities of a persistent space and a cosmic time. Prerelativity physics assumed that if two events happen in different places, the question of their simultaneity can be answered easily. It is now held that each series of events has its own time order, and it is difficult to relate the one to the other since there is no one common standard time. Unless we take into account the relative motion of the observer and the object that is under inquiry, exact measurements cannot be made. There is not and cannot be any constant unit of measurement. What a thing is in its nature depends not only on the nature of the thing itself, but also on the nature of the observer relative to the object. Distances, lengths, volumes are all relative to particular frames of reference.[1] The law of relativity applies to all natural events, from radioactive atoms to celestial bodies.

We can distinguish in events two aspects, the normal and

1 'A distance as reckoned by an observer on one star is as good as the distance reckoned by an observer on another star. We must not expect them to agree. The one is a distance relative to one frame, the other is a distance relative to another frame. Absolute distance not relative to some special frame is meaningless' (Eddington: *The Nature of the Physical World* (1928), p. 21).

the material. Space-time refers to the formal aspect. Each event, whatever be its quality, has its own endurance, its spatio--temporal character. It is limited and not absolute; it is temporary, not everlasting. Space-time is the natural condition of finiteness, limitation; change which characterizes all events. It is not a real homogeneous structure, but an integral aspect of reality. It is not a sort of stage on which different kinds of material exhibit their dance, but refers only to certain rules and modes of expressing the broadest features and relationships within a universe of mobile events. A space-time relatedness applies to the whole of nature and confers unity on it. Since relatedness is not by itself a fact, the ultimate fact of nature is conceived as a process, a passage, single and not multiple. The name 'event' is applied to the parts or aspects of the process. Nature is an essentially unanalysable and individual process of change in which certain formal attributes called space-time and certain material characteristics called objects, as matter, life, etc., exhibit themselves as standing in many relations to each other and the whole.

The mathematical sciences deal with the formal stuff of events. Their study is of ideal abstractions, and their logic is formal, one of implication. Pure mathematics abstracts from even the space-time conditions, and deals with the pure concept of order or structure in its most abstract possible form. The units are characterless and can be shuffled and manipulated with the least interference with their inner nature. Mathematics is thus a model science.

It is more akin to logic than to physics. The discovery of the non-Euclidean geometry, algebra and arithmetic, the rise of the non-quantitative subjects like the theory of groups and projective geometry, show the purely formal nature of mathematics. Whitehead says that 'mathematics in its widest signification is the development of all types of

formal, necessary, deductive reasoning.'[1] Such a view conflicts with Kant's belief that mathematical propositions are
synthetic while logical propositions are formal and analytic.
There seems to be a confusion here between pure and applied mathematics. Since Kant does not accept the possibility of purely logical intuitions, he suggests *a priori*
intuitions of space and time which have a reference to the
sensible world. Russell and Whitehead argue in their *Prin-
cipia Mathematica* that the proof of the proposition $7 + 5 = 12$
is as strictly logical as any other proof. Though many of us
cannot understand mathematical demonstrations without
reference to images and diagrams, these are not however a
part of the demonstrations. Mathematics cannot be
regarded as of the same character as physics.

There are some who believe that space-time is not a
formal abstraction from experience, but is itself the most
elementary fact of existence. Eddington seems to think that
matter is reducible without remainder to space-time relations.[2] Space-time according to him is the ultimate fact, in
terms of which alone everything else can be defined. The
ultimate in nature is not physical but logical or mathematical. The real, which is independent of the observer, is not a
series of events which can be grasped by the senses, but a
system of relations which can only be conceived by thought.
The roots of reality are the eternal, changeless, mathematical relations. Masses and forces are purely psychological
appearances resulting from the interaction between the observer and the eternal relations which are their condition.
Matter is reduced to thought: physics to mathematics.[3]

1 *Universal Algebra*, p. vi.
2 *Space, Time and Gravitation* (1921), p. 197.
3 Sir James Jeans: *The Mysterious Universe*. Cp. also the Hindu
   mathematician who says: 'What is the good of elaborating it all?
   Whatever there is in all the three worlds containing moving and
   unmoving beings, nothing of all this can assuredly exist apart from

For Alexander, space-time is the ultimate reality from which both space and time are abstractions. Space-time is a kind of universal motion, and concrete things are differentiated complexes of motion within this universal scheme. Space-time has certain pervasive or categorical properties like existences, universality and order, which characterize all things. Other empirical qualities which distinguish different classes of objects emerge only under special conditions. Space-time, according to Alexander, spontaneously differentiates into finite collocations of point-instants. The simplest of these consists of motions of different velocities and extents of motion. When these objects form certain patterns the quality of materiality emerges; when other conditions are added, colours, etc., emerge.

Physical experience is not the same as knowledge of mathematical equations. The perception of light or colour is not the same as the perception of an identity. Spatio-temporal relatedness is incapable of existence apart from events. In the most primordial form events are not only spatio-temporal but physical also. There is a definite content in addition to space-time relatedness. It may be a flash of lightning, a thing of beauty, or an object of knowledge. We seem to touch the rock-bottom in the empirical universe in the physical events of the world. Space-time quality is the stuff of all events. None of them is by itself existent. They are distinct ideas, but existentially they are intrinsic factors in the process of being, and are abstracted by thought from the concrete process. Like all other events, the physical ones occur only in space-time. They occur here and not there, now and not then.

The displacement of hard indivisible matter by electric influences is of the greatest importance from the philosophical

measurement.'

point of view. Matter is not a thing, but a system of inter-related events. The old view of matter as a permanent substance having certain qualities and standing in various relations and performing definite functions is displaced by the conception of matter as a cluster of unstable events. The contrast between matter as insert and life as active, matter as reversible and life as irreversible, disappears. The difference between life and matter is not one of activity and passivity, but between two different kinds of activity. The inertia of matter which Newton exalted in his first law is itself the result of its internal activity. Radio-activity in matter is analogous to organic descent in life, though the former is regressive and the latter progressive activity. We can apply the concepts of families, genera and species to both the periodic table of Chemistry and the systems of Botany and Zoology. There is no impassable gulf between matter and life.[1] Atom, molecule, colloid, protoplasm, cell seem to be more or less continuous phases of a single process. Matter is concentrated structural energy which makes possible the creation of fresh forms, structures and types. It is as truly creative as living organism or mind. When atoms combine into a molecule they acquire a new status. In virtue of the whole to which they belong, they acquire new qualities, which could not be deduced from their nature before combination.

6. Substance

The whole history of philosophy may in a sense be regarded as the criticism of the category of substance. Though Greek philosophy started with the conception of a permanent being, which is present identically in all transformations,

1 Science is to-day 'the study of organisms. Biology is the study of the larger organisms, whereas physics is the study of the smaller organisms'(Whitehead:*Science and the Modern World* (1926), p. 145).

it soon gave place to a different view in Pythagoras and Heraclitus. The real consists not in an unchangeable substance, but in certain constant properties which persist in all becoming. The essence of things is number according to Pythagoras. For Heraclitus substance is not something which lies outside becoming, but is the immanent law or the logos which pervades all becoming and gives it its form. For Kant substance is a concept of the understanding, and Hume traces it to empirical habit and association. It is imagination which combines what occur together frequently in a regular order, into one idea. Avenarius and Mach look upon substance as a conceptual device for simplifying thought. The unity of substance is a nominal one. The identity of a thing is a fiction. The constancy of certain relations is all that is meant by it. Our minds are so made that they regard a number of conditions linked together as a unity, and treat the conditions themselves as properties belonging to it. We distinguish things by their properties. We speak of a thing as the same only so long as it has the same properties. The most satisfactory view of substance is what is expressed in a memorable phrase by Lotze, that a thing is what it does. Its nature is the way it behaves. In his *Metaphysics*, Lotze exposes the futility of the conception of a substantial reality, 'communicating to the properties gathered about it the fixedness and consistency of a thing'.[1] What the inner essence of a thing is we do not know. We call a thing real, substantive or identical when it behaves in a certain specific way, when it changes in a certain regular order. The substantiality of a thing is the law according to which the changing events are connected with one another, the formula which sums up its history, the pattern which expresses its behaviour. Lotze compares the essence of a

1 E. T., Book i, chap. iii, pp. 57-75.

thing to a melody where the successive sounds obey a law of consecutiveness. We speak of a substance when its qualities are coherent, when its successive changes follow a historic route. The being of a thing is constituted by its becoming. Whitehead tells us that what is permanent in the organism is not 'substance' but 'form', and forms suffer changing relations.[1] Limited regions of space-time often have more or less clearly distinguishable qualities that tend to persist through time, or if they change, they do so in an orderly and gradual way. In other words, changes take place within the limits of a type. The fundamental structure is not altered. The term 'physical object' refers to such extended, qualitative, space-time regions. The things of the physical world are 'substances' only in this sense. We do not have in them any permanent substratum supporting adventures of changing qualities and relations, and surviving identically in the course of these adventures. A string of events is what we mean by a substance.

The quantum theory makes the notion of an enduring substance irrelevant to physics. A thing is a set of influences from a locality or a centre, which is itself purely hypothetical. Strictly speaking, we have a set of events as scenes in a drama or notes in a tune. There is no thing which exists entire any moment, or survives throughout. Not even an electron can be conceived as a particle of matter self-identical through time and occupying a sharply defined region of space. Self-identity results from an averaging process taken over a relatively long period of time. An electron is a sort of a statistical invariant. Its substantiality is traced to some superior co-ordinating force, for each continuant is held to be the activity of a co-ordinating force. The unity of a thing is the unity of its history.[2] The causal connection

1 *Process and Reality* (1929), p. 40.
2 Bertrand Russel says: 'We have to change our notions both of

confers sufficient unity to deserve a distinct name. Unfortunately the single name suggests a single thing, and if the events concerned do not occur in the same place, we say the thing has moved.

If things are a series of events, then identity means connected continuity. If the changes are gradual and do not involve any structural alterations, we have the continuity which is mistaken for identity. If the changes are sudden and entire, so as to involve structural alterations, we say the identity is violated, the thing has altered. There is persistence of plan or pattern for a certain extent of time. The longer it persists, the more substantial is a thing said to be. But it does not mean persistence of stuff. We say it is the same thing so long as there is persistence of form in addition to the usual change of stuff. Take the human body. The stuff in it is not exactly the same for two moments, and yet we call it the same body so long as the outward form and characteristic ways of behaviour are maintained. There are cases where we do not observe continuity, but attribute it. We hold that we are the same selves and that our environment is the same, even though we do not notice the environment and there are gaps in our conscious life as in sleep. Sometimes our ideas of continuity are confused. Jerky events seem continuous in a cinema. Rapid vibrations are taken for steady colours. That there are ultimate discontinuities in nature is the teaching of the quantum hypothesis. However, a substance which is a logical category is a continuant which we either observe or infer.

What we regard as substance depends on our interests.

substance and of cause. To say that an atom persists is like saying that a tune persists. If a tune takes five minutes to play, we do not conceive of it as a single thing which exists throughout that time, but as a series of notes, so related as to form a unity. In the case of the tune, the unity is aesthetic; in the case of the atom, it is causal' (*An Outline of Philosophy* (1927), p. 118).

For some purposes the human individual is a substance; for others any part of his body may be a substance; for philosophical purposes nature as a whole may be the substance. If independence of existence is the mark of substantiality, no finite particular is a substance, though we can mark off any set of events as an individual for conventional purposes. Matter is the name for a cluster of events, possessing certain relatively persistent habits and potencies.

7. Cause

The conception of cause also requires revision. That there is a real connection between events which present themselves to us and not a mere subjective association is the condition of the possibility of any science. Kant gives us a simple illustration. My perceptions, he said, in apprehending a house may begin anywhere and end anywhere, may begin at the top and end at the bottom, or vice versa, but when we apprehend a ship going down a stream the sequence of perceptions is determined. We cannot vary or reverse the other. Kant explained that causality was a synthetic *a priori* principle. It is sometimes argued that the idea arises in the immediate experience of effort which we use as an interpretative principle in objective science. If conative efficiency is the basis of the causal concept, inanimate objects cannot be regarded as efficient. Besides, conative efficiency, however familiar, is not easily explicable. It implies rigid contact, which is absent even in densely packed situations. Again, the causal concept seems to imply that the world is a collection of distinct things which it is not. Simply because the concepts are hard and precise, it does not follow that the situations to which they apply are equally hard and precise. By applying mathematical formulas to concrete existence, we suggest that there is no more in the effect than is in the cause. If cause and effect are identical or equivalent, then all progress and creativeness will be ruled out. Events happen according to certain rules. There is no necessity why they should happen that way, but they do happen. Why water should be formed when oxygen and hydrogen combine, and not any other element, we do not know. It seems to be quite arbitrary. Things do not exist in nature by necessity. Nothing *must* be, nor is there any sufficient reason why anything *should* be. The fact is that things *are*. Hume long ago showed that there is no more reason for belief in cause and effect than that we constantly see one thing happen after another. No matter how often we may see events occur in a regular order, we are no wiser. The laws of succession are observed facts, and there is no logical necessity about them. When we say that A is necessarily followed by B, all that we mean is that this rule of connection between A and B is found in a large number of instances, and we know of no case to the contrary. To say that B rises out oi A is to note a fact of sequence. It does not mean that B is or is equivalent to A. The effect is not the cause in a different form. The end is not the beginning in disguise. We cannot speak of causes, for there are no causes, but only causal laws, selected uniformities of sequence, observed laws of succession. Events are connected and causal laws tell us of the correlations of events.

8. *Order and progress*

A scientific treatment of the universe is possible because nature is a network of interconnected events. Every event has both an individual and a social character. It has an irreducible specificality, a unique itselfness, as also a connection with other events. Each event is just what it is, but it cannot be what it is without the influence and assistance

of the other events. The events are by no means windowless,
lonely and cut off. The environment is not separate from or
external to the individual. The old conception of atoms
made them entirely independent as to their character and
their relations were external and contingent. An atom would
remain the same whether there was an environment or not.
The conception of the electron brings out the 'social' character. We cannot understand it, if we take it as an abstract
individual. The electrons form groups or wholes, and their
relations can be understood only if they are viewed as
members of wholes. An electrons within a living body is
different from one outside it, owing to its share in the plan
and arrangement of the body. The atoms and molecules
which are wholes have individual patterns of their own. The
relations of the protons and electrons in their wholes are not
external and accidental, but are due to the general structure
of the atom itself. The more complex structures like
molecules determine their characteristic properties. Even at
the physical level, reality is not a collection of independent
things, but a whole, and as such it has a structure which
prescribes the relations as well as the properties of the
parts. Control by the whole is the striking fact. We can infer
from one part to another since events form a world of
intercourse and association. At any one stage the whole
universe represents a cosmic situation, and any part of it
represents the whole background.

There is not only order, but what one might call progress.
The two striking features of the physical world are continuity and change, connection with the past and creative
advance into the future. Time is connection, not mere succession. The past never dies, but lives in the present, and the
present flows into the future. Every event has not only a
retrospective but a prospective reference. At the conscious
level we have memory of the past as well as anticipation of

the future. We have at the physical level also what answers to memory and anticipation, a physical memory and blind anticipation. No event is complete. It seeks for its completion in an undetermined future. Throughout the process of nature we have creativity, or the coming into being of the new, which is not reducible to or deducible from the old. We cannot forecast the future on the basis of our knowledge of the present. The atomic processes of radiation and chemical combination produce stable compounds. Two hydrogen atoms some distance apart, with the total energy necessary to make a molecule, move towards one another under an irresistible law of attraction if outside influences do not interfere. The two atoms work towards a definite goal, though they are unconscious of it. Something new is perpetually happening in the course of nature. Every event seems to actualize a fresh possibility not contained in the past. Matter effects in its onward march new structural grouping and combinations which are not only valuable to us, but valuable in the order of the universe. Lloyd Morgan tells us that there are 'emergents' in nature--using an expression of G.H.Lewes--whose character cannot be foretold from the nature of their several constituents as they are in themselves. The nature of the new structures or the emergents can be discerned only by observation and experiment after they have come into being. In mere 'resultants' the nature of the product resembles the nature of the assembled parts; in 'emergents', on the other hand, we have a new and unforeseen structure and character. If evolution means an unfolding of what is already in being, emergence can only be the emerging or the coming into view of what is already contained in it, though hidden. But evolution now is interpreted as the coming into existence of something new, which is unpredictable before its occurrence.

While each event is different from every other and has its

own distinctive nature, we concentrate attention on the form, pattern or structural organization, and so long as it remains the same we do not concern ourselves with the differences which are negligible from the point of view of scientific classification. But when a new mode of organization arises, it attracts our attention, and we say that a new form has emerged. The difference between resultant advance and emergent evolution is methodological and not metaphysical. There is always creative advance in time, small or great. Matter is essentially creative in character, and its processes are irreversible. That is why it is regarded as the mother of the universe. Creativeness is not confined to the vital and psychological aspects, but matter also is creative change. Its irreversible processes mean plans and ends, however unconscious matter may be of them. The physical world itself prepares for an unfulfilled future. At a certain time there came to be on the surface of the earth abundant supplies of carbon, hydrogen and oxygen, which provided suitable conditions for the rise of life. The processes of the physical environment cannot be accounted for without a reference to the end of life, for which they were a preparation.

The past cannot account for the present. Every occurrence is a mystery. Existence is a continuous miracle. Physical science fails if it attempts to transform a miracle into an equation. It describes the way in which bodies behave, and not why they do so. Our physical and chemical symbolism is a necessary working instrument which is exceedingly useful. But it is only a rough representation of reality in one of its aspects. We may feel that we know all about matter, that its existence is undoubted, and that its nature is intelligible, but all that we know about it is the effect it produces on us. When we come to think of it, it reduces itself to certain feelings and relations among them. It is experience and possible experience.

9. *Physical science and subjectivism*

Matter may be far more complex in its structure and far subtler in its possibilities than we ever imagined, yet it is matter and not anything else. To reduce it to electric energy is not to equate it with mind. There is, however, a tendency to interpret the physical in terms of the psychological in the writings of some scientific metaphysicians. The two chief doctrines of modern physics, relativity and quantum theory, are mainly responsible for it. In the history of thought, relativity and subjectivism generally get mixed up. The variable characters are often attributed to the subject. A classical illustration of it is found in the distinction of primary and secondary qualities. The latter, representing variable features, are traced to the activity of the subject. Now that even the 'primary' features are said to be relative, it is inferred they are also subjective. All properties which belong to an entity or system under specific conditions of relation to some other term or terms are said to be relative, while those which follow form the self-enclosed nature of an entity without reference to anything outside it are said to be absolute. Characters which were once regarded as absolute and intrinsic are now known to be relative and variable. They are not properly characters of the real, and are traced to subjective contexts. Besides, the analogy of human perspective is best adapted to the exposition of the relativity of events. If physical relations are characterized by relativity, then the subjectivity of human perspectives must also be present in them.[1] If we believe in uniformity of

1 Eddington says: 'We ourselves, our conventions, the kind of thing that attracts our interest, are much more concerned than we realize in any account that we give of how the objects of the physical world are behaving. An object which, viewed through our frame

nature, it is due to our desire for simplicity and not any natural necessity. Our laws are no part of nature's plan or structure. 'The fact that a predictable path through space and time is laid down for the earth is not a genuine restriction on its conduct, but is imposed by the formal scheme in which we draw up our account of its conduct.'[1] Consciousness is not a mere 'unessential complication occasionally found in the midst of inorganic nature at a late stage of evolutionary history', but is essential to all experience. The properties which physical science ascribes to its objects are largely the product of thinking minds. The science of physics is a structure we build on the basis of mental phenomena which we receive and the laws which we form. Besides, there seems to be an element of spontaneity in the physical world itself. Indeterminacy or contingency is generally associated with human volition. Natural events are known to be indeterminate. Referring to the Heisenberg principle of indeterminacy, Eddington says, 'Physics is no longer pledged to a scheme of determinate law'.[2] Quoting Einstein on the conflict between physical reality and structural causality, he argues that 'the future is a combination of the causal influences of the past, together with unpredictable elements--unpredictable not merely because it is impracticable to obtain the data of prediction, but because no data connecting causality with our experience exist'.[3] Eddington is inclined to believe that this indeterminacy is a sign of mental activity, an expression of freedom of choice. As the laws of physics are not strictly causal, as there is

of conventions, may seem to be behaving in a very special and remarkable way, may, viewed according to another set of conventions, be doing nothing to excite particular comment'. (*The Nature of the Physical World*, 1928, p. 152).

1 *Ibid.*, p. 148.
2 *Ibid.*, p. 294.
3 *Ibid.*, pp. 294- 295.

nothing which predetermines the quantum principles of the atom which seem to be more or less like the choice of the brain, what is below the atom may be said to be continuous with what is below the brain. 'In the case of the brain we have an insight into a mental world behind the world of pointer readings, and in that world we get a new picture of the fact of decision which must be taken as revealing its real nature--if the words "real nature" have any meaning. For the atom we have no such insight as to what is behind the pointer readings. We believe that behind all pointer readings there is a background continuous with the background of the brain.'[1]

Another argument which Eddington employs is that scientific truths are verifiable only in concrete and complex occurrences whose total character is not deducible from mere equations. The laws of physics deal with abstractions, quantitative correlations of 'pointer readings' which might apply within any one of a number of possible worlds. 'Of the infinite number of worlds which are examples of what might be possible under the laws of nature, there is one which does something more than fulfil those laws of nature. This property, which is evidently not definable with respect to any of the laws of nature, we describe as "actuality", generally using the word as a kind of halo of indefinite import. We recognize the actuality of a particular world because it is that world alone with which consciousness interacts.'[2] 'The differentiation of the actual from the non-actual is only explicable by reference to mind.'[3] The actual non-metrical stuff of events is mind-stuff. 'The stuff of the world is mind-stuff.'[4] Mind is taken in an extensive sense.

1 *The Nature of the Physical World*, pp. 311-312.
2 *Ibid.*, pp. 265-266.
3 *Ibid.*, p. 267.
4 *Ibid.*, p. 276.

'Consciousness is not sharply defined, but fades into subconsciousness, and beyond that we must postulate something indefinite, but yet continuous with our mental nature. This I take to be the world-stuff'.[1] From the evidence of the mystics, the oneness of the physical world with consciousness is also inferred.[2]

The feature which are relative and variable are not necessarily subjective. Special and variable features are as much real as the general and pervasive ones. The theory of relativity attempts to establish equations which hold for all observers, and which are independent of the personal positions. The new physics puts objectivity in a new setting, but does not cancel the distinction between the subjective and the objective. Again, it is difficult to accept the view that human convenience determines the occurrence or non-occurrence of such apparently objective facts as the relative position of the earth. The sun does not conform to Einstein's prediction simply because he would have it so. The actual and determinate motions of heavenly bodies are due to determinate physical causes. To hold that the general laws of physics do not determine the actual conditions of events, but only describe them, is not to deprive them of their objectivity. Our measurements of time, seconds and minutes and hours, may be human conventions, but the rhythmic processes of nature are not in any way disturbed by the way in which we happen to look at them. The solar system is objective, even though it is discerned by us from

1 *Ibid.*, p. 280.
2 'Our minds are not apart from the world and the feelings that we have of gladness and melancholy, and our yet deeper feelings are not of ourselves alone, but are glimpses of a reality transcending the narrow limits of our particular consciousness--the harmony and beauty of the face of Nature is at root one with the gladness that transfigures the face of man' (*The Nature of the Physical World*, p. 321).

various points of view and is able to enter into a number of astronomical systems. In a very real sense we make nature. We attach a value to permanence and create a world of apparent substance. But this does not justify us in overlooking the compulsion of fact. It is under the control of fact that we build our sciences. If we ignore it, thought becomes mere imagination. The human mind is responsible for the concept of matter, but it is not the creator of matter as well.

From indeterminacy we cannot infer human freedom. Natural events are indeterminate in some respects, even when the laws of their general structure are fully specified. But this indeterminacy does not mean irrationality of nature or arbitrariness such as we associate with human preference. The principle of indeterminacy shows us that no one set of physical measurements can completely determine the complexity of natural fact. Heisenberg's principle of indeterminacy is an expression of the limits of practical measurement. It does not mean the absence of determination. All abstract determinations are partial as regards the total event. Even the freedom of man is not helped in any way by freaks within the atom. To suggest that electrons possess free will is to degrade freedom itself.

It is true that the conclusions of science are verified only in the context of experience. But appeal to the contingent actuality of what happens is not an appeal to the subjective mind. The experience to which science appeals is not a private system of mental data. Actuality is discoverable in the course of events, and not in our feelings or notions about the inner character of events. There is an unknown content deep within the world of physics unreachable by the methods which the physicists use. But it does not follow that the content is the stuff of consciousness simply because we have a direct knowledge of intrinsic nature only in conscious life.

While we can sympathize with Eddington's anxiety to mentalize the experienced world which cannot be reduced to equations of physics on the ground that chance, contingent actuality and indetermination are characteristics of mental phenomena, it is difficult to ignore those persistent aspects of experience which refuse to be reduced to mere sentience. A stone is not a self any more than a self is a stone. From the empirical point of view their characters are so different that any attempt to reduce the one to the other is illegitimate. The experiences of the human mind are a feature of the natural world quite as much as the movements of molecules.[1] The concept of matter stands for an aspect of the experienced world which is set over against the mental as its medium for expression. The relative solidity of matter helps the expression of mind, and at the same time limits and restrains its activity. The negative function of matter has received great emphasis in the history of thought. The decay of the flesh entails the failure of spirit. The body is the tomb of the soul, as Plato urged. The threats of modern scientists that the sands of the physical universe are running out, and that no race of men or supermen can live for ever are based on the negative function of matter. In concrete experience mind and matter are in relation, but the concreteness of the relation is prejudiced by the assimilation of the one to the other. Matter and mind both belong to nature, but matter is not mind. Its otherness to mind is unaffected, however much it may be etherealized.

1 Cp. Max Planck: 'Reason tells us that both the individual man and mankind as a whole, together with the entire world which we apprehend through our senses, is no more than a tiny fragment in the vastness of Nature, whose laws are in no way affected by any human brain. On the contrary, they existed long before there was any life on earth, and will continue to exist long after the last physicist has perished' (*The Universe in the Light of Modern Physics*, E. T., 1931, p. 8).

Sir James Jeans in *The Mysterious Universe* (1930) thinks that as the behaviour of nature seems to be most adequately described by 'pure' mathematical relations, the reality of nature must behave like the mind of the mathematician. Since mind consists of thoughts, nature may be regarded as made up of thoughts. Such an exaltation of the physical into the mystical is not supported by science. Sir James seems to forget that the type of analysis exemplified by mathematical physics is not the most adequate method of dealing with physical facts. It is incomplete, derivative and abstract. The mathematical properties of events do not tell us of their intrinsic nature. We start with sensible phenomena as the reality to be explained and construct from them scientific entities like electrons and energies which are abstractions from the perceived. If the abstract is interpreted as the real and the concrete as the appearance, it requires further proof than Sir James offers.

Terms like 'feeling', 'experience', 'value', generally reserved for psychological contexts, are used by Whitehead in a wider sense.[1] Physical events are spoken of us percipient. Each occasion is a concrescence. It 'prehends' all other occasions into itself. The world 'prehension' is suggested by Descartes' mental 'cogitations' and Locke's 'ideas'. Even physical relatedness becomes a sort of apprehension. 'The most individual actual entity is a definite act of perceptivity'[2] and since this perceptivity is immediate and non-cognitive, ' the actual fact is a fact of aesthetic ex perience.'[3] The event as the most concrete actual something has value. Value is present in the electrons as truly as in the mind, though in a different way.[4]

1 Nothing is to be received into the physical scheme which is not discoverable as an element in subjective experience (Whitehead *Process and Reality* 1929 , p. 253).
2 *Religion in the Making* (1926), p. 108.
3 *Ibid.*, p. 113.
4 *Ibid.*, p. 109.

If consciousness and selectivity are to be regarded as the defining features of human experience, all events do not possess them, and it is rather confusing to use terms in a wider sense. Conscious experience is a natural occurrence just where, when and as it has been found to occur. It is a late and limited factor in a world of nature which it did not create, and whose more pervasive features it cannot seriously alter.

We may sum up the general characteristics of the physical world: (1) What was regarded as a passive immutable particle is now known to be a complex system of seething energy. An atom is an organism whose members are protons and electrons. Molecules and human society are more complex organisms. (2) Physical nature is an ordered whole and operates as such, and its members are interdependent. There is thus an interactive union between every organism and its environment. (3) Every event has both caused and creative aspects. Its changes are thus trans-mechanical. (4) Scientific explanation finds its limits when we reach the creative side. Science cannot explain why matter should exist, nor why there should be two species of electrons and protons.

10. *Life*

It is in the context of matter that life is found fumbling for light. Biological sciences deal with the distinctive phenomena presented by living organisms from microbes to mammals and their activities. Though something life-like might be found in other parts of the universe, biologists study life in the region of the earth's surface, seas and atmosphere. Though the higher organisms exhibit the feature of consciousness, biological sciences do not concern themselves with it.

There is something specific in the behaviour of living organisms which is not traceable in the non-living. The processes of assimilation, respiration, reproduction, growth and development are different from physico-chemical reactions. A living organism maintains its specific structure and activities throughout all changes. The stability of form is maintained in a living organism through an inner activity, and not mere passive resistance to changes in the environment. In the activity of respiration, for example, the processes which regulate with the utmost accuracy the pressure of oxygen in the blood and of carbon dioxide in the lungs are intelligible only as a means of preserving the equilibrium of the organism as a whole. The dream of the whole, the idea of the object is the active influence operative in all life phenomena. Life is a dynamic equilibrium which tends to maintain itself. The parts of a living organism are less independent than those of a physical one. The removal of any part from a physical body does not involve any essential change of properties, but in living organisms, form, structure and composition are interdependent. The living organ is a whole, doing things that no atomic systems could ever do. They register the results of their experience, and in a sense form habits. The changes which they present in response to outward circumstances are retained and built into the organism.

An atom can neither mend itself nor reproduce itself. A living organism adapts itself to its environment. It does not simply react to the changes of the environment, but replies to them. As soon as a living organism is injured, the healing process sets in. A plant develops a new sprout in the place of one cut off. The changes which occur in the process of development are of a specific kind. The process of reproduction starts in a part of the organism itself. There is the hereditary transmission of enormously complicated

physico-chemical structures. In a sense the environment is
not foreign to the organism, but enters into its very life. The
organism nourishes itself by assimilating materials from its
environment. The two are so well adapted to each other that
they may be regarded as expressions of a larger whole. The
two are inextricably intertwined. There is a specific inner
direction in living organisms which grow, repair, reproduce
themselves, and mould the outer circumstances into their
own patterns. What we know of matter does not help us to
understand the co-ordinated maintenance of life. Life is a
different order of fact.

11. *Vitalism*

The striking difference between the living and the non-
living suggested to some physiologists the hypothesis that
a new principle called an 'entelechy' or an unconscious 'soul'
takes control of the physical processes. There are souls or
entelechies hidden in living things. Hans Driesch bases such
a view on his experiments with the eggs of the sea urchin,
in which the eggs were dissected and yet produced *whole*
organisms of a small size.[1]

As a protest against the view which treats living organisms as mere machines or as complexes of physico-
chemical processes, the vitalist hypothesis is useful. The
strikingly specific behaviour of living beings cannot be confused with atomic activity. vitalism stresses the fact of
co-ordinated activity in the phenomena of life by which the
individual parts are adapted to the maintenance and
functioning of the whole. The cause of the particular mode
of existence of each part lies in the whole. Life experiences
are the expressions of a persistent and indivisible unity. But
this vital principle cannot be a non-physical entity influencing

1 *Science and Philosophy of the Organism.*

physical experience. Professor Loeb has shown that the prick of a needle or some such disturbance starts the process of division and furthers normal development in an unfertilized ovum which would not otherwise divide and develop. We do not know the relation between the prick and the marvellously co-ordinated developmental changes. He also traces the activity of the simpler organisms to tropisms, direct reactions to light, heat, pressure, etc.[1] It is obvious, however, that physico-chemical stimuli start various kinds of vital activity. In reply the vitalist say that the vital principle operates only in conjunction with physico-chemical causes. It is only a regulative principle demanding for its operation a suitable physico-chemical process. But while phenomena of life depend on physical conditions, we do not know how physical conditions determine the phenomena of life. From a strictly scientific point of view, vitalism is unsatisfactory, since it attempts to explain every thing which occurs in a living organism, and we are unable to test its truth. As observers of experience we must be content with a statement of facts, a description of nature as it appears in the phenomena of life. In living organisms there is a new organization of structure and a specific co-ordination of activity, a design in them, and inward determination of all the parts by the function and purpose of the whole, which cannot be interpreted physically. The only point relevant to science is that the kind of correlation needed for the biological facts is different from that needed for physical phenomena.

The science of biology does not account for life, but assumes it as beyond all explanation. Life is a part of nature, differing in kind from matter, though there is scope in living organisms for the application of both the physical and

1 *The Mechanistic Conception of Life* (1912).

biological explanations.

12. *Evolution*

Answering to the qualities of continuity and change, or conservation and advance in the physical world, we have in the world of life heredity and variation. Living organisms inherit a plan of organization, and also vary it. New structures and organs, new functions and powers appear. Living creatures have arisen, apparently by gradual change, from simpler ancestors. The hypothesis of evolution is suggested as an explanation for the origin of the new species.

If we leave aside the ancient philosophies of India and Greece, the modern theory of evolution is mainly the work of Linnaeus (1707-1778), Buffon (1707-1788), Erasmus Darwin (1731-1802), Lamarck (1744-1829), Charles Darwin and his followers. While Linnaeus believed in the separate creation of each species of plant and animal, he admitted in his later work that in certain cases new forms might have come into being through crosses between the original species. He was, however, of opinion that the change was a degeneration since it tended to obscure the perfection of the original type. Buffon started with a belief in the fixity of species, though he questioned the perfection of the plan on which the species were originally built. From his knowledge of comparative anatomy he argued that the original plan was not to be viewed as perfect since it had parts which were of little or no use to the animal, and which seemed to be taken from other animals. This led to the conception that the members of a group of species showed striking family resemblance, and might have been derived from a common ancestor either by progressive change or degeneration. He made valuable suggestions about the changes in the plant and animal induced by the environment. Both Erasmus

Darwin and Lamarck argued that changed circumstances in an animal's life led to alterations in its habits. These changes of habits resulted in the increased use of some organs and decreased use of others, eventually producing a change of form. They thought that such 'acquired characters' were inherited.

Malthus's *Essay on the Principle of Population* (1798) suggested to Darwin the importance of the principle of natural selection as a factor by which progressive changes are brought about. In his *Origin of Species* (1859) he gave details and demonstrations of his view of evolution, that life on this planet evolved by a gradual and yet continuous process from the earliest forms of living organs to the latest product, man. Natural selection, variation and heredity are said to be the factors through the operation of which new species arise out of existing ones. Natural selection by itself cannot account for the new changes. It is a sifting process, and assumes the two other factors of variation and heredity. According to the former, no two animals or plants are quite alike. Even the offspring of the same parent or parents tend to vary in greater or less degree both from their parents and from one another. The novelties or the new departures are called the variations. If a new variation is not inherited by the progeny, it is of little direct value in evolutionary change. The principle of heredity tells us that the peculiarities exhibited by the parents tend to be transmitted to the offspring in greater or less degree. When the new characters are produced by the variability of organisms, natural selection decides their survival or death. If the characters are not adapted to the environment, they are eliminated in the competition. If, on the other hand, they equip their possessors better for the struggle, they tend to survive. The offspring of the successful tend to resemble the parents in exhibiting the favoured variation to a greater degree than the parents, and a new type becomes established by a continuous piling up of small useful accretions through many generations.

After Darwin and Spencer, it was realized that the stages of development were not gradual, but abrupt. Bateson showed that variations, in many cases, were of a discontinuous nature. According to Hugo de Vries, variations may arise either suddenly or gradually. The former are called mutations, the latter fluctuations. De Vries attributed all specific advance to large well-marked variations or mutations. Mutations are independently heritable and illustrate the principles of Mendelian inheritance.

Weismann opposed Lamarck's theory of the transmission of acquired characters, in which both Darwin and Spencer had faith. He distinguished between germ-plasm or reproductive tissue and somato-plasm or bodily tissue, and held that changes induced in the organism could be transmitted only if the germ–plasm was affected. Heritable variations are represented in the germ-cells, and the non-heritable ones are not.

How do we account for the variations, small or great, gradual or abrupt? We cannot trace them to the influence of the environment, for the types without the variations seems to be just as well adapted as those with them. Weismann's theory of physical necessity cannot account for them. Darwin's view of chance variations is a confession of inability to explain the source of variations. Complex organs like the eye do not seem to be produced by a series of fortuitous variations, and still more fortuitous survival. Modifications and variations do not come singly but in complexes, involving many minor and consequential modifications and variations. Each single small variation is not independently selected. In other words, the organism seems to 'vary' as a whole.

Bergson finds that the molluscs in the order of evolution proceed by steady steps to develop an eye, which resembles very much the eye developed by the independent line of vertebrates. How does it happen that similar effects appear in different lines of evolution brought about by different means? How could the same small variations occur in two independent lines of evolution if they were purely accidental? The two series must have been governed by a common vital impulse to this useful end. There is something more in evolution than merely mechanical urges. Bergson is inclined to attribute a 'rudiment of choice'[1] to the species which, travelling by different paths, reach the same goal. Given a new situation, the 'urge' common to all members leads them to meet it by a new method. If this relatively new mode of behaviour becomes fixed, natural selection perpetuates the congruent variations and eliminates those of an opposite kind. According to Bergson, it is the inner urge, or life force, or an upward drive, that incites the whole species in a definite direction. His view is nearer Lamarck's position. According to Lamarck, new surroundings produce new needs, and these evoke new functions. Animals striving to improve their conditions acquire modifications which they transmit to their successors. We cannot account for the origin of new organs, for the co-ordination of variations or even their rise when their utility is not perceived unless we assume with Lamarck and Bergson that there is a deeper law of inward striving after higher forms of life. The striving of the organism is the creative effort to which evolution is due. The hormic theory asserts that each animal has a special nature, by which it strives towards a limited number of goals. The hormic tendencies of the different species are differentiations of a primaeval urge to live. The variations

1 *Creative Evolution*, English Translation (1911), p. 96.

are the creatures' efforts to meet the new situations.

Lamarck's theory of the transmission of acquired characters is questioned on the grounds that there is no mechanism by which the changes in an organism, such as increase of size, could be represented by changes in the structure of the germ-cell, and that there is no experimental evidence in support of the inheritability of the effects of use and disuse. Our ignorance of the way in which the germ-cell reacts to the bodily changes does not compel us to deny all changes in the germ-cell as the result of bodily changes. The conditions under which alone experiments are possible are not favourable to decisive conclusions. We have to induce changes in the organism by more or less unnatural interference from without, and our observations regarding such artificially induced characters need not be true of naturally developed changes. Besides, evidence in favour of the Lamarckian hypothesis is steadily increasing.[1]

Besides, the functioning of the whole in which organism and environment are parts accounts for the action and interaction of the parts themselves, such as the systematic co-operation between organs of different species. Protoplasm develops into the two main lines of the vegetable and the animal. Their mutual dependence is another illustration of the social and integral character of the universe.

All biologists accept the evolution idea as a broadly satisfactory account of the mode of change that has actually taken place. There is a great difference of opinion in regard to the causal factors which operated in the evolution. In

1 Professor Mc Dougall says: 'Since 1920 I have conducted an experiment on strictly Lamarckian principles, and have found clear-cut evidence of increasing facility in successive generations of animals trained to execute a particular task. This very great increase of facility seems explicable in no other way than by transmission of the modifications acquired by the efforts of individuals'(*Psychologies of 1930*, 1930, p. 27n.).

spite of the great advance of our knowledge, what Darwin said in his *Origin of Species* is still true. 'The laws governing inheritance are for the most part unknown.' 'Our ignorance of the laws of variation is profound.' The known facts of biology can be summed up in the statement that there is deep within life itself a power of variation and a persistent tendency to perfect itself.

Darwin's theory was confined to the biological field. He noted the changes within the different forms of life, but he assumed that life always came from life. He broke down only the lines between species, between the lower and the higher forms of life. Herbert Spencer made a philosophy out of Darwin's observations, and seemed to account for the rise of the living from the non-living, the mental from the non-mental. The difference between these is reduced to the degree of the complexity of the organization.

Evolution is no explanation. It does not say why the process should have ever occurred, why life should occur at all. Survival of the fittest does not carry us far. Life has little survival value as compared with matter from which it is supposed to have sprung. A rock survives for hundreds of millions of years, while even the oldest tree is only a few thousand years old. If survival was the aim of nature, life would never have appeared. A strict science of biology merely notes the facts that in life we have a different set of phenomena and novelties occur right through, that plants and animals are not fixed, and have evolved or developed from other forms, and that in fact the whole organic kingdom has suffered a gradual evolution, moulded by inner urge and pressure of outer circumstances.

What we find to be the characteristic features of the physical world are found true of living organisms in a higher degree. They represent a different order of fact than atomic systems, and seem to be nearer to reality than the latter.

They are individual wholes, and act as such. They maintain a constancy in the external and internal environment. There is no division between the organism and the environment. They are expressions of a larger whole, which includes them both. While they tend to preserve the pattern and continue the form, there is also creative change in them. Neither physics nor biology can account for these specific features.

13. Mind

Mental phenomena are different from vital activities. Though the living organism maintains its activity and reproduces its structure as an organized whole, its responses manifest only the organic wholeness and persistence. Each step in its activity is an immediate response to the conditions existing at the moment. What we have is unconscious organic activity. Though the organisms seem to have a 'mind' of their own, it is only seeming. The growth of an embryo realizes a plan, but its stages of development are only immediate responses to the conditions of the environment. The relation between the organism and the environment which we discovered in the physical and biological worlds becomes more intimate in the mental world through the organs of sense and of action. Through the organs of vision and hearing an animal is able to keep in touch with distant environment. Animals learn from experience. They modify behaviour in the light of previous results. So long as the end is not secured, the activity does not cease. It ceases the moment the end is achieved. The animal looks out for stimuli, and when they occur it reacts to them in a special way. The presence of consciousness makes a real distinction to the behaviour. Self-preservation becomes consciously directed through the feelings of pleasure and pain, of benefit and injury to the organism. The activities possess a unity and a co-ordination. The animal acts as a whole and not simply in its various parts. However primitive consciousness may be, it means a sense of direction. Conscious behaviour, adaptive and selective, is different from physical reactions or life adjustments. It is something *sui generis*, new and distinctive, unique and creative. Its appearance marks a new departure of a far-reaching character. It cannot be reduced to neurological happenings in the brain. It is a function of a later evolved and special integration of life.

Though the connection between nervous and physical events is intimate, one cannot be reduced to the other. Professor Watson attempts to reduce conscious behaviour to a derivative of reflex action. A few native reflexes common to all the individuals of the species form the basis on which all types of behaviour are built. Physiological traits are inherited and complicated behaviour results through habit-formation by way of conditioning. Professor Pavlov's experimental work on 'conditioned reflexes' is utilized in support of this view. If we bring food near a dog, his mouth waters. The stimulus of food causes the response of salivation, which is an unconditioned or absolute reflex. If just before or simultaneously with the presentation of food a bell is rung and if this is repeated often there is established a conditioned reflex, so that a dog will salivate when the bell is rung, even when food is not presented. The response of salivation is now produced by a new stimulus which has come to be associated with the original stimulus. The activities of the mind, like the movements of the body, are traced to the complex conditioning of primitive responses. Consciousness is an accidental accompaniment of physiological activity.

But a conditioned reflex is not an intelligent adaptation. The latter is not a random process, nor a result built up by many repetitions, but it is hit upon in a more direct way. It is not a mechanized habit, but a creative power. Behaviour is not what we observe, but only movements. To treat them as behaviour is to assume a unity of direction and activity on the part of the organism as a whole. A conscious organism expresses a meaning with which it is identified. Animals whose cerebrum is destroyed, and other centres are intact, are capable of complex reflex activity, but not conditioned reflexes.[1] Conditioned reflexes seem to be purposive. Though mind is a continuation on a higher plane of the organic regulation and co-ordination which characterize the mindless organisms, its presence is the primary fact. It is a new level of reality with its own peculiarities and laws. Though there are aspects in conscious organisms which are physico-chemical or biological, their behaviour is different from that of unconscious organisms.

The *Gestalt* Psychology, by insisting on the fact that there is more in the whole than in the mere sum of its parts, implies that the introduction of consciousness makes a difference to the activity. The belief grew up that the difference between conscious and unconscious activity is due to the presence in the body of something which is different from body, viz. 'soul'. It is given a local habitation in the body, the pineal gland or the brain. The observed phenomena are not consistent with the existence of a soul independent of the body. The mind of an animal is not an 'anima' in control of its body, but is the organization of its acts which are mental. Conscious phenomena are determined by physiological influences. When the heart ceases to beat, consciousness lapses. Three or four deep inhalations of nitrogen mean loss of consciousness; restore oxygen in the lungs, consciousness reappears. We discern the activity of

1 McDougall: *An Outline of Psychology* (1923). pp. 55-56.

the mind in relation to physical change in complex parts of the body, though we have no direct knowledge of the nature of this relation. But the soul is not independent of the body and its environment. It must either include the body, or become a function of the body. The truth of animism is that conscious behaviour is different in kind from the behaviour of physical bodies. Even the greatest extension of physiological knowledge will not help us to infer mental activity from brain structure. Just as a living organism is a whole with a far higher degree of internal relatedness than any non-living system, the mental represents a higher degree of self-regulation and control than the body. It cannot be understood by a study of the living organism. Aristotle says that the soul is to the body as vision is to the eye, or axeness is to the axe. The most detailed examination of the physical and physiological constitution of the eye will not explain the phenomenon of sight, even as the examination of the form and material of the axe will not explain the act of cutting. The soul is the actuality of the organic body in man, even as vision is the actuality of the eye. We cannot reduce psychology to physics or physiology. While the conscious arises from or emerges out of the vital or the biological, it is as real as the biological, from which it emerges, and represents a kind of interaction with things different from the vital.

The environment is not something unrelated to the conscious organisms. It belongs to them. The world in which they live is not a physical world. The individuals and the environment form together one whole. The individuals exist among others and struggle with them.

Answering to the physical principles of causation and creativity, the biological ones of heredity and variation we have at this level the pervasive characters of *horme* (T. P. Nunn) and *Mneme* (Semon), which correspond to conation

and memory at the human level. The development of new
traits of activity, new methods of discrimination are all due
to the hormic tendencies. The suggestion that the variations
of the hereditary nature of the species are due to the efforts
of the organisms which are required to develop new powers
and functions in the varying situations of the environment
receives support at this level.

CHAPTER VII

Human Personality and its Destiny

1. *Self-consciousness*

IN self-conscious beings, we meet with a set of phenomena quite distinct from the physical or the vital or the merely conscious. Reflective mind is different from the unreflective mind of the infant or the animal. When the plain man protests that men are not to be confused with apes, he declares that however primitive man may be, he is still distinctly human. Man had been on earth for hundreds of thousands of years. Early specimens such as Pithecan-thropus were dug up in Java and the skull of Eoanthropus was found at Piltdown. However strange and brutish they may seem, they were distinctly men. They not only used tools which were ready to hand, but made tools for their use. They had reason which was distinct from instinct, however highly developed the latter may be. The reflective capacity of the human mind and its power of free invention are not mere complications of lower instincts. It is the es-sence of self-conscious intelligence to look before and after and vary action according to circumstances. Instinct does neither. When we pass from animal to man, we find not a gradual development but a sudden break, a leap into a new form of experience. Man is able to dominate nature. If he is the master of the world today it is not because his physical frame is more powerful or his movements quicker or his instincts sharper than those of other animals. It is because of his intelligence which enables him to adapt himself to new and varying situations. Pascal urged that the minute human being who *knows* he is crushed is infinitely higher than the unknowing mass, however vast, which crushes him. Knowledge is the distinguishing feature of human consciousness and it is an ultimate fact incapable of derivation from anything else. We can describe and analyse the contents of knowledge but we cannot explain why there is knowledge.

Man is not, however, an altogether separate and peculiar being. He bears the marks of his origin in his organism, his fragile body, limited life and bounded mind. He has grown out of the physical, vital and animal life into the power of manhood. He is a part of universal nature, a whole carved out of nature's continuum. But man is not simply the animal gone up any more than an animal is a man gone down. Between the two there is a gulf. No amount of scientific observation can help us to explain the astonishing change.

Attempts are sometimes made to reduce man to the level of an animal. Behaviourist psychology assumes that human behaviour can be observed like the phenomena studied by natural sciences. Psychology as a science should restrict itself to direct experimental observation. It has little to do with personal experiences, values and purposes.

The inadequacy of beahviourism becomes more pointed at the human level. To reduce human behaviour to reflex action is a travesty of the facts. The material provided by introspection is relevant to the science of psychology. The body as perceived from the inside is different from the body externally observed. The observation of the external manifestations of behaviour does not tell us of the individual who is living through his experiences. The latter are immediate data and can be conveyed to others only mediately. Again, while the organism strives to preserve its health and wholeness of being and struggles to achieve a harmony of its essential parts in their full development man alone has to do it with effort and will. What other objects of nature possess as a natural quality, man has to achieve through effort and endeavour. The theory of conditioned reflexes cannot account for intelligent behaviour.[1] If the behaviourist account were true, then man is a slave to his environment without any dignity or freedom. He will be automatically responding to the varying situations with reflexes conditioned and unconditioned. Deliberate attempts to lift himself by struggle and suffering, by self-discipline and self-development are futile. If a fount of type is shaken by in a bag, the text of Watson's *Behaviourism* would result if only the time allowed is indefinite. Such a view robs mentality of its meaning and stultifies its own truth. If a man thinks even as a stone runs downhill, his thought is absolutely determined and cannot be judged as either true or false.

In psychoanalysis, we seem to have an opposite story where mental phenomena are causal factors and physical behaviour can be explained in terms of personal history. An objective treatment is not of much use and we have to cross-examine the individual about his dreams and associations. The greater part of our mind is hidden from us. It is buried or repressed and yet affects our waking consciousness. It is not possible to equate the 'unconscious' of the psychologist with the 'biological' of the behaviourist. It suggests that the unconscious and the conscious are parts of one whole.

While the behaviourist and the psychoanalyst treat of body and mind as distinct, the supporters of the *Gestalttheorie* look upon mind-body as a whole. They lay stress on

1 Professor Pavlov writes: 'It would be the height of presumption to regard these first steps in elucidating the physiology of the cortex as solving the intricate problems of the higher psychic activities in man when in fact at the present stage of our work no detailed application of its results to man is yet permissible' (*Behaviourism: A Symposium, ed.* by King (1930), p. 40).

the importance of patterns or configurations in the psycho-physical realm. Strictly speaking, there is only one whole, the totality of being. For practical convenience, we isolate wholes of varying degrees of completeness. If we take the process of walking, we can account for it only if we consider the nature of the organism and the nature of the world with which it is interacting. We cannot walk on water. Yet for practical purposes we distinguish the self as a system functioning in a larger whole. The psychological whole is distinguished into two elements of the self and the environment. Psychology studies the nature of the self which is also a whole in a relative sense. The human individual is not a corpse added to a ghost (Epictetus) or a soul *plus* an automaton (Descartes). It acts as a whole and not with its dissociated parts.

The atomistic psychology, which analyses the stream of consciousness into separate units and accounts for the course of the stream by the interplay of these units, is now obsolete. The physiological evidence is against such a theory. The brain functions cannot be broken up into elementary units, occurring in distinct areas. The specific character of any brain process involved in any particular activity of the organism is a quality of the total process, a peculiarity of the total field and not a putting together of specific processes occuring in special areas. The *Gestalt* psychology holds that the stream of consciousness is not a sum of elements but a configuration in which every distinguishable part determines and is determined by the nature of the whole. Thoughts and their relations are unified wholes of subordinate parts and not mechanically added sums of independent units. The self is a unity which is more than a sum of its subordinate parts.[1] It is an active living whole, a

1 Even Behaviourism tells against the atomistic view of mind. Cp. Watson: 'Let me start by saying that man to the behaviourist is a

body-mind, the latest term in the evolutionary process.

2. *The self an organized whole*

The human self is an emergent aspect of the world proce ss and not a substance different in kind from the process itself. Persistence of pattern constitutes unity of a thing or a self. Though every one of the constituents of the body is changing, the bodily system as an organized totality endures. It is the same with regard to the human self which is a unity of diverse parts with an enduring structure. Transient as many of its elements are, the plan of organization, however, is preserved.

In the history of thought the individual self has often been conceived on the analogy of a physical thing. It is said to possess an ultimate core of reality which remains unchanged throughout the changes of its qualities or states. It is viewed as a simple self-identical somewhat distinct from its experiences which are attached to it. Western philosophy owes to Plato the idea of an indestructible soul substance inherently immortal. Since the soul is not composite it cannot be disintegrated. Scholastics argue from the unity and simplicity of the soul to its indestructibility and immortality. Descartes revived the classic formula of the soul as a thinking substance. Those who adopt this view argue that it can explain the possibility of personal identity and immortality.

Reality is everywhere complex. It is so even in the atom. The self as real need not be simple. Locke confesses that a simple substance distinct from its manifestations could be 'a hidden something, I know not what, in behind'. Hume's arguments against the theory of self as a being or a substance

whole animal. When he reacts, he reacts with each and every part of his body' (*The Nursery and Instincts. The Psychologies of 1925*, 1926, p. 2).

which in some inexplicable way transcends the totality of its content still hold good. Such a substance is not observable and there is no evidence that it exists. Kant urges that the notion is self-contradictory, for all we know is an object of the self and never the self itself. If the soul were of the indestructible, atomic character, its existence would be of no value at all, much less its continuance. The self has no element which is self-identical throughout. The body is continuously changing. It is a scene of unending waste made good by repair. Thoughts and emotions are constantly changing. There is nothing concrete in the individual which is not produced and which will not pass away, nothing from which there is no escape, or change. The distinctiveness of selfhood does not lie in its simplicity but in the specific organization of its contents.

Often, the self is confused with a series of mental states. Buddha opposed the two extreme views that the self is an unchanging essence and that is it absolutely different each moment. He held to the middle position that the self arises through the past as its cause.[1] It is a system of responses to environmental situations. It is a connected whole, whose parts work together. Even the most primitive individual faces the world to a unity. The self is not a collection of mental states but is characterized by organization. It is an organization which is active as a whole. It s activity is not as Gentile thinks, within a world of its own, where the mind creates its own environment and is uncontrolled by external facts. The self is not encased in a hard shell. It is constantly interacting with the environment.

The organization of the self, however, is a matter of degree. The lower animals which are tied to immediate situations do not have the unity and organization characteristic

1 *Saṁyukta Nikāya* ii. 20; see *Visuddhimagga*, ch. xvii.

of the human self, though they also have an instinctive unity. By the ability to use symbols and reflect on experience, a higher synthesis is rendered possible at the human level, where the organization is not simply external. The instinctive control of animal behaviour yields to the rational determination of the self. The human self is able to save the past, bind it with the present, and face the future. Plato tells us that in the self of man are found three types of function, appetites and desires, emotional reactions and intellectual ideals. It is the last which organize experience into more or less permanent unities. Each of us tries to control his life by a main life-purpose to which all others are subordinated. This choice limits the direction and scope of the development of the self. The self is a teleological unity, which is the only thing constant in the concrete, busy, active, dynamic self. Each soul has its life's star, its main purpose. 'Man is altogether formed of his desires'.[1] In all his transformations, certain persistent and distinguishable characters remain. As the unity of a single melody is realized in the passage of time, the unity of self is realized in the series of stages, towards the attainment of ends.

What we call a person at any stage is the cross-section of the growing entity. We speak of the person as the same so long as certain determinable characteristics are found for a definite period of time. The organization of the contents has a specific character which constitutes the individual's uniqueness. As the whole is more than the sum of its parts, it determines the nature of the parts and their functioning. The individual carries his uniqueness even unto his thumb prints, as criminals know to their cost.

In a true sense, therefore, personality is a mask. It is the part we play in the drama of life, an imperfect expression of

1 Kāmamayam evāyaṁ puruṣaḥ (Brh. Up. iv. 4-5).

the groundswell of our nature. Each looks at the world from a characteristic point of view. The mental data can be systematized in different ways and so long as they are fused into a single whole, we have a single self. The phenomena of multiple personality point out that for the same period or different periods we may have different conceptions of our self due to loss of consciousness or discontinuity. If the experiences are not sufficiently integrated, selfhood becomes loose and is often broken up into a series of relatively unconnected systems of behaviour and we have cases of many selves.

3. *The self as subject*

The self as an organized whole is to be distinguished from the self as subject. The former is the problem for psychology, the latter for metaphysics. In all experience we have the duality between the subject experiencing and the object experienced. The subject of experience is said to be distinct from every moment of the experience. It is the persistent substratum which makes all knowledge, recognition and retention possible. However much such a substratum may be essential as a principle of explanation, psychology does not tell us of it.

It is sometimes argued that the series of experiences is aware of itself as a series. The whole series is involved in the knowledge of each item, which is difficult to understand. Hume reduces the subject to the object and makes the self a bundle of conscious happenings, for he could not find the 'I' among his mental states. But the impressions cannot be made into a whole without the activity of the self. There is no explanation as to why the rapidly passing experiences hang together as the experiences of one and the same individual. The laws of association cannot account for this fact. Kant rightly contends that the laws of association mean a self which is more than a mere haphazard bundle of experiences.

William James looks upon the passing thought as the subject of the experience. It gathers up into self all that has previously occurred and grows on by assimilating the new. The thought is the thinker. But we cannot understand how one state can absorb another.

James Ward believes that William James confuses process and content, subject and object. He argues that every moment of experience has the three aspects of attention, feeling and presentation. While the first two are subjective, presentation is the object of experience. For Ward, the successive acts of attention manifest the subject's existence. Ward is correct in making out that the nature of self is constituted more by the acts of remembering, thinking and willing than by the materials or contents remembered, thought or willed. The activities, rather than the contents with which they deal form the self, though the two are inseparable. The active self is held to be more persistent than the contents which are ever changing. Ward's 'subject' is far too abstract and is postulated for the purpose of explaining experience.

Ward's view reminds us of Kant's 'I think', which must accompany all experiences. The 'I think' of Kant is often represented as a mere logical form which accompanies all objects of consciousness. Though the relation of such a changeless passive entity, which remains the same yesterday, today and for ever, to the constantly changing experiences is not easy to conceive, such a 'subject' is assumed to account for the synthesis involved in experience. It is said to be the ground of all categories, that which makes possible the empirical unity of consciousness. The deeper strand of Kant's teaching does not favour the view of the self as an abstraction.

The subject and object of consciousness are elements which are distinguishable but not separable in experience, which is one. The distinction between the two comes before us as a distinction within a whole. If the two were independent of each other, knowledge would become a mystery. They are ideal factors in the whole of experience and not opposite divisions or separate parts of it. We cannot build knowledge from out of them, for it is the ultimate fact behind which we cannot go. The true subject or the self is not an object which we can find in knowledge for it is the very condition of knowledge. It is different from all objects, the body, the senses, the empirical self itself. We cannot make the subject the property of any substance or the effect of any cause, for it is the basis of all such relations. It is not the empirical self but the reality without which there could be no such thing as an empirical self. The individuals are able to have common experience, know a real world as identical for all because there is an ideal self operative in all. The individual who is aware of himself as limited has the direct consciousness of something which limits him and his purposes. The consciousness of limit involves the action of the greater unlimited self in us. In order to assign a limit to our thought, we must in some sense be beyond that limit. To confuse the subject with the mind immersed in bodily experience prevents us from attaining complete comprehension of the object that appears to confront us. The true subject is the simple, self-subsistent, universal spirit which cannot be directly presented as the object. When Plato says that the mind in man is the offspring of the eternal world-mind, when Aristotle speaks of an 'active reason', at the apex of the apex of the soul, which is divine and creative, when Kant distinguishes the synthetic principle from the merely empirical self, they are referring to the self as subject. The deeper unity is what Kant refers to as the transcendental self. Only in calling it the self he is applying to noumenal reality a category of the phenomenal world. It is not an abstract form of selfhood, for it is that which manifests itself in the organization of the empirical self. It is within this universal spirit that the distinction of subject and object arises. While the empirical self is always correlated with a not-self, the universal self includes all and has nothing outside to limit it. The Hindu thinkers call it the *ātman* as distinguished from the empirical self or the *jīvātman*.

When we raise the question about the unifying agency in selfhood we are raising the more general question of the principle of unity in all existents, physical and biological included. Their unity is of the same character as the unity of selfhood, though less complex and less personal, but in principle it is the same.

4. *The self and the environment*

The integral relationship between the organism and its environment which we found to be true of the subhuman grades of reality is also true of the human world. Human individuals are not unchanging substrata of change with accidental qualities and related to one another externally but are elements in an interrelated system. They are centres of experience or processes of becoming through a creative synthesis of their relations. They possess a certain relative independence though the general nature of the system conditions them all. Instead of being a self-contained individual, each empirical self is the expression or focussing of something beyond itself.[1] The real whole or individual is that which includes persons and their environment and

1 Professor J. S. Haldane writes: 'Personality is not something confined and completed in itself separately from an environment in space and time, but extends over that environment' (*The Sciences and Philosophy*, 1929, p. 303).

these exist in themselves by a process of abstraction. However self-conscious or self-determining, the human being is not absolutely individual. From the first his world is equally real with himself and his interactions with it influence the growth of his individuality. The individual and the world co-exist and subsist together.

At the biological level, there is no such thing as an individual centre of life. The cells in an organism are unintelligible apart from the whole. Their life is centred in the life of the whole. While plants and animals lead 'whole' lives harmoniously, human beings set up discords between themselves and their environment. The unity between the organism and the environment, which is a striking point in the subhuman world becomes sundered in the human. While the human being belongs to a larger world which penetrates him at every pore and lives through his interactions with it, his self-consciousness sets up a dualism which is untrue to fact and opposed to his whole nature. He forgets that his interests are not private to himself and believes himself to be distinct with his own form of individuality. While this strong sense of individuality is necessary for action, it is confused with individualism. He is in a state of unstable equilibrium. His conscience is the sign of a divided life. He is a flame of unrest full of uncertain seeking and disorder. So long as the individual suffers from separateness he is restive and homesick. He is always striving to get beyond his separateness.

Human progress lies in an increasing awareness of the universal working in man. Through the exploring of nature, the striving after wisdom and the seeking of God, the individual struggles to achieve a harmony between himself and his environment. He finds his goodness in what is more than himself. He realizes that his fragmentariness will be cured only if he is devoted to the whole. Fulness of life means service to the whole. So he strives after values, frames ideals and struggles to build up a world of unity and harmony. He forms associations, develops common interests by organizing families, tribes, churches and countries. Knowledge, art, morality and religion are the devices employed by man to realize his destiny as a member of a spiritual fellowship, a kingdom in which each is in the whole and the whole is in some measure in each. 'That they all may be one as Thou Father art in me and I in Thee that they also may be one in us.' Such a union based on knowledge, love and service is closer and more intimate than any represented by the lower orders of existence.

The peculiar privilege of the human self is that he can consciously join and work for the whole and embody in his own life the purpose of the whole. This embodiment differs vastly in degree from individual to individual. It is the source of the difference between superior and inferior souls. The two elements of selfhood, uniqueness (each-ness) and universality (all-ness) grow together until at last the most unique becomes the most universal. While every individual fulfils his real function in the whole and obtains value and dignity, no one individual is as wide as the whole itself. It is limited because it is only one individual element in what is much greater than itself.

There is a tendency, especially in the West, to over-estimate the place of the human self. Descartes attempts to derive everything from the certainty of his own isolated selfhood. It is not realized that the thought of the self which wants to explain everything, the will of the self which wants to subjugate everything, are themselves the expression of a deeper whole, which includes the self and its object. If the self is not widened into the universal spirit, the values themselves become merely subjective and the self itself will collapse into nothing. Man's continual striving for perfection in spite of all error and misunderstanding, defeat and disappointment, his perpetual attempt to transform all occurrences into harmony, to make the external express the inward and the partial success which has attended his efforts show that the task he is attempting is one in line with the genius of reality. The values we strive for are organic to existence. The whole course of nature is an expression of meaning to be understood by man. Interaction with individuals, knowledge of one another and social relations with one another are possible because we all form parts of one system.

5. *Karma and freedom*

The two pervasive features of all nature, connection with the past and creation of the future, are present in the human level. The connection with the past at the human stage is denoted by the word *Karma* in the Hindu systems. The human individual is a self-conscious, efficient portion of universal nature with his own uniqueness. His history stretching back to an indefinite period of time binds him with the physical and vital conditions of the world. Human life is an organic whole where each successive phase grows out of what has gone before. We are what we are on account of our affinity with the past. Human growth is an ordered one and its orderedness is indicated by saying that it is governed by the law of Karma.

Karma literally means action, deed. All acts produce their effects which are recorded both in the organism and the environment. Their physical effects may be short-lived but their moral effects (*saṃskāra*) are worked into the character of the self. Every single thought, word and deed enters into the living chain of causes which makes us what we are. Our life is not at the mercy of blind chance or capricious fate.

The conception is not peculiar to the Oriental creeds. The Christian Scriptures refer to it. 'Be not deceived; God is not mocked: for whatsoever a man soweth, that shall he also reap.'[1] Jesus is reported to have said on the Mount, 'Judge not that ye be not judged, for with what judgment ye judge, ye shall be judged, and with what measure ye mete, it shall be measured to you again.'

Karma is not so much a principle of retribution as one of continuity. Good produces good, evil evil. Love increases our power of love, hatred our power of hatred. It emphasizes the great importance of right action. Man is continuously shaping his own self. The law of Karma is not to be confused with either a hedonistic or a juridical theory of rewards and punishments. The reward for virtue is not a life of pleasure nor is the punishment for sin pain. Pleasure and pain may govern the animal nature of man but not his human. Love which is a joy in itself suffers; hatred too often means a perverse kind of satisfaction. Good and evil are not to be confused with material well-being and physical suffering.

All things in the world are at once causes and effects. They embody the energy of the past and exert energy on the future. Karma or connection with the past is not inconsistent with creative freedom. On the other hand it is implied by it. The law that links us with the past also asserts that it can be subjugated by our free action. Though the past may present obstacles, they must all yield to the creative power in man in proportion to its sincerity and insistence. The law of Karma says that each individual will get the return according to the energy he puts forth. The universe will respond to and implement the demands of the self. Nature will reply to the insistent call of spirit. 'As is his desire, such

---

1 Galatians vi. 7. Cp. Ezekiel: 'The soul that sinneth it shall die' (xviii).

is his purpose; as is his purpose, such is the action he performs; what action he performs, that he procures for himself.'[1] 'Verily I say unto you that whoever shall say to this mountain, "Be lifted up and cast into the sea," and shall not doubt in his heart but believe fully that what he says shall be, it shall be done for him.' When Jesus said, 'Destroy this temple and I will raise it again in three days', he is asserting the truth that the spirit within us is mightier than the world of things. There is nothing we cannot achieve if we want it enough. Subjection to spirit is the law of universal nature. The principle of Karma has thus two aspects, a retrospective and a prospective, continuity with the past and creative freedom of the self.

The urge in nature which seeks not only to maintain itself at a particular level but advance to a higher becomes conscious in man who deliberately seeks after rules of life and principles of progress. 'My father worketh hitherto, and I work.'[2] Human beings are the first among nature's children who can say 'I' and consciously collaborate with the 'father' the power that controls and directs nature, in the fashioning of the world. They can substitute rational direction for the slow, dark, blundering growth of the subhuman world. We cannot deny the free action of human beings however much their origin may be veiled in darkness. The self has conative tendencies, impulses to change by its efforts the given conditions, inner and outer, and shape them to its own purpose.

The problem of human freedom is confused somewhat by the distinction between the self and the will. The will is only the self in its active side and freedom of the will really means the freedom of the self. It is determination by the self.

It is argued that self-determination is not really freedom. It makes little difference whether the self is moved from

1 *Brh. Up.* iv. 4. 5.
2 John v. 17.

without or from within. A spinning top moved from within by a spring is as mechanical a top as one whipped into motion from without. The self may well be an animated automaton. A drunkard who takes to his glass habitually does so in obediences to an element in his nature. The habit has become a part of his self. If we analyse the contents of the self, many of them are traceable to the influence of the environment and the inheritance from the past. If the individual's view and character are the product of a long evolution, his actions which are the outcome of these cannot be free. The feeling of freedom may be an illusion of the self, which lives in each moment of the present, ignoring the determining past. In answer to these difficulties, it may be said that the self represents a form of relatedness or organization, closer and more intimate than that which is found in animal, plant or atom. Self-determination means not determination by any fragment of the self's nature but by the whole of it. Unless the individual employs his whole nature, searches the different possibilities and selects one which commends itself to his whole self, the act is not really free.

Sheer necessity is not to be found in any aspect of nature; complete freedom is divine and possible only when the self becomes co-extensive with the whole. Human freedom is a matter of degree. We are most free when our whole self is active and not merely a fragment of it. We generally act according to our conventional or habitual self and sometimes we sink to the level of our subnormal self.

Freedom is not caprice, nor is Karma necessity. Human choice is not unmotived or uncaused. If our acts were irrelevant to our past, then there would be no moral responsibiltiy or scope for improvement. Undetermined beginnings, upstart events are impossible either in the physical or the human world. Free acts cannot negate continuity. They arise within the order of nature. Freedom is not caprice since we carry our past with us. The character, at any given point, is the condensation of our previous history. What we have been enters in the 'me' which is not active and choosing. The range of one's natural freedom of action is limited. No man has the universal field of possibilities for himself. The varied possibilities of our nature do not all get a chance and the cosmic has its influence in permitting the development of certain possibilities and closing down others. Again, freedom is dogged by automatism. When we make up our mind to do a thing, our mind is different from what it was before. When a possibility becomes an actuality, it assumes the character of necessity. The past can never be cancelled, though it may be utilized. Mere defiance of the given may mean disaster, though we can make a new life spring up from the past. Only the possible is the sphere of freedom. We have a good deal of present constraint and previous necessity in human life. But necessity is not to be mistaken for destiny, which we can neither defy nor delude. Though the self is not free from the bonds of determination, it can subjugate the past to a certain extent and turn it into a new course. Choice is the assertion of freedom over necessity by which it converts necessity to its own use and thus frees itself from it. 'The human agent is free.[1] He is not the plaything of fate or driftwood on the tide of uncontrolled events. He can actively mould the future instead of passively suffering the past. The past may become either an opportunity or an obstacle. Everything depends on what we make of it and not what it makes of us. Life is not bound to move in a specific direction. Life is a growth and a growth is undetermined in a measure. Though the future is the sequel of the past, we cannot say what it will be. If there is no indetermination, then human consciousness

1 *Pāṇini*. i. 4. 54.

is an unnecessary luxury.

Our demand for freedom must reckon with a universe that is marked by order and regularity. Life is like a game of bridge. The cards in the game are given to us. We do not select them. They are traced to past Karma but we are free to make any call as we think fit and lead any suit. Only we are limited by the rules of the game. We are more free when we start the game than later on when the game has developed and our choices become restricted. But till the very end there is always a choice. A good player will see possibilities which a bad one does not. The more skilled a player the more alternatives does he perceive. A good hand may be cut to pieces by unskilful play and the bad play need not be attributed to the frowns of fortune. Even though we may not like the way in which the cards are shuffled, we like the game and we want to play. Sometimes wind and tide may prove too strong for us and even the most noble may come down. The great souls find profound peace in the consciousness that the stately order of the world, now lovely and luminous, now dark and terrible, in which man finds his duty and destiny, cannot be subdued to known aims. It seems to have a purpose of its own of which we are ignorant. Misfortune is not fate but providence.

The law of Karma does not support the doctrine of predestination. There are some who believe that only the predestination of certain souls to destruction is consistent with divine sovereignty. God has a perfect right to deal with his creatures even as a potter does with his clay. St Paul speaks of 'vessels of wrath fitted to destruction'. Life eternal is a gracious gift of God. Such a view of divine sovereignty is unethical. God's love is manifested in and through law.

In our relations with human failures, belief in Karma inclines us to take a sympathetic attitude and develop reverence before the mystery of misfortune. The more understanding we are, the less do we pride ourselves on our superiority. Faith in Karma induces in us the mood of true justice or charity which is the essence of spirituality. We realize how infinitely helpless and frail human beings are. When we look at the warped lives of the poor, we see how much the law of Karma is true. If they are lazy and criminal, let us ask what chance they had of choosing to be different. They are more unfortunate than wicked. Again, failures are due not so much to 'sin' as to errors which lead us to our doom. In Greek tragedy man is held individually less responsible and circumstances or the decisions of Moira more so. The tale of Oedipus Rex tells us how he could not avoid his fate to kill his father and marry his mother, in spite of his best efforts. The parting of Hector and Andromache in Homer is another illustration. In Shakespeare again, we see the artist leading on his characters to their destined ends by what seems a very natural develcpment of their foibles, criminal folly in Lear or personal ambition in Macbeth. The artist shows us these souls in pain. Hamlet's reason is puzzled, his will confounded. He looks at life and at death and wonders which is worse. Goaded by personal ambition, Macbeth makes a mess of it all. Othello kills his wife and kills himself because a jealous villain shows him a handkerchief. When these noble souls crash battling with adverse forces we feel with them and for them; for it might happen to any of us. We are not free from the weaknesses that broke them, whatever we call them, stupidity, disorder, vacillation or, if you please, insane ambition and self-seeking. Today the evil stars of the Greek tragedians are replaced by the almighty laws of economics. Thousands of young men the world over are breaking their heads in vain against the iron walls of society like trapped birds in cages. We see in them the essence of all tragedy, something noble breaking down, something sublime falling with a crash. We can only bow our heads in the presence of those broken beneath the burden of their destiny. The capacity of the human soul for suffering and isolation is immense. Take the poor creatures whom the world passes by as the lowly and the lost. If only we had known what they passed through, we would have been glad of their company. It is utterly wrong to think that misfortune comes only to those who deserve it. The world is a whole and we are members one of another, and we must suffer one for another. In Christianity, it needed a divine soul to reveal how much grace there is in suffering. To bear pain, to endure suffering, is the quality of the strong in spirit. It adds to the spiritual resources of humanity.

6. *Future life*

Though the most influential philosophies and religion have been vague if not reticent on the question of life after death, some of our modern cults make one believe that the future of the self is lit as by the footlights of a theatre. Everything seems to be clear. The depths are charted. Hell hath no secret terrors nor heaven any unpainted joys. The problem of life after death has no interest for those who believe that it is a fact divinely revealed to us as well as for those who affirm that there is nothing in us apart from the body. The crude theory of materialism which denies future life is inconsistent with the emergent view of self. If the self is not produced by the body, it need not be ended when the body is destroyed.

Difficulties arise when we try to define the nature of the future life. Before we take up the theory of rebirth, we may briefly refer to two doctrines, viz. personal immortality and conditional immortality.

7. *Personal immortality*

Those who seek for personal immortality do not know clearly what it means. We long to have the touch of the vanished hand, the sound of the voice that is still. In other words, we want the person to be preserved in his entirety, bodily presence as well as mind and purpose, the house we can see and touch, and the dweller in the house. It will not satisfy us if the house is ruined and only the tenant alive. We want to see the lost child and not the little angel, the person we loved and not one clothed in spirit and transfigured in the glory of God, who will startle us out of our wits. Supposing we are allowed the choice, which grade of one's earthly existence is to be perpetuated, the body as it was at the dying moment or in the prime of life or the baby at birth. We do not want endless youth or endless old age. Whatever it be, if it is endlessly continued, we will be sick unto death. The famous chorus of Euripides' *Heracles* wished to have their flaming youth over again. Some of us would like to combine the ardours of youth with the insight of age, little knowing that one is inconsistent with the other. We do not know what we want and we do not want what we know.

8. *Conditional immortality*

The doctrine of conditional immortality is becoming popular, especially among Christian thinkers. Lotze claims immortality only for those who realize in themselves nature of such high value that on account of it they cannot be lost to the whole. Professor Pringle-Pattison follows Lotze in this respect. Immortality, he contends, is not 'an inherent possession of every human soul, or a talismanic gift conferred indiscriminately on every being born in human shape. A true self comes into being as the result of continuous effort and the same effort is needed to hold it together and ensure its maintenance, for the danger of disintegration is always present'[1]. As adaptation to environment is the condition of survival of organisms, even so, the self of man can survive only if it is adapted to the divine environment. Immortality is not our natural birthright, a thing to which we are entitled but a prize to be won.

The plausibility of this theory is due to the fact that we are confusing here immortality with survival, eternal life with durational continuance. At death almost all of us are below that degree of perfection which entitles us to immortality. While we may admit that immortality in the sense of eternal life is conditional on the possession of the requisite perfection, we need not admit that the vast majority of mankind who are not fit for immortality do not survive at all. Though only the saints may be fit for immortality, both the saintly and the sinful may continue after death. It is not fair to contend that in Christian theology conscious existence terminates at death for the wicked and the malignant. Catholic Christianity assumes an unending existence even for those who miss beatitude. Eternal life and annihilation are not the only alternatives.

Professor Pringle-Pattison believes that the importance of moral life requires the conditional nature of immortality. 'To assure people that, whatever they do, all will come right in the end, is not an effective method of awakening them to the gravity of decisions here and now, which bind upon the soul the fetters of habit and make it even more difficult to find the way back.'[2] This is not a valid argument. The law of Karma insists on the great importance of our acts here and now, and yet demands survival. If the human self fails in this life to achieve integration of its mental contents by imposing on them a persistent purpose it need not disappear

1 *The Idea of Immortality* (1922), pp. 195-196
2 *Ibid.*, pp. 203-204.

altogether. On such a view it will be difficult to conceive what would happen to the innumerable infants and young children who have passed out of this life without any opportunity of achieving a real selfhood. Even many adults are really children when they die. It will not be easy to decide whether the coherence achieved is enough to warrant survival or not. Most of us at death would not have had such a sufficient glimpse of the eternal values as to deserve its fuller realization in other chances of life. We learn how to live only at the time when life is all spent. Professor Pringle-Pattison may have no room for 'the continued existence of those who made no use of life while they had it'[1] and view with little concern the total disappearance of the major portion of humanity, but we may well conceive the possibility of the general rise of mankind to the vision of love and goodness if they have a few more chances. Besides, the power of deep love may rouse even the most degraded souls to the hideousness of their condition so that they need not be regarded as hopelessly lost. History is full of instances of 'sinners' who suddenly turn to the light, but if death ends their life, their lives will constitute a dead loss and a frustration of divine purpose.

Professor Pringle-Pattison does not seem to recognize the ineffaceable worth of individuals and the need for letting them have other opportunities. In the *Timaeus* Plato argues that since God cannot wish to destroy his own work and since nothing else can destroy it, the souls which are made by God in his own image cannot be destroyed, though the process by which man achieves his end of likeness to God may be an endless one. Professor J. Estlin Carpenter writes: 'The Buddhist scheme proclaims the ultimate salvation of all beings. Christianity in its most widespread historic forms

1 *Ibid.*, p. 197.

still condemns an uncounted number to endless torment and unceasing sin.'[1] The teaching concerning ultimate damnation is continuous and widespread in the history of the Christian Church, though universalist emphasis is to be met with in Origen and the Christian Platonists. Origen held that indeed all will be saved, including the Arch-Enemy of God. The roman Catholic Church is bound to the idea of Hell by the Council of Trent. We may cut out the harsher sayings of Jesus as unauthentic. The punishment of Dives may be interpreted as remedial. The weeping and gnashing of teeth in the parable of the drag-net as well as the assertion that the sin against the Holy Spirit will not be forgiven 'neither in this world nor in that to come' may be dismissed as eschatological exaggerations. And yet there seems to be an inconvenient amount of undisputed teaching that became exaggerated in the hands of the Apocalyptists. If we are unwilling to cut off the offending hand or foot, Gehenna is the only place for us. In the story of the Celestial Banquet as well as that of the Sheep and the Goats utter rejection is set forth as a real possibility. But the modern mind cannot accept the idea of endless punishment which leads to no improvement. Even the man of ill-will will eventually be enlightened and saved. We need not believe that such a doctrine dulls the fine edge of moral effort. Some authority for a universalist view may be found in the riper saying of Jesus. The infinite value of every individual soul to God as Father[2] is an assurance that he will not suffer the loss in death of any of his children. On the eve of the Crucifixion, Jesus is reported to have said: 'I am the good shepherd. The good shepherd lays down his life so that not one of the sheep might be lost.' God's patience is not likely to be exhausted in the short span of a single life. If every soul is precious to

1 *Buddhism and Christianity*, p. 306.
2 Luke xv. 2.

God, universal salvation is a certainty. If some souls are lost, God's omnipotence becomes problematical.

If we mean by immortality not survival but eternal life, what counts is personal effort. While the goal may be fixed, the attainment of it depends on the active co-operation of the selves. If we believe that even the most hardened soul will shape in the right direction, it is merely an assertion of the omnipotence of the spirit and the all-compelling character of goodness. No being is wholly evil or impenetrable by good. None can for long resist the influence of spirit and the individuals who perfect themselves with effort and discipline are the remnant that will redeem the race.

9. *Rebirth*

The doctrine of rebirth has had a long and influential history. It is a cardinal belief of the Orphic religion that the wheel of birth revolves inexorably. Pythagoras, Plato and Empedocles regard rebirth as almost axiomatic. For them pre-existence and survival stand or fall together. It persists down to the later classical thinkers, Plotinus and the Neo-Platonists. If we turn to the Hebrews, there are traces of it in Philo and it was definitely adopted in the Kabbala. The Sufi writers accept it. About the beginning of the Christian era it was current in Palestine. Herod, for instance, thinks that Jesus may be John the Baptist risen from the dead.[1] Jesus's disciples tell him of the rumours that he is John the Baptist or Elijah or Jeremiah. When he treats a man who was born blind, his followers ask whether the blindness was in consequence of his sins in a previous life.[2] Julius Caesar finds the belief in rebirth among the ancestors of the British, for in his *History of the Gallic Wars* he writes that the Druids

1 Matthew xiv. 2.
2 John ix. 2. See also Matthew xi. 14-15.

'inculcate this as one of their leading tenets--that souls do not become extinct but pass after death from one body to another and they think that men by this tenet are in a great degree incited to valour, the fear of death being disregarded.' Within the Christian Church it was held during the first centuries by isolated Gnostic sets and the Manichaeans in the fourth and fifth centuries. Origen believed in it. In the Middle Ages the tradition was continued by the numerous sects collectively known as Cathari. At the Renaissance Bruno upheld it, and Van Helmont in the seventeenth century adopted it. Swedenborg states it in a modified form. Goethe played with it, while Lessing and Herder believed in it seriously. Hume and Schopenhauer mentioned it with respect and among contemporary philosophers there are at least half a dozen who believe in it, though they are not prepared to avow it in view of inadequate evidence and proof.[1]

The emergent view of the self makes the hypothesis of rebirth a reasonable one. Throughout nature life is preserved and continued through incessant renewal. Life is a perpetual going on, never resting, always straining forward for something that has not been but should be. While at the zoological level the perpetuation of the species is the end, at the human level development of unique individuality seems to be the end in view. The self of man is not an abstract quality or essence which remains the same for all time. It is a living experience of which duration is an intrinsic characteristic. If everything else in nature arises from something continuous with it and passes into something also continuous with it, the self need not be an exception to the general scheme. 'Like corn the mortal grows; like corn is born again.'[2] The way of nature is continuity within a certain

1 Mc Taggart: *The Nature of Existence*, Vol II (1927), Ch. LXIII.
2 *Kaṭha Up.* I. 6.

general pattern. If the general plan of consecutiveness is not to be violated, the human selves must continue after death. They carry on past threads, weave out something in the present and prepare for the future.

Continuity here cannot be of the same type as in the subhuman stages; for the organization and control the self possesses are of a unique character. The unity in the subhuman world is looser than in the human. While a wall is broken up, its units of bricks may remain intact. But if a self is destroyed, its elements of thought, emotions and volitions are also destroyed. The form and the matter, the pattern and the material are so closely knit that if there is a drastic separation, the self is destroyed. The continuance of the self is not, therefore, of the same type as the continuance of the other organisms.

The self aims at fulfilment of function or development of individuality. It can grow indefinitely in depth, richness and comprehensiveness. We cannot in one life exercise all the powers we possess or exhaust all the values we strain after. The capacity of the self for endless improvement, and the pervasive facts of continuance point to a future where the self's 'with- held completions' obtain a chance. The broken lives that require to be renewed are the forces that integrate creation. The successive lives are a closely connected sequence where the acts of one life determine the basis and opportunities of the next.[1] There are no blind rushes to the goal. The children of a God in whose eyes a thousand years are as a day need not be disheartened if the goal of perfection is not attained in one life. The individual has appeared and disappeared times without number, in the long past and will continue to be dissolved and reformed through unimaginable centuries to come. The bodily life is an episode

1 *Chān. Up.* iii. 14. I.

in the larger career of the individual soul which precedes birth and proceeds after death.

It is an admitted principle of science that if we see a certain stage of development in time, we may infer a past to it. It is not true that we 'brought nothing into this world.'[1] The self enters this life with a certain nature and inheritance. We commonly speak of talents that are inherited, an eye for beauty, a taste for music, which are not common qualities of the species but individual variations. So the self must have had a past history here and elsewhere. We cannot believe that the rise of self with a definite nature is simply fortuitous. Mc Taggart refers to certain facts which are not explicable on any other hypothesis than that of pre-existence. 'Two people who have seen but little of each other are often drawn together by a force equal to that which is generated in other cases by years of mutual trust and mutual assistance.'[2] The capriciousness of sex desire is not the whole explanation of love at first sight. Again, characteristics which we have to acquire through toil and effort, others seem to possess as natural gifts.[3] Infant prodigies are

1 I Timothy, vi. 7.
2 *Some Dogmas of Religion* (1906), p. 121.
3 'One man seems to start with an impotence to resist some particular temptation which exactly resembles the impotence which has been produced in another man by continual yielding to the same temptation. One man, again, has through life a calm and serene virtue which another gains only by years of strenuous effort. Others, again, have innate powers of judging character, or of acting with decision in emergencies, which give them while yet inexperienced advantages which the less fortunate men attain, if they attain at all, only by experience of years. Here, then, we have characteristics which are born with us and which closely resemble characteristics which in other cases we know to be due to the condensed results of experience. If we hold the doctrine of pre-existence we shall naturally explain these also as being the condensed results of experience, in this case, of experience in an earlier life' (*ibid.*, p. 122).

fairly familiar in the East. In the West also we meet with them now and then. When Yehudi Menuhin, as a twelve-year-old violinist, amazed music critics at the Albert Hall by the fully adult nature of his technique and, above all, of his interpretation, when the Belgian baby, André Lenoir, multiplied in a flash any five figure number with any other five figure number and performed prodigies of mathematics before the astounded professors of Brussels, may not these be traced to faculties acquired in earlier lives?

If we do not admit pre-existence, we must say that the soul is created at the birth of the body. Such a view makes all education and experience superfluous. If the soul is said to be created with a definite nature, it is difficult to understand why such varied natures should be imposed on the souls. Our fates seem to be due to caprice and cruelty. God, if not nature, places us in different circumstances and then judges us as if we were responsible for our lots. It must be a strangely whimsical deity who enjoys our adventures. He endows Jesus and Judas with different 'complexes' and then complains that while Jesus succeeds in striving for heaven, Judas fails. Judgment seems to be utterly wrong when caprice is king.

If the law of continuity is not a broken dream, the future life must be of the same nature as the present. Since the self is not an atomic nucleus quite separate from the organism as a whole, it will continue to be of the same character after death. The main intention of the soul-substance theory is to maintain the unity of the self even though many changes may happen to it. The unitary character of the self is preserved if we look upon it as the organized or consolidated unity of all our experience. Rebirth is change within a general structural progression. Death is not a unique event in our progress. It is part of a continually recurring rhythm of nature, marking a crisis in the history of the individual. It is the moment when the self assumes a new set of conditions.

The question is whether the death of the body does not mean an essential change in the nature of the self. Though the self-conscious mind may have developed out of simpler forms of biological process, it achieves gradually a degree of independence and is able to react on the body with an increased degree of freedom. The life of the human self does not centre in the body, though it uses the latter for the promotion of its purpose. 'It is the body which dies when left by the self; the self does not die.'[1] The death of the physical body does not mean dissipation of the self. If the self wakes up after dreamless sleep and feels its continuity with the self that went to sleep, death need not mean discontinuity. If it is argued that the self has its materials through its connection with a body and when it ceases the contents of the self will disappear, we may say that the self is dependent on the body for his material only so long as it is connected with it. But an empirical conjunction is not a metaphysical necessity. If we require brains to think when we are embodied, it does not follow that we require brains to think even when we are disembodied. The instrumental theory that the self is an entity distinct from the body which it uses as an instrument cannot account for the observed dependence of mental states on bodily disturbances. An injury to the body affects not only the manifestations of the self but the self itself. There are cases where men's characters are changed by bodily injuries. We cannot say that the character remains unchanged while only the behaviour changes. The self is a complex of mind-body, however much the mind may be superior to the body. So, it is said, that the death of the gross body does not mean a complete destruction of all physical connection. The Hindus believe in the

1 *Chān. Up.* vi. ii. 3.

vehicle of self, a body which differs from the present gross one though not completely discontinuous with it. In other words, there is an organic relationship between the self and its body. The ancient theory of a finer ethereal body seems to receive some support from the psychical research. Even when due allowance is made for fraud, error and chance co-incidences, there is enough evidence to justify the belief that apparitions are due to the action of the dead persons whose bodies they represent.

If there is a close bond between the self and the body, then we cannot say that any self can inhabit any body. If the contents and conditions of the self-existence must be similar to those which obtain here, rebirth in the form of animals or angels becomes an extravagance.[1] The kind of life after death cannot be completely different from the present one. Death cannot alter so profoundly the life of the self. No human being can take birth in a body foreign to its evolved characteristics. It is possible for man to degenerate into a savage being but he is still a man. If retrogression is referred to, then it is spread over long ages. While it is theoretically possible that the life process which has now reached the human level may so operate as to sink into the animal, from which it may again spring forward on a different line of evolution altogether or continue to sink below the animal world, we are not concerned with such speculative possibilities. While we need not dogmatically deny the possibility of reversion to animal births, we are now concerned with the normal changes which are within a type. It is possible that rebirth in animal form is a figure of speech for rebirth

1 The Hindu Scriptures affirm rebirth in animal forms (See *Chān. Up.* v. 10. 7; *Manu* I. 56 among others). Plato's *Republic* refers to lives of men in the form of animals. Empedocles believes that souls pass into animal and plant lives.

with animal qualities.[1]

The juridical theory associated in the popular mind with the doctrine of Karma is responsible for this mistaken view of rebirth in the form of animals, as also for the notions of heaven and hell as places of resort where we receive our rewards or punishments. It is not, however, a fair representation of the Hindu view, though much popular support can be produced for it. The theory of *saṁsāra* is quite inconsistent with any permanent abodes of bliss or suffering.

The human instinct for justice naturally associates the thought of suffering and pain with vice and wickedness. Suffering is the shadow thrown by the power of evil. Even Kant is inclined to look upon God as a sort of paymaster-in-chief working out a compensatory system of justice. For Kant, while virtue is the supreme good (*supremum bonum*), is not the complete good (*summum bonum*). The latter includes happiness also. But the universe is such that this *summum bonum*, consisting of both virtue and happiness, is unattainable. If normal life is not to be dismissed as a vain pursuit of imaginary ends, we must assume that virtue is attainable by all rational beings and happiness accompanies virtue in exact proportion. Since complete virtue is not attained in this life and experience shows that virtue does not lead to proportionate happiness, it is certain that man has an endless life and there is a God who shall see to it that virtue and happiness are rightly apportioned. Kant assumes in the argument that it is a supreme requirement of morality that the virtuous individual should be made happy in exact proportion to his goodness. In a just order of the world virtue must receive the reward of happiness and vice the punishment

1 Tylor in his *Primitive Culture* says; 'The beast is the very incarnation of familiar qualities of man; and such names as lion, bear, fox, owl, parrot, viper, worm, when we apply them as epithets to man, condense into a word some leading feature of a human life' (ii. 17).

of pain. Traditional Christian theory asks us to do good 'in obedience to the will of God and for the sake of everlasting happiness.'[1] Plato in his *Republic* scorns the religious teachers who describe the righteous dead 'as reclining on couches at a banquet of the pious and with garlands on their heads, spending all eternity in wine-bibbing, the fullest reward of virtue being in their estimation an everlasting carousal'[2]. We find in many systems ideas of the moral government of the world confused with those of retribution and it is not surprising that belief in the systematic distribution of rewards and punishments after death for the deeds done in this life was current in India and assumed crude and questionable forms. The Hindu thinkers, however, who accept the view of Karma equate it with the will of God. God is in man and his law is organic to man's nature. [3] God is the universal background providing scope and expression for the different possibilities but the actualization of them depends on the will of man. [4] Heaven and hell are states of the self and not places of resort.[5] Even the most ghastly inferno comes to an end one day. An eternity of torment is inconsistent with a God of love. Virtue is heaven, self-sufficiency

1 Paley: *Principles of Moral and Political Philosophy* (1785), Bk. I, ch. vii.
2 (363). Spinoza turns on 'those who expect to be decorated by God with high rewards for their virtue and their best action, as for having done the direst slavery--as if virtue and the service of God were not in itself happiness and perfect freedom' (*Ethics* ii. 49, Sch.; cp. also v. 41, sch.).
3 Rāmānuja says: 'That man who acts with the determination to be wholly on the side of the Supreme, the Lord blesses by creating in him a taste for such actions only as are a means of attaining him and are extremely good. But he punishes the man who acts with the determination to be wholly against him by creating in him a taste for such actions as stand in the way of attaining him and lead him downward' (Commentary on the *Brahma Sūtra* ii. 3. 41).
4 See Śaṁkara on *Brahma Sūtra* ii. I. 34.
5 *Vishnupurāṇa*.

and health of the soul, and vice hell, suffering and disease of the soul. Goodness is its own reward and evil-doing carries its own penalty with it. It is not a question of the expediency or profitableness of virtue.

How does the self find a new home after death? The mechanism of rebirth is difficult to know, if not impossible to conceive. But simply because we do not understand the process we cannot deny the facts. We know that mental qualities are transmitted from parents to offspring but we do not know how. While the parents may be regarded as producing new bodies, they do not produce new selves. Again, it is held that the self is not altogether discarnate. It is invested in a finer vehicle, the subtle body (*sūkṣhma śarīra*) when it leaves the gross one.[1] The necessary physical basis is secured by the subtle body. The *lingaśarīra* or subtle body which is said to accompany one throughout one's empirical existence is the form on which the physical body is moulded. It is this which assumes the body necessary for its efficiency at its next birth by attracting physical elements to itself. At physical death, only the gross, outer form perishes. The rest of the self is not disturbed. Rebirth is only the renewal of the instrument through which the self works. The self is not at each birth a new entity but a continuous process. A transition is conceived from one situation to another at physical death. 'As a man might cross a ditch by swinging himself as he hangs to a rope from a tree on this bank, so does mind (*vijñāna*) at death proceed onward in causal relation to objects and so on.'[2] There is such a thing as psychic gravitation by which souls find their level, i.e. their proper environment. Birth is incarnation of the psyche and death disincarnation of it. When the machinery we use

1 *Chān. Up.* v. 3. 3; v. 9. I. *Brh. Up.* iv. 3 and 5; vi. 2. 14-15. *Bhagavadgītā* xv. 7 and 8. *Brahma Sūtra*, iii. I. I-7.
2 *Visuddhimagga*, p. 554 (Pali Text Society, 1920-1921).

becomes useless, it is scrapped and another set up in its place. The Pauline metaphor has it, 'to every seed his own body'.[1] It is stated in the Hindu Scriptures that the dying thought has great significance for the next life. Not that the thoughts at death are more important than the thoughts at a prior stage of development, but that they represent the culmination of the process of self-development. The dying thought resumes in itself all thoughts and states that went before. It is the sum total of its predecessors, the inheritor of its past and the point for future growth.

The difficulty of the congruence of the self with the body it acquires is not peculiar to the theory of rebirth. So long as we do not believe that the character of the self is produced by the body, the question of the linking up of a particular self with a particular body is a problem. How does the self become connected with a body such that its character resembles the characters of the ancestors of that body? If the parents do not produce the self at the time they produce the body and if it is attributed to God, the case for rebirth is not worse. Parents provide the matter for the new clothing of life.

The theory of rebirth is said to be inconsistent with the principle of heredity. The child seems to be a product of the parents whom it resembles in body and mind. It is unnecessary to assume that it comes from another life. If parents really make the child, heredity will be the universal law. This difficulty will hold for every theory except that of materialism. If the soul is 'created' by God, there is no reason why it should be like the parents. If God first fixes upon the character of the self and then selects the physical basis by

---

1 Cp. *Anguttara Nikāya* i, p. 223. Action is the seed field, consciousness the seed. Cp. John Masefield in his poem entitled *A Creed*: 'I hold that when a person dies His soul returns again to earth.'

choosing the parents, the theory seems to be far-fetched and is open to other criticisms. It is simpler to hold that the self seeking for rebirth obtains embodiment in the frame offering the necessary conditions. The physical body derived from the parents according to the laws of heredity is appropriated by the conscious self. If this theory is not acceptable, much less is the other view which holds that a sort of supernatural essence is thrust into the bodily context at the appropriate moment. The self selects the frame which fits it even as we pick the hat which suits the shape of our head. We are reborn in families where the qualities we possess and seek to embody are well developed. Even as the determining factor is the shape of the head and not the size of the hat, so also in rebirth the deciding factor is the nature of the self and not the parents of the body. The soul draws around it the forces necessary for its proper embodiment. It is therefore natural that the child should be like the parents.

As a matter of fact all children are not like their parents. They manifest qualities which are not possessed by a long line of ancestors and it is no answer to say that some remote ancestor might have had them.

The view of the correlativity of self and body suggests the presumption that the life hereafter is akin to the life on earth and is subject to the law of change. Future life is not one deathless existence but a process marked by periodic mortality of the body. So long as the self is growing, periodic death is also a fact. The Catholic doctrine of Purgatory teaches that those who are not yet prepared for heaven are purified in it. Purgatory is sometimes conceived as continued moral progress after death. Religious conceptions of heaven and hell suggest a deathless life after this. If heaven is a state where perfection prevails and improvement and progress are impossible, even the noblest of us are not in a fit condition to enter heaven. While the best of us are not quite prepared for the sudden splendour of bliss, the worst of us are not so bad as to be cast aside into eternal doom. Eternal states after death are improbable. The process of gradual improvement must go on after the death of our present bodies and it is reasonable to assume that this life is followed by others like it, each separate from its predecessor and successor by death and rebirth. Though it is conceivable and the life after death may be so indefinitely long as to admit of a continuous development of the process begun in this life, it is not probable that there will be such a change from the present order of experience. At any rate when we come to the state of hell, it is absolutely necessary to assume that there is an end to it, unless god wants to play the devil. None of us is so completely dead to the divine in us as to deserve eternal hell. Whatever we may think about the compatibility of death with absolute perfection, it is certainly compatible with absolute imperfection. Life after death is continuous with our present existence.

William James in his lecture on *Immortality* argues that if future life be true, then there would be vast numbers on the other side and the question of accommodation may become a real inconvenience. 'The very heavens themselves and the cosmic times and spaces would stand aghast ... at the notion of preserving eternally such an ever-swelling plethora and glut of it.'[1] A constant supply of new souls none of which ever perished would mean a real difficulty. Even those who take this objection seriously will be more at ease if future life is conceived in terms of rebirth.

The theory of a soul without a past but with a future is not easy of acceptance. If the soul is created by the birth of the body, then the death of the body destroys it. Tertullian, who holds that 'soul is nothing if not body', believes that the

1 P. 36; see also Bradley: *Appearance and Reality*, p. 502.

soul dies with the body and the two are raised again by miracle. If we disallow miracles, then there is no necessity why a created being should endure for all time. If the soul has a beginning, it must have an end. It is difficult to admit that a being which begins to exist at a certain definite point of time is immortal in the future like a string with only one end. It is contended that human souls, when once they are produced, happen to be of value not only in themselves but also to the universe. Their destruction will be inconsistent with the goodness of the universe. But 'goodness' does not mean exclusion of all evil. In that case the meaningless misery and the pointless suffering which life so often brings with it are enough to damn it. If goodness is not inconsistent with the existence of certain evils, then the destruction of human souls need not be inconsistent with the goodness of the universe. Dr Mc Taggart adopts the doctrine of the native immortality of the human soul.[1] This view secures both the past and the future existence of the soul, though it is not quite satisfactory as it seems to make al' progress illusory.

A common objection to the hypothesis of rebirth is the lack of memory of the past. If I am not able to own the past and profit by it, future life seems to be meaningless. Rebirth of an individual without a memory of his precious life would mean the annihilation of the past person and the creation of a second with a similar character. An unbroken conscious experience in a durational sequence constitutes the meaning and value of future life.

A little examination tells us that this objection cannot be seriously pressed. If the theory of rebirth is well grounded otherwise, the question of lapse of memory does not touch it. Memory may be necessary for a retributive theory of the

---

1 *Some Dogmas of Religion* (1906).

universe but not for moral continuity. Death may destroy memory of our deeds but not their effects on us. The metaphysical question of the continuity of the self is not in any way affected by the discontinuity of memory. The nature of each individual is moulded by the experiences of the past. Every state is conditioned by the prior and leads on the another. Simply because we do not have a memory of to early phases of our life or of our existence in the mother's body, we do not deny them. Even in this life we forget a great deal.

The purpose of memory is to enable us to grow wiser by experience, and virtuous by effort. Wisdom and virtue are not acquired by the storing of facts in memory but only by the training of the mind and will. The facts we learn and the acts we do may be forgotten but the cultivated mind and the fashioned will remain. Culture is that which remains when we forget everything that we learn, even as character is what remains when we forget all the deeds we did. What matter is the experience, not what we do, but how we do it. The knowledge we acquire and the possessions we gain may not remain with us, but the patience and the care we develop in acquiring them will stick to us. The hours spent in idleness or suffering are more fruitful for the growth of the soul than the waste of time in ambitious self-seeking. The Upaniṣad says that when self leaves the body its 'knowledge, work and experience (pūrvaprajña) accompany it'.[1] Hegel tells us that at death we have a 'collapse into immediacy'. All our experience consolidate themselves in giving a twist to ourself, a bias to our mind, and it is this we carry across. It remains with us though we have no memory of how we acquired it.

If the present life is valuable without any memory of its

1 *Brh. Up.* iv. 4. 2.

past, a future life need not be less valuable simply because it has no memory of its past. Besides, if we did not lose memory, it might turn out a positive nuisance. Our relations with our fellow-men are sufficiently complex without adding to them reminiscences of past lives. Again, things may be in the self though not in consciousness. Our past experiences even in this life when they are forgotten leave their traces in the mind. Consciousness is confined to mental processes of which the subject becomes aware in normal introspection. The 'unconscious' mind includes the relations with the world of which the subject is not normally conscious. Yet the individual lives not by his consciousness alone but by his whole mind, whose contents sometimes become accessible to introspection. Socrates is reported in the *Meno* as eliciting from a slave boy by a series of appropriate questions a geometrical theorem of which the boy had no previous conscious knowledge.[1] There is an ancient tradition in India that one can remember one's past lives by means of 'the constant study of the scriptures, by purification, by austerity, by the love of all creation.'[2]

Future life depends on a great many other conditions; for the self at any stage expresses the cosmic situation also. It is obvious that rebirth is not an eternal recurrence leading nowhere but is a movement with a meaning. It is not a mere rediscovery of the status which we have and always had. It is a genuine growth into personality and character from the humblest beginnings in the subhuman world. It recognizes that the values won and character achieved are conserved as mind and purpose which accompany us even through death. The future depends on what we make of this

1 85.
2 *Manu*. iv. 148.
   Dr Besant tells us that the Spanish inquisitors were always reborn deformed. Where exactly she learned that one cannot tell.

plastic raw material which receives determination by our free choice. Our life is not a puppet show but a real growth. The human soul represents an order of reality different from that of atoms, plants and animals. It is a more complex organization with its own specific nature. It is more intimately bound up with its environment. It has the two features of continuity with the past (karma) and creative advance into the future (freedom). It is as incomplete as any other organism and so perpetually moves on. There is no scientific explanation of the origin of intelligent beings or their specific characteristics.

10. *Spirit*

Besides consciousness in the animal world (perception and action), and self-consciousness in the human (intelligence and will), we have spiritual consciousness or super-consciousness, a level of experience at which new aspects of reality reveal themselves. While in the first case we have a psychological unity between the animal and the environment, in the second we have a logical unity and in the third a spiritual unity. At the spiritual level, the individual becomes aware of the substance of spirit, not as an object of intellectual cognition but as an awareness in which the subject becomes its own object, in which the timeless and the spaceless is aware of itself as the basis and reality of all experience. The spirit which is inclusive of both self and object is self-subsistent and self-consistent. Nothing in our experience can be said to be real or individual without qualification except spirit. There is nothing within it to divide it, nothing outside to limit it. It alone satisfies our total desire and whole intelligence. It is all that there is, all being and all value.

Many of us may not be made the mystic way and spiritual

experience may not interest us. But it cannot be said that what our minds fail to grasp is unthinkable and what does not interest us is unreal. Supposing we shut our eyes to spiritual experience, it does not cease to be the truth. Though we may not understand, with all our efforts, Einstein's relativity, conscious ignorance or inability should not become unbelief.

It is because the universal spirit, which is higher than the self-conscious individual, is present and operative in self-conscious mind that the latter is dissatisfied with any finite form it may assume. When self-consciousness knows itself to be finite and limited, it is a greater-than-self that judges that which is less than itself in its wholeness. The reality of universal spirit is not an uncriticized intuition or a postulate of philosophy but the obvious implication of our daily life. At the human level the secret tendency of man's nature to be a superman is found at work. The destiny of man is to manifest this secret aspiration. While for the self-conscious individual, religion is only faith in values, for the spiritual being it is vital contact with reality which is the source of all values. So long as the human consciousness is on the pathway to reality, the spirit is an *other* to it. It is remote, like Plato's 'Idea' of another world apparent to our eyes only as a shadow on a wall, but to one who has risen to the level of spirit, it is of the world, present here and now. The awakened man draws back from his mind, life and body and all else that is not his true being and knows himself to be one with the eternal spirit which is the soul of all phenomena. Spirit is something essentially and purely inward to be known only from within, and yet when it is known it leaves nothing outside. In the language of religion, spirit is God, the ultimate reality which is one and all-comprehensive. The spiritualized man is a new genus of man exhibiting a new quality of life. His self becomes as wide as the world itself, as he feels that the one spirit is present in all minds, lives and bodies. The supermen, the masters of life, enter into conscious possession of this truth and act from it. They represent the eternal norms of humanity. They are the saved souls.

11. What is salvation?

Salvation is different from survival, liberation (*mokṣa*) from rebirth (*saṁsāra*), life eternal from durational continuance. It is the difference between two levels, the self-conscious and the spiritual. So long as the self occupies the human standpoint, it is bound to a task which is self-contradictory and cannot therefore be realized. It is only a question of indefinite progress in time and not of final attainment. For Kant the ethical plane is the highest and so he looks upon moral life as an infinite process of approximation to perfect virtue. The self can never attain the goal, though it is perpetually tending towards it. The self is always in a state of growth and self-enlargement. As soon as one goal is reached, others attract it and the series seems to be limitless.

For those who do not look upon the plane of ethics, the individualism of morality, the passage in time as the highest, survival indicates only the proximate future of the self and there is an ultimate goal which is beyond the conditions of progress and decline or mere passage in time. The Hindu thinkers affirm the reality of life eternal or release from rebirth. It is a supreme status of being in which the individual knows himself to be superior to time, to birth and death. It is not a life merely future or endless but a new mode of being, a transfigured life here and now. Rebirth is subject to time and it is inevitable so long as we stick to the individualistic position. If we transcend individualism, we rise superior to the phenomena of time and thus escape from rebirth. When the Hindu thinkers ask us to attain release from rebirth, they are asking us to transcend the standpoint of mere individualism and rise to an impersonal universalism. To seek for liberation from the wheel of births and deaths is nothing more than to rise to the spiritual level from the merely ethical. The spiritual is not the extension of the ethical. It is a new dimension altogether, dealing with things eternal. The saints who worship God do not worship man enlarged. As a new creation in the order of the universe, the spiritual is not a mere unfolding of the human.

The Hindu theory has many analogies in the West. The Orphics refer to the feeling of ecstasy or possession by God, when the individual seems to pass out of himself and feel himself to be one with the universal God. In the cult of Dionysus, the chief aim of the ritual is the identification of the worshipping individual with God. In the *Symposium* Plato gives us the doctrine of a timeless existence attainable here and now by an escape from time and form. Islam describes the bliss of saints as consisting in union with God, a state which the mystics and dervishes wish to attain even in this life. The Neo-Platonists and Spinoza and the mystics of Christianity adopt a similar view.

Cosmic history is working towards its highest moment when the universal tendency towards spiritual life becomes realized in one and all, when the ethical experience of non-attainment yields to participation by the creatures in life eternal, when the powerful will of the individual yields in love to the spirit of the universe. As matter was delivered of life and life of mind, so is man to be delivered of the spirit. That is his destiny. Our logical consciousness attempts to arrive at truth but succeeds only to a limited extent; our ethical will achieves only a partial realization of its aims; our heart's aspirations to seize and enjoy the delights of its aims; our heart's aspirations to seize and enjoy the delights of existence meet with limited success. If the deeper spirit in us sees the truth unveiled and enjoys freely the delight of being then it and not self-conscious mind is the original and fundamental intention of nature which must emerge eventually. As matter was instinct with life which could emerge only when the necessary natural conditions were properly organized, as life was instinct with mind, waiting for its proper moment in vital organization to emerge, even so human consciousness is instinct with the stuff of spirit or supermind, though it could emerge only when the necessary effort and conditions are ready. Human life is being prepared for this end with the same advances and retardings, forward leaps and backslidings.

Hindu thinkers claim that the transition from the ethical individualism to the spiritual universalism is effected by means of *jñāna* or wisdom, intuitive understanding. The moralistic individualism is based on an imperfect outlook which is the root of our finiteness. We see ourselves as we are not, when we regard ourselves as individuals cut off from the rest of the universe. Though the pluralistic outlook is not a fiction framed by the individual self, but a grade of the growing universe, it has to be transcended. Hence the supreme importance of self-knowledge (*ātmajñāna*) or truth of the nature of things (*tattvajñāna*).

The state of freedom has been differently conceived. It is said to be atonement with God or continuous contemplation of the ideal world, an enjoyment of the redeemer's face or an extinction of the individual. The central question is whether the self loses or retains its individuality. Admitting that there are limits to our thinking on this remote and difficult subject, we offer a few considerations, general and tentative, and perhaps not quite self-consistent.

Theistic thinkers, whether in the East or West, believe

that the communion with God which was in the empirical condition transitory, intermittent and somewhat obscure becomes in the state of perfection continuous, permanent and unclouded. Struggle and progress yield to peace and joy, but there is no loss of individuality; the life of the individual is lifted into the light and largeness of spirit. It is a state of unimpeded energy and activity and not inaction and immobility. 'He becomes the lord himself; his movements are unfettered in all the worlds.'[1]

Saṁkara is generally regarded as favouring the hypothesis of the absorption of the individual in the eternal Brahman, when release is attained. It seems to be an inference from his repeated assertions that eternity means non-temporality. If temporality is the mark of the finite individuality, anything non-temporal is non-individual. But we find a large number of passages in Saṁkara which indicate that while the released soul attains at tne very moment of release a universality of spirit, it yet retains its individuality as a centre of action as long as the cosmic process continues.[2] The loss of individuality happens only when the world is redeemed, when the multiple values figured out in it are achieved. The world fulfils itself by self-destruction. The freed soul, so long as the cosmic process continues, participates in it and returns to embodied existence not for its own sake but for the sake of the whole. He has the feelings of kinship with all (sarvātmabhāva). He identifies himself with the universal movement and follows its course. As eternal life is a changed mode of living, it has little to do with the assumption of a body. The freed souls touch the fringe but do not enter the cloud; or, to use another famous metaphor, they enter the light but do not touch the

1 Chān. Up. vii. 25-32.
2 Saṁkara on Brahma Sūtra iii. 3. 32. See also Indian Philosophy, vol.ii, 2nd ed. (1931), pp. 642 ff.

flame. Coherence within the individual and harmony with the environment are both essentials for salvation. If we establish harmony within ourselves, overcome the struggle between the flesh and the spirit, we fulfil the first requirement. But harmony with the environment is not possible so long as there are unredeemed elements in it. We are not truly saved until the warring elements of our nature and the rivalries of individuals are both subdued into unity of life and spiritual fellowship. Perfect freedom is impossible in an imperfect world, and so those who have secured a vision of spirit work in the world so long as there is wrong to be set right, error to be corrected and ugliness to be banished from life. The individual who achieves unity within himself sets other men forward in desiring the same good. In a true sense the ideal individual and the perfect community arise together.

All individuals are destined to gain life eternal, for as a Hindu text says, we are the children of immortality. An apostolic writer observes: 'Now we are sons of God and we know not what we shall be'. When this condition is attained, we have a divine community (*brahmaloka*) where the individual is transformed by contemplation on the being of God into the likeness of that which he beholds. It is a life in which the individuals are united by a perfect interpenetration of mind by mind. Salvation in Plato's phrase is 'to be filled with reality'. Such a state of perfection or spiritualized harmony is the end of the world.

While it is not possible for us to describe that mode of being in logical terms, it is obvious that it is a condition of fulfilled desire. Life as we know it is kept going by lack of perfect adjustment. As Hobbes expressed it, 'Nor can a man any more live whose desires are at an end, than he whose senses and imagination are at a stand'.[1] Where everything is being and nothing becomes, where everything is finally

made and nothing is in the making, activity is inconceiv ble.
When movement reaches its fulfilment, life is not a going
concern. The historical process terminates and individuals
cease to exist as historical beings. We cannot conceive how
such a state of perfection is consistent with activity. There
is a lesson for us in the philosophy of Gilbert's king Gama,
who put it to us:

> Oh, don't the days seem lank and long
> When all goes right and nothing goes wrong,
> And isn't your life extremely flat
> With nothing at all to grumble at?

In Strindberg's play, *Master Olaf*, when at one point the
great Reformer of Sweden realizes that his goal is nearer to
him than he has supposed, he exclaims, 'What a frightful
thought! No further struggles--that would be death. It wasn't
victory then I was wanting.' A state where all individuals are
perfected and dwell in heaven enjoying the glory of God is
difficult to conceive. An English hymn describes heaven as
a place 'where congregations ne'er break up and sabbaths
have no end'. Whatever it may be for us laymen, it is certainly not heaven for ministers of religion. If what awaits us
is eternal idleness, it is no use to anybody. We all know how
the 'Soda-water paradise' of Chautauqua wrung from William James the cry, on emerging once more into the dark and
wicked world, 'Ouf, what a relief! Now for something primordial and savage, even although it were as bad as an
Armenian massacre, to set the balance straight again.' Aristotle says, 'Endless duration makes good no better nor white
any whiter.'

To evade this difficulty, it is sometimes argued that the
historical process will never terminate. It is possible for
individuals here and there to get released but the world as

6 *Leviathan*, ch. xi.

a whole will never be redeemed. The world exists from everlasting to everlasting. It follows that no individual can attain a perfect harmony both within and without. Perfection is unthinkable. It is given to us to strive after perfection and actualize it at best in fragments. We have to rest in the idea of perpetual effort. But this view ignores the solidarity between man and nature, values and reality. It cannot be a question of perpetual travelling. We should also arrive. It cannot be interminable singing; there should also be such a thing as completion in a song. There must come a time when all individuals will become sons of God and be received into the glory of immortality. When the world is redeemed the end of the plot is reached. Earth and heaven would be no more; the timeless and the transcendent alone remains.

Professor A. E. Taylor believes that the condition of the saved has room for 'a very real and intense moral life'. 'In heaven itself, though there would be no longer progress *towards* fruition, there might well be progress *in* fruition. Life "there" would be as life "here" is not, living by vision as contrasted with living by faith and hope; but might not the vision itself be capable of ever-increasing enrichment?' [1] Professor Taylor believes that even though the saved may be in actual enjoyment of the 'beatific' vision, some of them may 'see more of the infinite wealth of the vision than other's while each receives according to the measure of his capacity. But between a merely vague apprehension of the reality and its perfect embodiment in the concrete life of personality there is a vast region which can only be traversed by years of toil. Until this perfect comprehension is reached one is not saved. As those who see more will serve those who see less, the fact of service would supply the necessary element of adventure. But the question remains whether one is saved

1 *The Faith of a Moralist* (1931), I. pp. 407-408.

at all so long as a full vision of God is not had. If, on account of its infinity, it is impossible for us to attain that, we are not truly saved. Even salvation becomes an endless process of approximation to an ideal which we never reach. 'Progress in fruition' is more a statement than a solution of the problem. It does not really reconcile perfect fruition with endless progress. Perfection belongs to another dimension than the ethical, though it may express itself on the ethical plane. The experience of the changeless may lead to a changing world, though it is not equivalent to it.

It may be argued that it is an utterly futile business for any one responsible for this world to have brought in-dividual souls into existence, spent infinite pains in their education, only to disintegrate them ultimately. Is the spirit of man to be brought into fruition only to be broken for ever? Are the spiritual fires lit only to be reduced to ashes? We need not assume that this cosmic process is an end in itself. When its end is reached, when its drama is played, the curtain is drawn and possibly some other plot may com-mence.

We have now briefly considered the different possibilities. It cannot be that certain individuals will remain for all time unredeemed. If they are all redeemed, it cannot be that they sit down in heaven, praising God and doing nothing. So long as some individuals are unredeemed, the other freed souls have work to do and so retain their individualities. But when the world as such is saved, when all are freed and nothing remains to be done, the time process comes to an end. The threats of science that the world will be wound up one day need not depress us. The universe though 'unbounded' is 'finite'. The end of time may mean the perfection of humanity, where the earth will be full of the knowledge of spirit. The cosmic purpose is consummated so far as the conditions of space and time allow.

A scientific description of the nature of experience takes us gradually out of the world of matter, life, mind and intelligence to a spirit utterly transcendent beyond the descriptions of the intellect, which manifests itself as the supreme self and the individual soul, the supreme reality and the universe. Here our quest ends. Human thought cannot go beyond it.

The immensities of the universe do not dishearten us. Physically we may be specks in a dust storm raging through the world; psychologically our intentions may be confined to this or that organism, but truly we are all. The immensities of space and time, the vast variety of the species of life; the stupendous achievements of science and art are not outside us, but within us. They are our own useful creations, though in reality abstract and to that extent unreal. Spirit includes within its own nature space and time and embraces the whole of experience, individual persons and things. Matter, life, consciousness are ideal constructions and when we are dealing with them we are dealing with phenomena and not with reality. The universe need not be broken up into a set of conflicting reals called matter, life, consciousness and thought. They are not hard and fast divisions of reality but grades of experience. The truth of the universe is not a mathematical equation or a kinematical system or a biological adjustment or a psychological pluralism or ethical individualism but a spiritual organism. The lower we descend the more clear may be our knowledge. Mathematical knowledge may be very much clearer than our knowledge of the world as a closed energetic system, which may be clearer than a knowledge of its as the environment of life and sentience. The knowledge of ourselves as ethical beings may be much clearer than that of the world as spirit and yet it is this mysterious, unclear and inarticulate knowledge that brings us closest to reality.

CHAPTER VIII

Ultimate Reality

1. *'The world we live in'*

We have seen that there are certain pervasive characteristics of the world. *First*, it is an ordered whole. We find an unbroken continuity, a complete unity from the changes in the atom to the movements of history. The system of nature is a cosmos, a system of relationships intimately interdependent. This orderedness expresses itself in different forms of determination according to the level of being that has been attained. *Secondly*, every existent is an organization with a specific mode of relatedness. The quantum theory, the mutations in biology and the *Gestalt* psychology declare the wholeness of forms. *Thirdly*, the organisms tend towards greater interactive union with their surroundings or environment. Molecules, atoms and electrons are parts of a unity interacting with one another not fortuitously, but in relation to a material system of which they form parts. Nature is one large whole with matter, life, mind and value as its constituents. While these remain utterly unlike each other, they yet intermingle and coexist. The atom and its surroundings, the organism and its environment, the self and not-self, the individual and society are expressions of a unity which they also seek. In existence and in experience they are a unity, and they must therefore be a unity for our knowledge as well. The essential wholeness of reality is recognized by Plato.[1] *Fourthly*, in the continuous flow of nature there is neither repose nor halt. Nature is never satisfied with the level it has reached. It always aspires to

1 *Timaeus* and *Laws* x.

other levels. While effects follow causes, causes do not repeat themselves. There is the constant emergence of new qualities which we cannot predict from a knowledge of the old. Unpredictable novelties occur. The successive production of novelties displays an abruptness and a discontinuity analogous to genius in art, science and morality. Theories of emergence note this fact, though they do not explain it. *Fifthly,* the changes are not meaningless. The physical world is not a futile play of senseless atoms engaged in a deadly conflict. They are making things, and by exerting our control we can make them do the things we desire. The earth and its contents prepared for life, though life had to fit itself for its setting to grow. While a few specific chemical elements and their compounds provide the materials of the body, specific molecular vibrations, such as light and sound waves, serve as the necessary stimuli to direct life in its career by enabling it to see, hear, smell and taste other things round about it and react to them in its own interests. When at a later stage life had to work out its destiny and self-betterment by its own efforts, consciousness and human reason were devised. From the barely existent void or waters (*apraketamsalilam*) all this has emerged and is making for a profound co-operative and spiritual commonwealth with freedom and harmony as its marks. In spite of the little ups and downs of change, there seems to be a compelling drift towards better things. The world never stood still on its tracks, nor does it go backwards. There is a universal tendency discernible in every state from its origin to its present condition. *Sixthly,* the highest kind of experience we have seems to be all-inclusive and to produce personalities possessing such experience seems to be the end of the cosmic process.

2. *Naturalism*

The fundamental line of division between naturalistic and idealistic solutions is marked by the attitude they adopt towards the problem of the reality of time. Is the temporal order of events a fundamental character of reality, or does it fall within reality and belong only to certain beings or worlds within it?[1] The naturalistic solution asserts the ultimate reality time, and refuses to go beyond the temporal process. There is nothing deeper than the historical process, either underlying it or existing beyond it. Naturalism assumes that it can explain the whole process of the universe which is all that is. It looks upon the world as a sort of automatic machine which goes on working in a blind haphazard way. It reduces the temporal world to unconscious forces, makes life, consciousness and value mere by-products. It believes that the world machine needs only to be taken to pieces to be comprehended. It conceives of one kind of stuff, matter, and one kind of change, change in the relative positions of the particles of the stuff according to fixed laws. The different kinds of matter differ only in the number, arrangement and movements of the constituent particles. Naturalism conflicts with the results and canons of scientific investigation. Up to the middle of the nineteenth century the stronghold of the mechanistic theory was to be found in the science of physics. The Newtonian philosophy seemed to be quite successful in explaining phenomena in terms of matter and motion. Little billiard balls in random motion were enough to build up the whole universe. The phenomena of life with the appearance of purpose and guidance seemed to present difficulties, but evolution in the hands of Darwin and Spencer went a long way towards

1 See Bosanquet: *The Meeting of Extremes in Contemporary Philosophy* (1920).

settling them. But today the situation is quite different. The old categories of physics are not adequate even in the physical world, and purely mechanistic explanations of even the simplest living organisms are found impossible. The utter inadequacy of the naturalist hypothesis becomes obvious if we consider its bearings on the general characteristics of the world. The order of the universe is not a mechanical one. Scientific laws represent working hypotheses, abstract devices for understanding concrete facts of nature. They do not constrain or dictate to nature.[1] The mechanical view believes that there is no more in the effect than there is in the cause. Relations are of the type of mere repetition or fundamental clockwork. The endless versatility of nature conflicts with this view. Unlike those of a mechanical producer, the products of nature are infinite and formless. There is certainly orderliness in nature, but it is quite different from that of a mechanical tyranny.

All existents are organisms, which reflect the whole, past, present and future. Even in the simplest physical entities the plan of the whole controls the character of the subordinate parts which enter into them. The changes in the material

1 Eddington distinguishes three types of laws, identical, statistical and transcendental. Identical laws which govern mathematical identities are not genuine laws. While events are variable, in identical laws 'there is neither variableness nor shadow of turning. They deal with mathematical quantities built by us. Statistical laws are also due to the mind's attempt to devise appropriate formuals for co-ordinating selected data of observation. These are empirical and based on averages. Causal laws are of this character and are deduced from observed measurement. The truth of the average is quite compatible with lawlessness in the individual. Predictions are possible simply because averages are predictable irrespective of the forces underlying events. If there are genuine laws which control the physical world, they are of a transcendental character (*The Nature of the Physical World*, 1928, 224- 246).

world are not merely external ones of position, velocity, etc. Though all physical objects may ultimately be of the same stuff and possess the same properties, their sensible qualities which are different, whether apparent or actual, are not accounted for by the laws of pure mechanism.

If mechanism were true, the writer of Ecclesiastes, who laments that 'the thing that hath been, it is that which shall be; and that which is done is that which shall be done; and there is no new thing under the sun,' would be faithful to facts, but the truth is nearer what the Book of Revelation declares: 'Behold, I make all things new.' If naturalism were true, time would make no difference to the facts. Aristotle said long ago, if nothing depended on time for its realization, everything would already have happened. It believes that given sufficient time, every conceivable form will be realized, but the history of the universe is a unique series of configurations from which every other series is excluded. Time introduces something new in the properties of things. The historical process has in it two elements of continuity and novelty. Every stage of it is at once a continuity and a crisis. Nature has its own rhythm and cannot be rushed. Its processes are irreversible. The view of mechanism that the world came into existence of its own and has come to be what it is, without any reason or purpose behind it all, does not seem to be quite satisfactory. Even if the world is a mechanism, the questions remain, what guides the mechanism? Who set it up? Again, machines are made for certain ends, and their structures are unintelligible apart from these ends. The world process where everything depends on something else is not self-sufficient. Each event is what it is because of its relation to other events. We seek for something that is its own explanation, but we never get it. The world is an infinite series of conditioned events, but science cannot say why it is what it is. The value of the causal argument lies in that it insists that the finite universe demands a principle beyond itself to explain it. Science is a system of second causes which cannot describe the world adequately, much less account for it.

The mystery of all existence in time as a whole is only deepened by science and naturalism does not help to dissipate it.

4. *The holistic evolution of Smuts*

General Smuts in his book on *Holism and Evolution*[1] affirms that the one universal principle which would comprehend the different sciences of physics, biology and psychology is that of *Holism*, or the tendency in the universe to the creation of greater and greater wholes. Every whole, whether it be an atom or an amoeba or a human personality, has an appropriate plan or organization which the parts serve. Each whole has a specific character, an inwardness of structure and function. The parts are not to be regarded as irreducible units with fixed characters forming fresh wholes by entering into new combinations. The molecules which form an amoeba, e.g., do not behave as they do in a mere collection of molecules. Smuts includes in the whole both past and future. The field of the whole is distributed in the space around it. Objects are not to be regarded as simply located in a definite part of space at a definite time. They are extended through space and time. Simple location is displaced by the idea of interconnection. He finds evidence of creative or 'holistic' activity even in inorganic matter. When we come to matter in the colloidal state, it discloses properties and behaviour which seem in some ways to anticipate the processes and activities of life in its most primitive forms. He holds that matter itself is a product of

1 1926.

evolution. From the simplest atom to the most complicated, and from these to the enormous complexity of colloids, the process is always in the direction of greater wholeness. The general process of the formation of greater and greater wholes is truly creative in the sense that the goal of the process is not implicit in the beginning.

As a piece of metaphysics, General Smuts' position does not seem to be quite satisfactory. (1) He believes that 'holism' is not a simple empirical generalization describing the trend of natural processes, but identifies it with an active force of nature. It is a real *vera causa*,[1] 'fundamental, synthetic, ordering, organizing, regulating activity in the universe'.[2] (2) The metaphysical principle which is postulated to account for the world is conceived not as a vague indefinable creative impulse of the character of Bergson's *élan vital*, but as a specific force with a definite character and creative of all wholes in the universe. (3) Since 'holism' is conceived as a directive and creative principle operating from first to last, and since it is held responsible for the creation of wholes long ages before life or mind appeared on the scene, he is unwilling to equate it with mind, purpose or personality, since these appear on the scene of empirical reality at a late stage. 'Mind is not at the beginning, but at the end, but Holism is everywhere and all in all.'[3] 'Where was the spirit when the vast Silurian seas covered the face of the earth, and the lower types of fishes and marine creatures still faced the crest of the evolutionary wave? Or, going still further back, where was the spirit when in the pre-cambrian system of the globe the first convulsive movements threw up the early mountains which have now entirely disappeared from the face of the earth, and when the living forms,

1 *Holism and Evolution*, p. 99.
2 *Ibid.*, p. 319.
3 *Ibid.*, p. 335.

if any, were of so low a type that none have been deciphered yet in the biological record? Where was the spirit when the solar system itself was still a diffuse fiery nebula?'[1] (4) If 'holism' becomes completely manifest in a supreme whole of which all lesser wholes are parts, it cannot be conceived on the analogy of any of the parts. The supreme whole being more than a sum of its parts cannot be considered to be of the same type as mind or personality, which are parts within the supreme whole. (5) Smuts is impressed by the reality of time and creative evolution, and is afraid that the identification of the active Holism with spiritual reality may prejudice the reality of cosmic evolution. For these reasons, Smuts asserts the reality of a holistic force, and yet declines to characterize it as anything else than a force which makes for wholes in the cosmic process.

If Smuts is unwilling to go further he cannot satisfy the inquiring mind. (1) He seems to overlook the difference between a descriptive statement of the general characteristics of the world process and a creative force universally operative in all nature. The former is the problem of science, while the latter is a postulate of metaphysics. The fact that he transforms an empirical feature into a metaphysical explanation shows the need for the latter. The characteristics of the universe call for an explanation. (2) What is the relation of the different classes of wholes to one another? He says, 'The four great series in reality, matter, life, mind and personality, are seen to be but steps in the progressive evolution of one and the same fundamental factor, whose path-way is the universe within us and around us. Holism constitutes them all, connects them all, and so far as explanations are at all possible, explains and accounts for them all.'[2] The series is not merely successive, but intimately

1 *Ibid.*, pp. 330-331.
2 *Ibid.*, p. 320.

continuous. What is the nature of the whole which includes all the others, and how is it related to the other wholes? (3) If the ideas of truth, beauty and goodness emerge finally and 'lay the foundations of a new order of the universe', what is their primal source and spring, and what provides the guarantee of their stability as foundations and their realization and maintenance in a new order? The idealists at any rate argue, to use the famous expression of Plato, that the order in time is the image of an order which is not in time. The temporal series is the scheme through which eternal values unfold themselves. (4) It is true that in the cosmic process matter, life, consciousness and value appear successively. Mind is a recent arrival, and the universe existed millions of years before its advent. The philosophy of idealism doe.. not deny the facts of evolution. It does not say that human beings were found before the earth was. When the idealist affirms the primacy of mind, it is not the mind of this or that individual that is so posited, but the supreme mind. Otherwise our only alternative is a crude naturalism which holds that the world process, apparently blind, somehow developed human beings who struggle blindly for a spiritual order which is a unified whole. To reduce God to a stream of tendency, however holistic it may be, is not to escape from naturalism. Smuts is quite correct in contending that the supreme reality cannot be described adequately if it is equated with mind or personality as we are aware of them. (5) Smuts does not tell us what the end of this whole-making universe and its likely nature are. (6) The question is inevitable whether time is all, or whether it is only a medium through which a higher purpose is working out its plans. If the cosmic process is a whole-building it may well be the scheme through which an eternal spirit is working out its plan. It is quite possible that the plan is one which has room for contingency and is dependent upon the initiative of the eternal and the return movement of nature. (7) If we give up spiritual direction of the universe altogether and make the 'holistic tendency' of Smuts responsible for the universe, the question remains whether this principle of 'holism' itself is in a process of development? If it is, it cannot serve as an explanation; if it is not, then it affects the real 'novelty' of the advance in time quite as much as any other view.

5. *Emergent evolution of Alexander and Lloyd Morgan*

Alexander gives us a picture of a growing universe in which matter, life, consciousness, etc., gradually arise from space-time or pure events. The universe according to him is a spatio-temporal system, working gradually towards the realization of that ultimate perfection which he calls deity. Space-time is the stuff out of which all existents are made. It is universe in its primordial form. Time is the mind of space. At the earliest level of existence, primary qualities like shape and numbers arise within the space-time structure. When these spatio-temporal configurations assume a certain complexity, we have matter or sub-matter. At a higher level of complexity certain material configurations 'emerge', such as complexes or conditions of bodies of which we become aware as colours, tastes and so forth. At certain critical points in the development of the spatio-temporal world new qualities appear which are based on the lower level of experiences and are yet qualified by a new character. When we have a certain complexity of physical and chemical processes, the quality of life arises. While Alexander confines the term 'emergence' to the large critical novelties, Lloyd Morgan applies it more freely to any change that can be called a change of character. Alexander makes out that the whole process of the universe is a historic growth from space-time. 'In the course of time, which is the principle of movement, the matrix of space-time breaks up into finites of ever-increasing complexity. At certain points in the history of things finites assume new empirical qualities which are distinctive of levels of experience, primary qualities, matter; secondary qualities, life, mind.'[1] The cosmic process has now reached the human level, and man is looking forward to the next higher quality of deity. The men of religious genius are preparing us for this next stage of development. Religion, for Alexander, is the yearning for this final advent. The divine quality or deity is a stage in time beyond the human. The whole world is now engaged in the production of deity. As time is the very substance of reality, no being can exhaust the future. Even God is a creature of time.

Alexander's brilliant attempt to frame a general metaphysical schemes in consonance with modern scientific developments suffers from certain fundamental disabilities. An anti-metaphysical bias governs the whole enterprise, though it is one of the most impressive metaphysical efforts of our time. The position of space-time in his metaphysics is ambiguous. It is an abstraction, an assumption made to account for concrete existence, and is not itself concrete existence. Yet it is called the stuff out of which existents are made. It once existed in its bareness, and only gradually became enriched by the appearance of qualities like form, colour, sound, beauty and goodness. In other words, it is the lowest level of existence. Since from it everything else arises, it becomes the absolute for Alexander. 'It is greater than all existent finites or infinites because it is their parent. But it has not as space-time their wealth of qualities, and being elementary is so far less than they

1 *Space, Time and Deity*, ii. p. 335.

are.[1] It is then a universal abstraction, and we are aware of it only as it is expressed in the finite existents of which it is said to be the parent. There is no proof that at the beginning there was a primordial condition of space-time from which all the richness of concrete experience was absent, and from which it has somehow emerged. If space-time were the ultimate reality, we do not know what it is.

The rise of matter from space-time is difficult to understand. Matter is not a piece of extension-duration. Alexander is not quite consistent when he says that every existent is 'expressible *without residue'* in terms of a lower order of existence. That would make his philosophy crudely naturalistic, and quite opposed to the 'emergence' view which he accepts.[2] Matter or mass is different from space-time. There is the same difficulty about the other items of the gallery. When physical structure assumes a certain complexity, life 'emerges' as something new. Its 'emergence' is just the problem. When the physical structure alters in complexity, as it does when it produces a central nervous system, 'mind' emerges and the gap between life and conscious behaviour is supposed to be covered. Alexander finds the explanation in a *nisus* or thirst of the universe for higher levels. It is the *nisus* that is creative, that satisfies the thirst. Primordial space-time and a *nisus* are Alexander's substitutes for the void and God of the Old Testament. Unless we assume the *nisus* to be a spiritual power ever drawing on its resources and ever expressing new forms, Alexander's whole account becomes unsatisfactory. The *nisus* cannot be an unconscious drive coming by degrees to consciousness in man. The creative spirit which is responsible for the *nisus* is not the result of the universe, as Alexander and others imagine, but its source as well, as the great

1 *Space, Time and Deity*, i. p. 342.
2 *Ibid.*, ii. pp. 45 ff.

religions and philosophies assert. If God is futu.e possibility, then religion as a human experience of worship of
God is the worship of a fiction. To look upon the *nisus* as
originally unconscious which has suddenly become conscious as the result of cosmic evolution is to mistake the
order of our consciousness for the order of reality. Our
unconsciousness of the Supreme need not be conclusive
proof of the non-existence of it. The first chapter cannot
account for the second simply because it comes before the
first. The author's mind is the real explanation.

There are occasions when Alexander feels that deity is
not simply some quality which emerges on this quite infinitesimal part of the universe. He says: 'God is the whole
world as possessing the quality of deity. Of such a being,
the whole world is the "body" and the deity is the "mind". But
this possessor of deity is not actual but ideal. As an actual
existent, God is the infinite world with its *nisus* towards
deity, or, to adapt a phrase of Leibniz, as big or in travail
with deity.'[1] May it not be that somewhere else in the vast
regions of space-time the quality of deity has been attained,
that long before our earth came into existence or humanity
emerged, a God far transcending our imagination has been
realized? The order of our knowledge is not the real order
of the universe. To us the world seems to come first and God
to emerge out of it, while God may in truth be the real of
which the world is the expression. That which is ultimate
for us is not the ultimate for reality. In creation the idea
precedes experience. God precedes the world if the empirical series is rooted in an order which is more than empirical.
If time were the ultimate reality, then the values we cherish
and by which we judge actual facts are passing fancies or
fluctuating ideas which contain parts of the process put

1 *Space, Time and Deity*, ii, p. 353.

forth. There are no absolute standards by which we can assign relative values to experience. If values are real, then their reality is not of the character of the things that change. They belong to a realm above all chance and change. To the extent they appear in our world, our world is real and our valuations have operative significance. In the stress of matter we have the striving of life to force an entrance. In the movement of life we have the deep urgence of mind to come to birth, and our conscious experience is one long endeavour to attain immortal being.

Lloyd Morgan,[1] who adopts a view almost similar to that of Alexander so far as the empirical universe is concerned, asserts that historical becoming cannot be intelligibly described in terms of temporal succession. He admits a hierarchical order of new modes of organization with attendant properties in the past evolution, and in the future also there may be such further steps upward in the orderly advance of nature, though we cannot deduce their character. The world is in the making, and at every stage of advance we find increasing complexity of stuff and richness in substance. For the explanation of this process Lloyd Morgan is not inclined to invoke a multitude of entelechies or souls, but he accepts God. He assumes 'something of the nature of a reality and directive Activity, of which the *de facto* relatedness and the observed changes of direction (with which science is concerned) are the manifestation.'[2] 'For better or for worse, I acknowledge God as the *Nisus* through whose activity emergents emerge, and the whole course of emergent evolution is directed.' God is not the emergent deity, but an Activity within which qualities emerge. God is the breath of the whole movement, the deep root which feeds the whole tree. He is the principle of all life, the unchangeable

1 *Emergent Evolution* (1923), *Life, Mind and Spirit* (1924).
2 *Contemporary British Philosophy*, First Series (1924), pp. 303-304.

good behind, or rather within, the temporal world, though
it is quite true that we could not have arrived at this creative
spirit until we saw the empirical universe which is its
explanation. The course of history is the gradual coming of
God to himself. Lloyd Morgan does not tell us whether the
emergence occurs according to a determinate rule, or is a
process of free creation. His allegiance to Spinoza makes
one suspect that the changes occur according to rule, and
there is no spontaneity. It is true that Lloyd Morgan contends that emergent evolution is unpredictable. But it is not
in the strict sense undetermined like Bergson's creative
evolution, not only unpredictable for human minds, but in
principle, or for all minds. Lloyd Morgan's acceptance of
Spinoza's metaphysical view makes it difficult for him to
believe in genuine emergence.

But while Lloyd Morgan infers the coming of divinity
from the purposeful direction of the universe, he is inclined
to make his God completely immanent. He believes in one
realm of reality that is both natural and spiritual, and
protests against the conception of two diverse orders of
being. 'The whole course of events subsumed under evolution is the expression of God's purpose.'[1] In distinguishing
the purpose from the cosmos, he implies that the purpose
is in a sense transcendent. In Whitehead we have an explicit
recognition of the element of transcendence.

6. *The ingressive evolution of Whitehead*

Whitehead is clearly conscious of the futility of all
naturalistic schemes, and falls back on the Platonic version
of the cosmic process. He agrees with Alexander in the view
that we get more out of the universe than is already contained in it, and yet nothing can emerge if its constituents

1 *Mind at the Crossways*, Preface.

and not already in existence. The qualities which are said
to emerge historically in Alexander, as the web of events
within the whole space-time assumes definite complexities
of configuration, are ingredient into events from the beginning according to Whitehead. The ingredience of eternal
objects into events is the explanation of the historical becoming. The universe is a developing series of events,
revealing a hierarchy of grades and values. At every step
we have the emergence of what is genuinely new, that was
not in existence in any previous phase of the line of advance.
Change is not a mere unfolding of what is implicit, or a
rearrangement of constituents with nothing new in the
whole they constitute. The higher cannot be adequately
explained in terms of the lower. Every event is a miracle, an
event from above. It embodies an idea from beyond and a
satisfactory cosmology should account for it. Whitehead
suggests an eternal order and a creative reality. The cosmic
series has a *nisus* towards the eternal order which is beyond
itself, though it is increasingly realized in the cosmic. Even
the simplest events are situations into which eternal objects
like red, sweet, which are not events, make ingression.
Whitehead holds that an independent possibility becomes
a definite actuality only through limitation. An essence becomes an existence, an object an event only by conforming
to the laws of the actual universe. An actual event is the
meeting-point of a world of actualities on the one side and
a world of ideal possibilities on the other. Eternal objects in
their interaction with creative passage issue in actuality,
reckoning with space-time, limitation, causal push or drag
of the past, and that ultimate irreducibility which we may
only call God. It is God who envisages the realm of possibilities and the world of settled fact so as to focus them on
each occasion for the creation of something new. It is he that
determines the ideal plans of events by the imposition of his

nature. Without such divine control, sheer unlimited activity taken with the infinite world of ideal forms would be unable to achieve anything specific. 'The universe exhibits a creativity with infinite freedom,' says Whitehead, 'and a realm of forms with infinite possibilities; but this creativity and these forms are together impotent to achieve actuality apart from the completed ideal harmony, which is God.'[1] God is the home of the universals and the ideal harmony.

There is a progressive incorporation into the cosmic series of the eternal order which God embraces in himself. The 'primordial' nature of God, by which Whitehead means God beyond time and not before time, is the conceptual consciousness of the possibilities capable of harmonious concurrent realization. These possibilities are called 'eternal objects'. Unlike Plato's ideas, they are not substances, but only forms. The view of forms as conceptually realized in God avoids the realism of independent existence as well as subsistence. The being of these eternal objects is not a ghostlike limitation of actuality, but consists in mere possibility. They are not metaphysical forces generating the world of existence, nor dynamic powers drawing men and things towards themselves. They are indifferent to their chance embodiment in existence, and many of them may not have been manifested at all in existence. They are eternal in their timeless being. They do not cease to be when all else perishes. They are not imaginary or abstract, but identical and individual, universal and non-existent. Some of them are apprehended as possibilities logically prior to their manifestation in existence, and others as symbols of values we pursue. Yet they are not efficient causes, since they belong to the realm of pure being. The relation of form to the temporal world is that of potentialities to actualities. The forms and the temporal process require each other. The process can attain order and determination only by participation in the forms, and the forms exist as relevant to the realization in the process of becoming. Actualities in the temporal world need to be described as processes of becoming by which sheer creativity governs determination, character, order. On the one hand, actuality arises from the background of the system of all other actualities, and is conditioned by them. On the other, it is a process of self-formation. It organizes the data presented to it in the light of ideas or purposes. The temporary actualities realize the possibilities surveyed in God's nature. We have thus creativity and God's primordial nature which is the vision of the possibilities before the temporal order. God is 'the actual but non-temporal entity whereby the indetermination of mere creativity is transmuted into a determinate freedom.'[1]

The relation between God and the world is for Whitehead one of immanence and interpenetration. As all relations are reciprocal, God is immanent in the world, and the world in God. As God transcends the world, the world transcends God. The order and purpose we see in the world is the result of actuality fulfilling the highest possibilities it sees before itself, which is the vision of God as relevant for it. God the consequent is distinct from the primordial nature of God. The order and the aesthetic harmony of the world become part of the nature of God as he is everlasting and so is conserved in him on the non-temporal side of valuation as everlasting. Whitehead says that God does not so much make the world as save it. As God transcends the world in that he holds before it the vision of an amazing wealth of possibilities at which it has yet scarcely begun to glimpse, so the world transcends God. The order in the world is not

1 *Ibid.*, p. 90

complete and all-pervasive. We have disorder and error due to the fragmentary shortsighted self-centred purposes from whence come evil.[1] God transcends as the vision of the order to be achieved, is immanent as the principle of the order achieved.

Whitehead distinguishes (1) an ultimate which he calls creativity, which is actual in virtue of its accidents, and (2) God who is the 'primordial non-temporal accident'.[2] God is not the Absolute, but only one of the accidental actualizations of the Absolute. It is difficult to conceive what this ultimate creativity which is said to be pure indetermination without any character of its own is. What is the source of limitation which turns this purely indeterminate creativity into a determinate freedom? Since God is only one of the accidents, he cannot be regarded as the source of the accident itself. He cannot be both the cause and the effect. Unless the ultimate reality is conceived in more satisfactory terms, on the lines of the Absolute mind which has ideal being and free creativity as its features, it becomes a mere logical abstraction. 'Creativity is without a character of its own in exactly the same sense in which the Aristotelian "matter" is without a character of its own.' 'It is always found under conditions and is described as conditioned.'[3] Since it is actual only in virtue of its accidents, it is hypostasized abstraction. It lives only in God. God is strictly speaking the highest reality, or the Absolute. He is the logical *prius* of the cosmic process which presupposes primordial nature, which does not presuppose it. That is why pure chaos is intrinsically impossible. The creative advance takes us to the realization of the conceptual plan. The whole plan of the cosmos has its adequate representation in the nature of

1 *Science and the Modern World*, p. 239.
2 *Process and Reality* (1929), p. 9.
3 *Ibid.*, pp. 42-43.

God, as it is the eternal completion of God's primordial conceptual nature. The 'consequent' nature of God evolves in its relationship to the evolving world. God occupies the status of an empirical event, for, says Whitehead, 'God is an actual entity and so is the most trivial puff of existence in far-off empty space.'[1] Even the 'primordial nature' of God, which is the entire multiplicity of eternal objects, is a created fact.[2] The unrealized eternal objects would be non-existent, but for God the 'primordial creature'. But being also consequent, He is the beginning and the end. He is the principle of concretion by which his conceptual plan becomes realized in fact. 'The consequent nature of God is His judgment on the world.' The actual world process requires for its explanation, according to Whitehead, a threefold character of God: (1) God as wisdom, the primordial nature; (2) God as love; and (3) God as judgment, a conception strangely reminiscent of the Hindu conception of God as Brahmā, Viṣṇu and Śiva. 'The universe includes a threefold creative act, composed of (i) the one infinite conceptual realization, (ii) the multiple solidarity of free physical realization in the temporal world,[3] and (iii) the ultimate unity of the multiplicity of actual fact with the primordial conceptual fact'.[4] God is the ground and the goal of the whole evolutionary scheme. Whitehead's view is strictly metaphysical, and the terms of love and tenderness he employs are not quite justified of cosmic elements. Again, God, in Whitehead's scheme, is affected by the process of reality. His nature finds completion only in terms of the world process. In any state he has a past which is irrevocable and a future which

1 *Process and Reality*, p. 24.
2 *Ibid.*, p. 42.
3 'The image--and it is but an image--the image under which this operative growth of God's nature is best conceived, is that of a tender care that nothing be lost.'
4 *Process and Reality*, p. 490.

is not yet. What happens to God when the plan is achieved, when the primordial nature becomes the consequent, when there is an identity between *natura naturans* and *natura naturata*, to use Spinoza's expression, is not clearly brought out.

7. *God*

The historical world of becoming is incapable of explanation from within itself. It is this fact that is brought out by the famous 'proofs' for the existence of God. They may not be able to offer a logical demonstration of the existence of God, but when the conviction arises otherwise they will help us to understand its rationality. The function of reasoning is not so much proof as the determination of an indeterminate object. The reality of God experienced by the mystics is found to be quite compatible with scientific facts and logical reasoning based on them.

The inadequacy of naturalism shows that the world process with its order and creativity requires for its explanation a creative power. For however far we may travel backwards in space or time, we cannot jump out of space or time, and we cannot account for space-time structure. The rationality of the universe suggests that the creative power is mind or spirit. There is no reason why we should identify it with vital force or life, as Bergson suggests, and not with spirit, for spirit is the highest we know. Descartes' argument is well known. Since we do not owe our own existence either originally or from moment to moment to ourselves or other beings like ourselves, there must be a primary and fundamental cause, God. God is not the cause in the ordinary sense, for that would be to make him an event within the series of events. The cause of the world creation lies in a sense outside itself. God is prior to the world, but not in any temporal sense. He is the logical *prius* of the world.

The ultimate creative energy of the universe is one and not many, for nature is too closely knit to be viewed as a scene of conflict between two or more powers. The first principle of the universe possesses unity, consciousness and priority of existence.

The teleological argument suggests that it is creative will and purpose. The endless variety of the world lends itself to the service of spirit. The argument against purpose in evolution is that the purpose or mind does not appear to learn from its mistakes. But if the end of the cosmic process is the perfecting of human personalities endowed with freedom through the process of trial and error, this element of uncertainty and adventurousness is bound to be present in the universe. The purpose is working within the frame of events. In spite of signs of lack of design, there is a general trend in evolution towards specific forms not yet realized. The immanent purposiveness of the world is not inconsistent with the presence of evil, ugliness and error. They are not, as Mc Taggart says, 'too bad to be true' or actual. Possibly they are necessary for the greater good of the reign of law in the universe. The overwhelming goodness of the universe requires its orderedness, and that may mean acute suffering and such other facts of experience which are seemingly irreconcilable with the purposiveness of the universe. If what we see of man's life is all there is to see, if there is no life before the cradle or beyond the grave, possibly we may not be able to establish the preponderant goodness of the world achieved at the cost of intense suffering and intolerable evil. The principles of Karma and rebirth suggest to us that the value of the world is not in any way affected by the actuality of evil, error and ugliness. The universe is one where these elements are transmuted into their opposites through a gradual process.

From the reality of spiritual experience and of the function of religion we can legitimately infer the reality of the
environment where the function finds its use. We have seen
that the object and the environment go together, and the two
may be regarded as expressions of a larger whole, which
includes them both. The religious activities of man cannot
be confined to the temporal environment. They require a
non-temporal good which is not an object of the temporal
world. The interaction of self and the universe has given rise
to these aspirations, which are their joint products. The
competitive world of claims and counter-claims cannot
satisfy the moral sense. The temporal world is not the only
or the ultimate world. The rational purposive character of
the universe gives us enough justification for presuming the
reality of a spiritual environment.

God as the universal mind working with a conscious
design, who is at once the beginning of the world, the author
of its order, the principle of its progress and the goal of its
evolution, is not the god of religion unless we take into
account the facts of religious consciousness. Our moral life
tells us that God is not only the goal but the spring and
sustainer of moral effort. Our spiritual experience reveals
to us the fact of the supreme all-comprehensive one. There
is an affinity between the structure of the world and the
mind of man. Our sense perceptions, our logical concepts,
our intuitive apprehensions are not forms superinduced on
reality, but are determinate forms of reality itself. From the
beginning we are in the presence of givenness, something
experienced. Because the objects are perceived only when
our minds are trained, it does not follow that the objects are
subjective. To see a rose we must turn our eyes in that
direction. To realize the supreme spirit, a certain purifying
of the mind is necessary. The reality of spirit is not

invalidated simply because it is seen only by those who are pure in heart.

Spirit is the reality of the cosmic process. Nothing of what comes in our personal experience can be predicted with complete truth of the ultimate reality, though no element in this experience is without meaning or value. No element of our experience is illusory, though every element of it has a degree of reality according to the extent to which it succeeds in expressing the nature of the real.

The conception of God as wisdom, love and goodness is not a mere abstract demand of thought but is the concrete reality which satisfies the religious demand. If we combine the ideas we are led to posit from the different directions of metaphysics, morals and religion, we obtain the character of God as the primordial mind, the loving redeemer and the holy judg ? of the universe. The Hindu conception of God as Brahmā, Viṣṇu and Śiva illustrates the triple character. Brahmā is the primordial nature of God. He is the 'home' of the conditions of the possibility of the world, or of the 'eternal objects' in Whitehead's phrase. If the rational order of the universe reflects the mind of God, that mind is prior to the world. But the thoughts of Brahmā,[1] or the primordial mind, should become the things of the world. This process of transformation of ideas into the plane of space-time is a gradual one which God assists by his power of productive and self-communicating life. In the world process all things yearn towards their ideal forms. They struggle to throw off their imperfections and reflect the patterns in the divine mind. As immanent in the process, God becomes the guide and the ground of the progress. He is not a mere spectator, but a sharer in the travail of the world. God as Viṣṇu is sacrifice. He is continuously engaged in opposing every

1 Brahmā, the Creator-God, is distinct from Brahman, the Absolute spirit.

tendency in the universe which makes for error, ugliness and evil, which are not mere abstract possibilities, but concrete forces giving reality to the cosmic strife. God pours forth the whole wealth of his love to actualize his intentions for us. He takes up the burden of helping us to resist the forces of evil, error and ugliness, and transmute them into truth, beauty and goodness. The Ṛg Veda says: 'All that is bare he covers; all that is sick he cures; By his grace the blind man sees and the lame walks.'[1] 'God is the refuge and friend of all.'[2] The Ṛg Veda says, 'Thou art ours and we are thine.'[3] God does not leave us in the wilderness to find our way back. Hindu mythology looks upon God as an eternal beggar waiting for the opening of the door that he may enter into the darkness and illumine the whole horizon of our being as with a lightning flash. It is not so much man seeking God as God seeking man. He goes out into the dangers of the wilderness to lead us out of it. God so loves the world that he gives himself to it. In communicating his nature to us, he makes us sharers in his creative power. He expects us to recognize and respond to his call and co-operate with him. He wants us to look upon him as our friend, lover and comrade. Our sin consists in distrusting God, in refusing to recognize his purpose and respond to his demand. Our virtue consists in assimilating the divine content and participating in his purpose. His love is his essential nature, and not a transitory quality. He is for ever saving the world.

While there is no risk that the world will tumble off into ruin so long as God's love is operative, yet the realization of the end of the world depends on our co-operation. As we are free beings, our co-operation is a free gift which we may withold. This possibility introduces an element of contingency

1 viii. 79. 2; viii. 4. 7.
2 Svetāśvatara Upaniṣad, iii. 17; see also Bhagavadgītā, ix. 18.
3 viii. 92. 32.

to the universe. The creative process, though orderly and progressive, is unpredictable. There is real indetermination, and God himself is in the making. If we say that God has a fixed plan which is being copied into matter, we are bound to cosmological determinism. Human co-operation is an essential condition of the progress of the world, and the freedom of man introduces an element of uncertainty. The struggle is not a parade, nor is history a mere pageant. Though God is ever ready to help us, our stupidity and selfishness erect barriers against and persistent operation of his love.

The view that God as love will see to it that the plan succeeds is not to be confused with the doctrine of absolute predestination, which may be interpreted as overthrowing human freedom and paralysing moral effort. After all, it is the fight that gives life its value and not the ultimate result, and even the consummation of the result is contingent on the passion with which human individuals work for the cause. The hope is there, that even the most wilful will respond to the long-suffering love of God. Though he is ever working in the hearts of men and drawing them towards himself, there are occasions when we withold the response and make the situation serious. When the hold of God on the world becomes precarious, his love, which is constant, manifests itself in a striking way. According to the Christian religion, when the situation became desperate it is said that God once sent a deluge which very nearly destroyed all mankind, and on another occasion sent his only-begotten Son. It does not mean that the love of God is an accidental quality brought into manifestation by the 'fall' of man. We need not think that God comes to our rescue simply because creation has gone off the rails. Love belongs to the very core of God's being. Utter and complete self-giving is the nature of divine activity, though the power to benefit by it depends

338   AN IDEALIST VIEW OF LIFE

on the capacity of the recipients.

The redemptive function of God is an incessant activity, though it becomes emphasized when the moral order is sharply disturbed. God manifests Himself in striking forms whenever new adjustments have to be brought about. These special revelations are called in Hindu mythology *avatārs*, or descents of God. The popular view holds that, when darkness gathers, the waters deepen and things threaten to collapse into chaos, God Himself becomes personally incarnate in a unique way. But the continuous urge of spiritual life, the growing revelation of ends in which the divine life comes to its own, the immanent law which constitutes the unity of the world and conditions the interaction of its several elements, are not consistent with the conception of unique revelations of complete Godhead on earth. The whole movement directed towards the realization of potentialities is a continuous incarnation of God. It is, however, true that the manifestation of spiritual values may be viewed either as the revelation of God, or the realization of the capacities of man. The two, God's revelation and man's realization, though distinguishable, are inseparable from one another. They are two aspects of one process. Lives like those of Buddha and Jesus, by revealing to us the great fact of God and the nature of the world as a temple of God, point out how we can overcome sin and selfishness. They achieve for human life what human life has done for nature below. The great story of life on earth is in a sense the 'martyrdom of God'.

Simply because there is the security that God's love will succeed, the struggle does not become unreal. God is not simply truth and love, but also justice. He is the perfection which rejects all evil. The sovereignty of God is indicated in the character of Śiva. God acts according to fixed laws. He does not break or suspend his own laws. The liberty to change one's mind is not true liberty. God cannot forgive the criminal, even when he repents, for the moral order which is conceived in love and not in hatred requires that wrongdoing should have its natural consequences. Plato, in words that seem to be an echo of Hindu texts, tells us that 'you shall assuredly never be passed over by God's judgment, not though you make yourself ;ever so small and hide in the bowels of the earth, or exalt yourself to heaven. You must pay the penalty due, either while you are still with us, or after your departure hence, in the house of Hades, or it may be, by removal to some still more desolate region.'[1] The one God creates as Brahmā, redeems as Viṣṇu, and judges as Śiva. These represent the three stages of the plan, the process, and the perfection. The source from which all things come, the spring by which they are sustained, and the good into which they enter are one.[2] God loves us, creates us, and rules us. Creation, redemption and judgment are different names for the fact of God.

So far as the world is concerned, God is organic with it. It is impossible to detach God from the world. The Hindu theologian Rāmanuja regards the relation of God to the world as one of soul to body. He brings out the organic and complete dependence of the world on God. God is the sustainer of the body as well as its inner guide. Struggle and growth are real in the life of God. Time is the essential form of the cosmic process, including the moral life, and it has a meaning to God also. Life eternal which carries us beyond the limits of temporal growth may take us to the Absolute, but God is essentially bound up with the life in time. Progress may be derogatory to the Absolute, but not to God, who is intensely interested in it. The process of the world is an emergence, but not of the type suggested by Alexander.

1 *Laws,*, 905A. Taylor: *The Faith of a Moralist,* i. pp. 325-326
2 *Tait. Up.* iii; *Bhagavadgītā* vii. 54.

It is an emergence under the guidance of God, who is
immanent in the process, though the goal is transcendent to
it. The process of the world is not a mere unfolding of what
is contained in the beginning. It is not a question of mere
preformation. The end of the world is not contained in the
beginning, such that God might retire from the process
altogether. Those who have any appreciation of this fact of
evolution cannot adopt the view of preformation, though
even a writer like Bergson, who emphasizes the creativity
of evolution, seems to think that the whole evolution of life
with its progressive manifestation of structure is latent in
life. He says: 'Life does not proceed by the assimilation and
addition of elements, but by dissociation and division.'[1] Such
a view is inconsistent with the main intention of Bergson's
teaching.[2] The world is in the making, and is being created
constantly, and the reality of change means a plastic world
and not a block universe. The creative impulse is present
from the beginning, but the forms created are due to the
cosmic stress. That alone can account for the ordered character of the world of varied tendencies. If matter, life, consciousness and value had each its own independent
evolution, the fact of their unity calls for an explanation, and
we may be obliged to use a principle somewhat like
Leibniz's pre-established harmony. Reality is a whole and
acts and advances as a whole. The control of the whole is
present in the growth of the parts, whether they are chemical compounds or cultural movements. The process of the
world is creative synthesis, where the formative energy,
local situation and cosmic control are all efficient factors.
The final end is not contained in the beginning. The interest
and attractiveness of the end cannot be divorced from the

1 *Creative Evolution* (E. T. 1911), p. 89.
2 For a criticism of Bergson's views, see the writer's book on *The Reign
  of Religion in Contemporary Philosophy* (1920).

process which leads up to it. A God who has arranged everything at the beginning of the world and can change nothing, create nothing new is not a God at all. If the universe is truly creative, God works as a creative genius does. The end grows with the process and assumes a definite shape through the characteristics of the parts of the process. There is thus an element of indetermination throughout the process, though it diminishes in degree as the amount of actuality increases. God the planner acts with real genius when confronted by actual situations.

God, though immanent, is not identical with the world until the very end. Throughout the process there is an unrealized residuum in God, but it vanishes when we reach the end; when the reign is absolute the kingdom comes. God who is organic with it recedes into the background of the Absolute. The beginning and the end are limiting conceptions, and the great interest of the world centres in the intermediate process from the beginning to the end. God is more the saviour and redeemer than creator and judge. As an essentially human phenomenon, religion insists on the 'otherness' of God. Without it, worship, love and repentance have no meaning. We seek union with God, a union of will and fellowship. God is a real living one who inspires trust and love, reverence and self-surrender. Salvation comes from the grace of God through *bhakti*, or trust in God, and surrender to him. In all true religion we have faith in and experience of a living God who saves and redeems us from our sins. The love of God is more central than either his wisdom or his sovereignty. These latter may lead to predestination theories which reduce the world process to a sham, where the freedom of man and the love of God are both illusory. If predestination is true, then the creation of novelties, the loving trust and surrender of man to God and the grace of God are illusions. In the ancient Epic of

Mahābhārata, Draupadi, the wife of Yudhiṣṭhira, declares bitterly against her fate, and suggests the probability of the predestination theory. The moral government of the world seems to her a mere fiction. She cites the authority of an ancient saga in support of her doubts. Looking at her husband deprived of his rightful throne and wandering in the wilderness pursued by want and adversity, she declares that the world is in the hands of purposeless omnipotence who bestows on his creatures according to his sweet pleasure happiness or misery, weal or woe. He plays with us as children with their toys, and we are deceived if we imagine that we have any choice in the matter. We play to the tunes set to us. Blind and powerless with regard to his weal or woe, man goes to heaven or hell as the Lord impels him. How can I believe that God acts according to law and not unjustly when noble men of integrity are disgraced and the wicked are flourishing? I see you in distress and Duryodhana in prosperity. I laugh at the God who acts so arbitrarily.' 'The Lord does not seem to act like father or mother to us, but acts as if impelled by wrath, and other people follow his example.' When Yudhiṣṭhira hears her lamentations and cries of despair, which remind us of the book of Job, her suggestion of a theory of predestination and dire omnipotence which is opposed to faith in a loving and just God, he rebukes her, saying that she is guilty of blasphemy. He criticizes her view, however ancient it may be, as atheistic (nāstika), and calls upon her to revile no more the supreme God, through whose grace the devotees of the world gain immortality. God wills the right and expects us to work with him and for him, and he is of inexhaustible grace. Love reveals the nature of God more than infinitude and sovereignty. The theory of predestination is repudiated in favour of the love of God and the freedom of man.

There are certain vital values of religion which are met

by the character of God as wisdom, love and goodness. Values acquire a cosmic importance and ethical life becomes meaningful. Till the completion of the cosmic process, the individual retains his centre as individual, and the completion is always transcendent to him, and so God is an 'other' over against him, evoking in him the sense of need. God is conceived as a personal being, towards whom the individual stands in a relation of co-operation and dependence. God is the final satisfaction, and in him man finds self-completion. He wants to grow into the image of God, perfect in power and wisdom.

8. *The absolute*

While the character of God as personal love meets certain religious needs, there are others which are not fulfilled by it. In the highest spiritual experience we have the sense of rest and fulfilment, of eternity and completeness. These needs provoked from the beginning of human reflection conceptions of the Absolute as pure and passionless being which transcends the restless turmoil of the cosmic life. If God is bound up with the world, subject to the category of time, if his work is limited by the freedom of man and the conditions of existence, however infinite he may be in the quality of his life, in power, knowledge and righteousness, he is but an expression of the Absolute. But man wants to know the truth of things in itself, in the beginning--nay, before time and before plurality, the one 'breathing breathless', as the *Ṛg Veda* has it, the pure, alone and unmanifest, nothing and all things, that which transcends any definite form of expression, and yet is the basis of all expression, the one in whom all is found and yet all is lost. The great problem of the philosophy of religion has been the reconciliation of the character of the Absolute as in a sense eternally complete with the character of God as a self-determining principle manifested in a temporal development which includes nature and man. The identification of the absolute life with the course of human history suggested by the Italian idealist may be true of the supreme god of the world, but not of the Absolute, the lord of all worlds. Creation neither adds to nor takes away from the reality of the Absolute. Evolution may be a part of our cosmic process, but the Absolute is not subject to it. The Absolute is incapable of increase.

While the absolute is pure consciousness and pure freedom and infinite possibility, it appears to be God from the point of view of the one specific possibility which has become actualized. While God is organically bound up with the universe, the Absolute is not. The world of pure being is not exhausted by the cosmic process which is only one of the ways in which the Absolute reality which transcends the series reveals itself. The Absolute is the foundation and *prius* of all actuality and possibility. This universe is for the Absolute only one possibility. Its existence is an act of free creation. Out of the infinite possibilities open to it, this one is chosen. When we analyse our sense of freedom we find that it consists in accepting or rejecting any one of a number of possibilities presented to us. The Absolute has an infinite number of possibilities to choose from, which are all determined by its nature. It has the power of saying yes or no to any of them. While the possible is determined by the nature of the Absolute, the actual is selected from out of the total amount of the possible, by the free activity of the Absolute without any determination whatsoever. It could have created a world different in every detail from that which is actual. If one drama is enacted and other possible ones postponed, it is due to the freedom of the Absolute.

It is not necessary for this universe to be an infinite and

endless process. The character of a finite universe is not incompatible with an infinite Absolute. We can have an infinite series of terms which are finite. The Absolute has so much more in it than is brought out by this world.

As to why there is realization of this possibility, we can only say that it is much too difficult for us in the pit to know what is happening behind the screens. It is *māya*, or a mystery which we have to accept reverently.

Sometimes it is argued that it is of the very nature of the Absolute to overflow and realize possibilities. The great symbol of the sun which is used in Hindu thought, Plato's system and Persian mythology signifies the generous self-giving and ecstasy of the Absolute, which overflows, and gives itself freely and generously to all. Timaeus says in Plato that the created world is there because the All-good wants his goodness to flow out upon it.[1] The Indian figure of *līlā* makes the creation of the universe an act of playfulness. Play is generally the expression of ideal possibilities. It is its own end and its own continuous reward. The Absolute mind has a perfect realm of ideal being, and is free creativity as well. Though the creation of the world is an incident in the never-ending activity of the Absolute, it satisfies a deep want in God. The world is as indispensable to God as God is to the world.

God, who is the creator, sustainer and judge of this world, is not totally unrelated to the Absolute. God is the Absolute from the human end. When we limit down the Absolute to its relation with the actual possibility, the Absolute appears as supreme Wisdom, Love and Goodness. The eternal becomes the first and the last. The abiding 'I am', the changeless centre and the cause of all change is envisaged as the first term and the last in the sequence of nature. He is the creative

1 29. E.I.

mind of the world, with a consciousness of the general plan and direction of the cosmos, even before it is actualized in space and time. He holds the successive details in proper perspective and draws all things together in bonds of love and harmony. He is the loving saviour of the world. As creator and saviour, God is transcendent to the true process, even as realization is transcendent to progress. This internal transcendence of God to the true process gives meaning to the distinctions of value, and makes struggle and effort real. We call the supreme the Absolute, when we view it apart from the cosmos, God in relation to the cosmos. The Absolute is the pre-cosmic nature of God, and God is the Absolute from the cosmic point of view.